Mastering Reverse Engineering

Re-engineer your ethical hacking skills

Reginald Wong

BIRMINGHAM - MUMBAI

Mastering Reverse Engineering

Copyright © 2018 Packt Publishing

Commissioning Editor: Vijin Boricha
Acquisition Editor: Heramb Bhavsar
Content Development Editor: Arjun Joshi
Technical Editor: Cymon Pereira
Copy Editor: Safis Editing
Project Coordinator: Kinjal Bari
Proofreader: Safis Editing
Indexer: Tejal Daruwale Soni
Graphics: Jisha Chirayil
Production Coordinator: Shraddha Falebhai

First published: October 2018

Production reference: 1311018

Published by Packt Publishing Ltd.
Livery Place
35 Livery Street
Birmingham
B3 2PB, UK.

ISBN 978-1-78883-884-9

www.packtpub.com

`mapt.io`

Mapt is an online digital library that gives you full access to over 5,000 books and videos, as well as industry leading tools to help you plan your personal development and advance your career. For more information, please visit our website.

Why subscribe?

- Spend less time learning and more time coding with practical eBooks and Videos from over 4,000 industry professionals

- Improve your learning with Skill Plans built especially for you

- Get a free eBook or video every month

- Mapt is fully searchable

- Copy and paste, print, and bookmark content

Packt.com

Did you know that Packt offers eBook versions of every book published, with PDF and ePub files available? You can upgrade to the eBook version at `www.packt.com` and as a print book customer, you are entitled to a discount on the eBook copy. Get in touch with us at `customercare@packtpub.com` for more details.

At `www.packt.com`, you can also read a collection of free technical articles, sign up for a range of free newsletters, and receive exclusive discounts and offers on Packt books and eBooks.

Contributors

About the author

Reginald Wong has been in the software security industry for more than 15 years. Currently, Reggie is a lead anti-malware researcher at Vipre Security, a J2 Global company, covering various security technologies focused on attacks and malware. He previously worked for Trend Micro as the lead for the Heuristics team, dealing with forward-looking malware detection. Aside from his core work, he has also conducted in-house anti-malware training for fresh graduates. He is currently affiliated with CSPCert.ph, Philippines' CERT, and is a reporter for Wildlist.org. He has also been invited to speak at local security events, including Rootcon.

About the reviewers

Berman Enconado is very passionate about everything relating to cyber security. Ever since he was a teenager, he has practiced, toyed with, and delved in the art of cracking and hacking. He started his professional career back in 2003 at Trend Micro. From then, he has shared his knowledge in reverse engineering and developed relevant malware-related systems with big companies such as eSoft, Sunbelt/GFI/ThreatTrack, NSSlabs, and currently Microsoft. He has been invited to be a speaker at conferences, educational institutions, and government sectors concerning malware and ways to efficiently subvert its progress.

Chiheb Chebbi is a Tunisian InfoSec enthusiast, author, and technical reviewer with experience of various aspects of information security, focusing on investigating advanced cyber attacks and researching cyber espionage. His core interests lie in penetration testing, machine learning, and threat hunting. He has been included in many Halls Of Fame. His talk proposals have been accepted by many world-class information security conferences.

I dedicate this book to every person who makes the security community awesome and fun!

Packt is searching for authors like you

If you're interested in becoming an author for Packt, please visit `authors.packtpub.com` and apply today. We have worked with thousands of developers and tech professionals, just like you, to help them share their insight with the global tech community. You can make a general application, apply for a specific hot topic that we are recruiting an author for, or submit your own idea.

Table of Contents

Preface

Reverse engineering is a tool used for analyzing software to exploit its weaknesses and strengthen its defenses. Hackers use reverse engineering as a tool to expose security flaws and questionable privacy practices. This book helps you to master the art of using reverse engineering.

Who this book is for

If you are a security engineer, analyst, or system programmer and want to use reverse engineering to improve your software and hardware, this is the book for you. You will also find this book useful if you are a developer who wants to explore and learn reverse engineering.

What this book covers

Chapter 1, *Preparing to Reverse*, shows how to obtain the samples used throughout the book and explains the journey we are about to embark on.

Chapter 2, *Identification and Extraction of Hidden Components*, covers basics of the operating system and malware installation behavior. We will learn where malware usually drops files and makes registry entries.

Chapter 3, *The Low-Level Language*, briefly covers the Assembly language and why we must understand it in order to reverse engineer.

Chapter 4, *Static and Dynamic Reversing*, explains how static and dynamic analysis are implemented. We will also have a brief discussion regarding reversing of a file using a few tools.

Chapter 5, *Tools of the Trade*, compares and contrasts tools of the trade and explains their weaknesses and when a tool won't work as intended, allowing you to change your tools and know where to turn to get the job done without blaming a tool for lacking a capability.

Chapter 6, *RE in Linux Platforms*, explains how to perform a static and dynamic Windows analysis in a Linux environment.

Chapter 7, *RE for Windows Platforms*, explains how to perform static and dynamic Windows analysis directly in a Windows environment.

Chapter 8, *Sandboxing: Virtualization as a Component for RE*, shows how to use emulation to inform reverse engineering and overcome obstacles when running on hardware other than the target binary supports.

Chapter 9, *Binary Obfuscation Techniques*, explains how to reverse engineer simple obfuscation techniques.

Chapter 10, *Packing and Encryption*, covers using debuggers to pause execution and dump the contents of memory for analysis using our disassembly tools.

Chapter 11, *Anti-analysis tricks*, shows how to identify and handle anti-reversing and anti-debugging tricks.

Chapter 12, *Practical Reverse Engineering of a Windows Executable*, covers practical use of the tools we are familiar with at this point.

Chapter 13, *Reversing Various File Types*, covers analyzing various file types using up-to-date tools.

To get the most out of this book

- Having some programming/shell scripting knowledge is an added bonus.
- Knowledge about information security and x86 assembly language is an advantage.
- Operating system used: Windows and Linux (version will depend on the requirements of VirtualBox)
- Processor with at least four cores, 4 GB of RAM, and 250 GB of disk space.
- You may need to download virtual machines from Microsoft in advance, as these may take some time to download. See the developers' page at `https://developer.microsoft.com/en-us/microsoft-edge/tools/vms/`.

Download the example code files

You can download the example code files for this book from your account at `www.packt.com`. If you purchased this book elsewhere, you can visit `www.packt.com/support` and register to have the files emailed directly to you.

You can download the code files by following these steps:

1. Log in or register at www.packt.com.
2. Select the **SUPPORT** tab.
3. Click on **Code Downloads & Errata**.
4. Enter the name of the book in the **Search** box and follow the onscreen instructions.

Once the file is downloaded, please make sure that you unzip or extract the folder using the latest version of:

- WinRAR/7-Zip for Windows
- Zipeg/iZip/UnRarX for Mac
- 7-Zip/PeaZip for Linux

The code bundle for the book is also hosted on GitHub at https://github.com/PacktPublishing/Mastering-Reverse-Engineering. In case there's an update to the code, it will be updated on the existing GitHub repository.

We also have other code bundles from our rich catalog of books and videos available at https://github.com/PacktPublishing/. Check them out!

Download the color images

We also provide a PDF file that has color images of the screenshots/diagrams used in this book. You can download it here: https://www.packtpub.com/sites/default/files/downloads/9781788838849_ColorImages.pdf

Conventions used

There are a number of text conventions used throughout this book.

CodeInText: Indicates code words in text, database table names, folder names, filenames, file extensions, pathnames, dummy URLs, user input, and Twitter handles. Here is an example: "The handle in hkResult is used by RegEnumValueA to begin enumerating each registry value under the registry key."

A block of code is set as follows:

```
while (true) {
    for (char i = 1; i <= 255; i++) {
        if (GetAsyncKeyState(i) & 1) {
            sprintf_s(lpBuffer, "\\x%02x", i);
            LogFile(lpBuffer, (char*)"log.txt");
        }
    }
}
```

When we wish to draw your attention to a particular part of a code block, the relevant lines or items are set in bold:

```
87 to base-2
87 divided by 2 is 43 remainder 1.
43 divided by 2 is 21 remainder 1.
21 divided by 2 is 10 remainder 1.
10 divided by 2 is 5 remainder 0.
5 divided by 2 is 2 remainder 1.
```

Bold: Indicates a new term, an important word, or words that you see onscreen. For example, words in menus or dialog boxes appear in the text like this. Here is an example: "In VirtualBox, click on **File|Import Appliance**."

 Warnings or important notes appear like this.

 Tips and tricks appear like this.

Get in touch

Feedback from our readers is always welcome.

General feedback: If you have questions about any aspect of this book, mention the book title in the subject of your message and email us at customercare@packtpub.com.

Errata: Although we have taken every care to ensure the accuracy of our content, mistakes do happen. If you have found a mistake in this book, we would be grateful if you would report this to us. Please visit www.packt.com/submit-errata, selecting your book, clicking on the Errata Submission Form link, and entering the details.

Piracy: If you come across any illegal copies of our works in any form on the Internet, we would be grateful if you would provide us with the location address or website name. Please contact us at copyright@packt.com with a link to the material.

If you are interested in becoming an author: If there is a topic that you have expertise in and you are interested in either writing or contributing to a book, please visit authors.packtpub.com.

Reviews

Please leave a review. Once you have read and used this book, why not leave a review on the site that you purchased it from? Potential readers can then see and use your unbiased opinion to make purchase decisions, we at Packt can understand what you think about our products, and our authors can see your feedback on their book. Thank you!

For more information about Packt, please visit packt.com.

1
Preparing to Reverse

In this first chapter, we will introduce reverse engineering and explain what it is for. We will begin by discussing some insights already being applied in various aspects that will help the reader understand what reverse engineering is. In this chapter, we will cover a brief introduction to the process and types of tools used in software reverse engineering. There are tips given here on the proper handling of malware. The last section of this chapter shows how easy it is to set up our initial analysis environment using tools that are readily available for download. The following topics will be covered:

- What reverse engineering is used for
- Applying reverse engineering
- Types of tools used in reverse engineering
- Guide to handling malware
- Setting up your reverse engineering environment

Reverse engineering

Breaking something down and putting it back together is a process that helps people understand how things were made. A person would be able to redo and reproduce an origami by unfolding it first. Knowing how cars work requires understanding each major and minor mechanical part and their purposes. The complex nature of the human anatomy requires people to understand each and every part of the body. How? By dissecting it. Reverse engineering is a way for us to understand how things were designed, why is it in its state, when it triggers, how it works, and what its purpose is. In effect, the information is used to redesign and improve for better performance and cost. It can even help fix defects.

However, reverse engineering entails ethical issues and is still a continuous debate. Similar to Frankenstein's case, there are existing issues that defy natural laws in a way that is not acceptable to humanity. Today, simple redesigning can raise copyright infringement if not thought through carefully. Some countries and states have laws governing against reverse engineering. However, in the software security industry, reverse engineering is a must and a common use case.

Imagine if the Trojan Horse was thoroughly inspected and torn down before it was allowed to enter the gates of a city. This would probably cause a few dead soldiers outside the gate fighting for the city. The next time the city is sent another Trojan Horse, archers would know where to point their arrows. And no dead soldiers this time. The same is true for malware analysis—by knowing the behaviors of a certain malware through reverse engineering, the analyst can recommend various safeguards for the network. Think of it as the Trojan Horse being the malware, the analyst being the soldier who initially inspected the horse, and the city being the network of computers.

Anyone seeking to become a reverse engineer or an analyst should have the trait of being resourceful. Searching the internet is part of reverse engineering. An analyst would not plainly rely on the tools and information we provide in this book. There are instances that an analysis would even require reverse engineer to develop their own tools.

Software auditing may require reverse engineering. Besides high-level code review processes, some software quality verification also involves implementing reverse engineering. The aim of these test activities is to ensure that vulnerabilities are found and fixed. There are a lot of factors that are not taken into consideration during the design and development of a piece of software. Most of these are random input and external factors that may cause leaks, leading to vulnerabilities. These vulnerabilities may be used for malicious intents that not only disrupt the software, but may cause damage and compromise the system environment it is installed in. System monitoring and fuzzing tools are commonly used when testing software. Today's operating systems have better safeguards to protect from crashing. Operating systems usually report any discrepancies found, such as memory or file corruption. Additional information, such as crash dumps, are also provided. From this information, a reverse engineer would be able to pinpoint where exactly in the software they have to inspect.

In the software security industry, one of the core skills required is reverse engineering. Every attack, usually in the form of malware, is reversed and analyzed. The first thing that is usually needed is to clean the network and systems from being compromised. An analyst determines how the malware installed itself and became persistent. Then, they develop steps for uninstalling the malware. In the anti-malware phase, these steps are used to develop the clean-up routine, once the anti-malware product is able to detect that the system has been compromised.

The analysis provides information about how the malware was able to compromise the system. With this information, network administrators are able to impose policies to mitigate the attack. If the malware was able to enter the system because of a user opening an email attachment that contains JavaScript code, the network administrator would implement the blocking of emails that contain a JavaScript attachment.

Some administrators are even advised to restructure their network infrastructure. Once a system gets compromised, the attackers may already have got all of the information about the network, and would easily be able to make another wave of the same attack. Making major changes will greatly help prevent the same attack from happening again.

Part of restructuring the infrastructure is education. The best way to prevent a system from being compromised is by educating its users about securing information, including their privacy. Knowing about social engineering and having experience of previous attacks makes users aware of security. It is important to know how attackers are able to compromise an institution and what damage they can cause. As a result, security policies are imposed, backups are set up, and continuous learning is implemented.

Going further, targeted companies can report the attack to authorities. Even a small piece of information can give authorities hints to help them hunt down the suspects and shut down malware communication servers.

Systems can be compromised by taking advantage of software vulnerabilities. After the attacker gets knowledge about the target, the attacker can craft code that exploits known software vulnerabilities. Besides making changes in the infrastructure, any software used should also be kept up to date with security features and patches. Reverse engineering is also needed to find vulnerable code. This helps pinpoint the vulnerable code by backtracking it to the source.

All of these activities are done based on the output of reverse engineering. The information gathered from reverse engineering affects how the infrastructure needs to be restructured.

Technical requirements

We will work in an environment that will make use of virtualization software. It is recommended that we have a physical machine with virtualization enabled and a processor with at least four cores, 4 GB of RAM, and 250 GB of disk space. Pre-install this physical machine with either the Windows or Linux operating system.

We will be using VirtualBox in our setup. The host operating system version of Windows or Linux will depend on the requirements of VirtualBox. See the latest version of VirtualBox at `https://www.virtualbox.org/` and look for the recommended requirements.

You may need to download virtual machines from Microsoft in advance, as these may take some time to download. See the developers' page at `https://developer.microsoft.com/en-us/microsoft-edge/tools/vms/`. Windows 10 can be downloaded from the following link: `https://www.microsoft.com/en-us/software-download/windows10`

Reverse engineering as a process

Like any other activity, reverse engineering is also a process. There is a guide that we can follow to help us generate information that can be helpful to both the analyst and stakeholders.

Seeking approval

Ethics requires anyone carrying out reverse engineering of software to have approval from the owner of the software. However, there are a lot of instances where software shows its bugs upfront, while the operating system reports it. Some companies are more lenient about their software getting reversed without approval, but it is customary today that any vulnerabilities found should be reported directly to the owner and not publicized. It is up to the owner to decide when to report the vulnerability to the community. This prevents attackers from using a vulnerability before a software patch gets released.

It is a different story when malware or hacking is involved. Of course, reversing malware doesn't need approval from the malware author. Rather, one of the goals of malware analysis is to catch the author. If not sure, always consult a lawyer or a company's legal department.

Static analysis

Without any execution, viewing the file's binary and parsing each and every byte provides much of the information needed to continue further. Simply knowing the type of file sets the mindset of the analyst in a way that helps them to prepare specific sets of tools and references that may be used. Searching text strings can also give clues about the author of the program, where it came from, and, most likely, what it does.

Dynamic analysis

This type of analysis is where the the object being analyzed gets executed. It requires an enclosed environment so that behaviors that may compromise production systems do not happen. Setting up enclosed environments are usually done using virtual machines, since they can then easily be controlled. Tools that monitor and log common environment actions are implemented during dynamic analysis.

Low-level analysis

There is some information that may be missed out during static and dynamic analyses. The flow of a program follows a path that depends of certain conditions. For example, a program will only create a file only if a specific process is running. Or, a program will create a registry entry in the `Wow6432Node` key only if it were running in a 64-bit Windows operating system. Debugging tools are usually used to analyze a program in low-level analysis.

Reporting

While doing analysis, every piece of information should be collected and documented. It is common practice to document a reverse engineered object to help future analysis. An analysis serves as a knowledge base for developers who want to secure their upcoming programs from flaws. For example, a simple input can now be secured by placing bounds validation, which is known about as a result of a prior reverse-engineered program that indicated possible buffer overflow.

A good report answers questions regarding the following:

- How a reversed engineered object works
- When specific behavior triggers
- Why specific codes were used in the program
- Where it was intended to work on
- What the whole program does

Tools

Doing reverse code engineering starts off with understanding the meaning of every bit and byte. Simply viewing the bytes contained requires developing tools that aid in the reading of files and objects. Parsing and adding meaning to every byte would require another tool. Reverse engineering has evolved with tools that are continuously updated when encountering new software technology. Here, we have categorized these tools into binary analysis tools, disassemblers, decompilers, debuggers, and monitoring tools.

Binary analysis tools

Binary analysis tools are used to parse binary files and extract information about the file. An analyst would be able to identify which applications are able to read or execute the binary. File types are generally identified from their magic header bytes. These Magic Header bytes are usually located at the beginning of a file. For example, a Microsoft executable file, an EXE file, begin with the MZ header (MZ is believed to be the initials of Mark Zbikowski, a developer from Microsoft during the DOS days). Microsoft Office Word documents, on the other hand, have these first four bytes as their Magic Header:

The hexadecimal bytes in the preceding screenshot read as DOCFILE Other information such as text string also give hints. The following screenshot shows information indicating that the program was most likely built using Window Forms:

```
A  0000000001A0   0000004001A0   0   .rsrc
A  0000000001C7   0000004001C7   0   @.reloc
A  000000006024   000000407E24   0   v4.0.30319
A  000000006048   000000407E48   0   #Strings
A  000000006068   000000407E68   0   #GUID
A  000000006078   000000407E78   0   #Blob
A  0000000080D9   000000409ED9   0   IEnumerable
A  0000000080E7   000000409EE7   0   addRFIDToDBToolStripMenuItem1
A  000000008105   000000409F05   0   Form1
A  00000000810B   000000409F0B   0   button1
A  000000008113   000000409F13   0   menuStrip1
A  00000000811E   000000409F1E   0   backgroundWorker1
A  000000008130   000000409F30   0   AboutBox1
A  00000000813A   000000409F3A   0   AddTextTo_richTextBox1
A  000000008151   000000409F51   0   textBox1
A  00000000815A   000000409F5A   0   UInt32
A  000000008161   000000409F61   0   Uint32
A  00000000816B   000000409F6B   0   PRINTER_INFO_2
A  000000008181   000000409F81   0   Form2
A  000000008187   000000409F87   0   button2
A  00000000818F   000000409F8F   0   textBox2
A  000000008198   000000409F98   0   Form3
A  00000000819E   000000409F9E   0   textBox3
A  0000000081A7   000000409FA7   0   Form4
A  0000000081AD   000000409FAD   0   textBox4
A  0000000081B6   000000409FB6   0   Form5
A  0000000081BC   000000409FBC   0   textBox5
A  0000000081C5   000000409FC5   0   Form6
A  0000000081CB   000000409FCB   0   Form7
A  0000000081D1   000000409FD1   0   textBox9
A  0000000081DA   000000409FDA   0   <Module>
A  0000000081E3   000000409FE3   0   GetPrinterA
A  0000000081EF   000000409FEF   0   AddTextTo_textRFID
A  000000008202   00000040A002   0   jobID
A  000000008208   00000040A008   0   PRINTER_CONTROL_PURGE
A  00000000821E   00000040A01E   0   PRINTER_CONTROL_RESUME
A  000000008235   00000040A035   0   PRINTER_STATUS_OFFLINE
A  00000000824C   00000040A04C   0   PRINTER_CONTROL_PAUSE
A  000000008262   00000040A062   0   MAX_RFID_DATA_SIZE
A  000000008275   00000040A075   0   SizeF
A  00000000827B   00000040A07B   0   AveragePPM
A  000000008286   00000040A086   0   System.IO
A  000000008290   00000040A090   0   PRINTER_ACCESS_ADMINISTER
A  0000000082AA   00000040A0AA   0   PRINTER_DEFAULTS
A  0000000082BB   00000040A0BB   0   PRINTER_CONTROL_SET_STATUS
```

Disassemblers

Disassemblers are used to view the low-level code of a program. Reading low-level code requires knowledge of assembly language. Analysis done with a disassembler gives information about the execution conditions and system interactions that a program will carry out when executed. However, the highlights when reading low-level code are when the program uses **Application Program Interface (API)** functions. The following screenshot shows a code snippet of a program module that uses the GetJob() API. This API is used to get information about the printer job, as shown here:

```
.text:10001010 ; int __cdecl GetPageCount(HANDLE hPrinter, DWORD JobId)
.text:10001010                 public GetPageCount
.text:10001010 GetPageCount   proc near            ; DATA XREF: .rdata:off_10002518↓o
.text:10001010
.text:10001010 var_C          = dword ptr -0Ch
.text:10001010 pcbNeeded      = dword ptr -8
.text:10001010 var_4          = dword ptr -4
.text:10001010 hPrinter       = dword ptr  8
.text:10001010 JobId          = dword ptr  0Ch
.text:10001010
.text:10001010                 push    ebp
.text:10001011                 mov     ebp, esp
.text:10001013                 sub     esp, 0Ch
.text:10001016                 mov     eax, ___security_cookie
.text:1000101B                 xor     eax, ebp
.text:1000101D                 mov     [ebp+var_4], eax
.text:10001020                 mov     eax, [ebp+hPrinter]
.text:10001023                 lea     ecx, [ebp+pcbNeeded]
.text:10001026                 push    esi
.text:10001027                 push    edi
.text:10001028                 push    ecx                 ; pcbNeeded
.text:10001029                 push    0                   ; cbBuf
.text:1000102B                 push    0                   ; pJob
.text:1000102D                 push    2                   ; Level
.text:1000102F                 push    [ebp+JobId]         ; JobId
.text:10001032                 mov     [ebp+var_C], eax
.text:10001035                 push    eax                 ; hPrinter
.text:10001036                 mov     [ebp+pcbNeeded], 0
.text:1000103D                 call    ds:GetJobW
.text:10001043                 mov     esi, [ebp+pcbNeeded]
.text:10001046                 push    esi                 ; Size
.text:10001047                 call    ds:malloc
.text:1000104D                 add     esp, 4
.text:10001050                 mov     edi, eax
.text:10001052                 lea     eax, [ebp+pcbNeeded]
.text:10001055                 push    eax                 ; pcbNeeded
.text:10001056                 push    esi                 ; cbBuf
.text:10001057                 push    edi                 ; pJob
.text:10001058                 push    2                   ; Level
.text:1000105A                 push    [ebp+JobId]         ; JobId
.text:1000105D                 push    [ebp+var_C]         ; hPrinter
.text:10001060                 call    ds:GetJobW
.text:10001066                 mov     ecx, [edi+28h]
```

Debuggers

Disassemblers can show the code tree, but the analyst can verify which branch the code flows to by using a debugger. A debugger does actual execution per line of code. The analyst can trace through codes such as loops, conditional statements, and API execution. Since debuggers are categorized under dynamic analysis and perform a step-wise execution of code, debugging is done in an enclosed environment. Various file types have different disassemblers. In a .NET compiled executable, it is best to instead disassemble the p-code and work out what each operator means.

Monitoring tools

Monitoring tools are used to monitor system behaviors regarding file, registry, memory, and network. These tools usually tap or hook on APIs or system calls, then log information such as newly created processes, updated files, new registry entries, and incoming SMB packets are generated by reporting tools.

Decompilers

Decompilers are similar to disassemblers. They are tools that attempt to restore the high-level source code of program unlike disassemblers that attempt to restore the low-level (assembly language) source code of a program.

These tools work hand in hand with each other. The logs generated from monitoring tools can be used to trace the actual code from the disassembled program. The same applies when debugging, where the analyst can see the overview of the low-level code from the disassembly, while being able to predict where to place breakpoints based on the monitoring tools' logs.

Malware handling

Readers of this book are required to take precautions when handling malware files. Here are some initial tips that can help us to prevent our host machine from being compromised:

- Do your analysis in an enclosed environment such as a separate computer or in a virtual machine.
- If network access is not required, cut it off.

- If internet access is not required, cut it off.
- When copying files manually, rename the file to a filename that doesn't execute. For example, rename `myfile.exe` to `myfile.foranalysis`.

Basic analysis lab setup

A typical setup would require a system that can run malware without it being compromised externally. However, there are instances that may require external information from the internet. For starters, we're going to mimic an environment of a home user. Our setup will, as much as possible, use free and open source tools. The following diagram shows an ideal analysis environment setup:

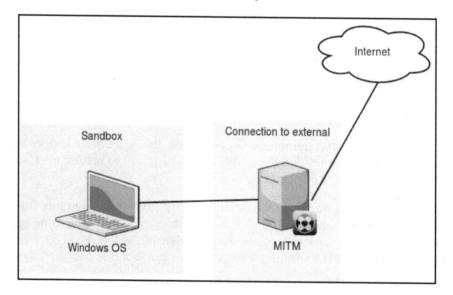

The sandbox environment here is where we do analysis of a file. **MITM**, mentioned on the right of the diagram, means the **man in the middle** environment, which is where we monitor incoming and outgoing network activities. The sandbox should be restored to its original state. This means that after every use, we should be able to revert or restore its unmodified state. The easiest way to set this up is to use virtualization technology, since it will then be easy to revert to cloned images. There are many virtualization programs to choose from, including VMware, VirtualBox, Virtual PC, and Bochs.

It should also be noted that there is software that can detect that it is being run, and doesn't like to be run in a virtualized environment. A physical machine setup may be needed for this case. Disk management software that can store images or re-image disks would be the best solution for us here. These programs include Fog, Clonezilla, DeepFreeze, and HDClone.

Our setup

In our setup, we will be using VirtualBox, which can be downloaded from `https://www.virtualbox.org/`. The Windows OS we will be using is Windows 7 32-bit, which can be downloaded from `https://developer.microsoft.com/en-us/microsoft-edge/tools/vms/`. In the following diagram, the system, which has an internet connection, is installed with two virtual machines, a guest sandbox and guest MITM:

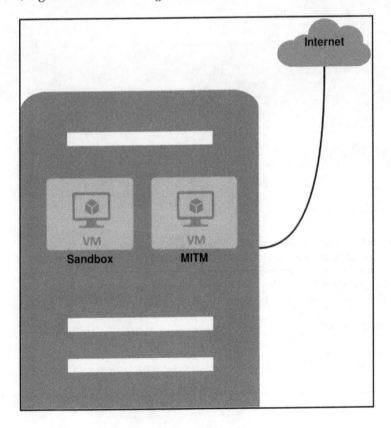

1. Download and install VirtualBox and run it. VirtualBox has installers for both Windows and Linux. Download the Windows 7 32-bit image, as shown here:

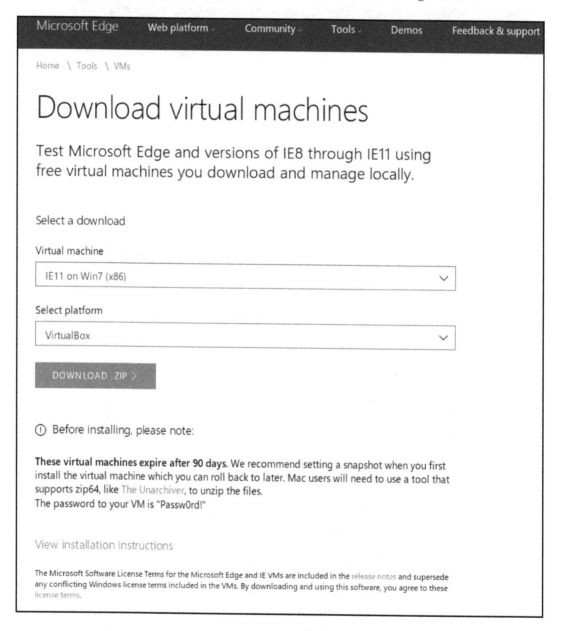

Microsoft Edge   Web platform   Community   Tools   Demos   Feedback & support

Home \ Tools \ VMs

Download virtual machines

Test Microsoft Edge and versions of IE8 through IE11 using free virtual machines you download and manage locally.

Select a download

Virtual machine

IE11 on Win7 (x86)   ⌄

Select platform

VirtualBox   ⌄

DOWNLOAD .ZIP >

ⓘ Before installing, please note:

These virtual machines expire after 90 days. We recommend setting a snapshot when you first install the virtual machine which you can roll back to later. Mac users will need to use a tool that supports zip64, like The Unarchiver, to unzip the files.
The password to your VM is "Passw0rd!"

View installation instructions

The Microsoft Software License Terms for the Microsoft Edge and IE VMs are included in the release notes and supersede any conflicting Windows license terms included in the VMs. By downloading and using this software, you agree to these license terms.

2. The image downloaded from the Microsoft website is zipped and should be extracted. In VirtualBox, click on **File|Import Appliance**. You should be shown a dialog where we can import the Windows 7 32-bit image.

3. Simply browse and select the OVA file that was extracted from the ZIP archive, then click on **Next**, as shown here:

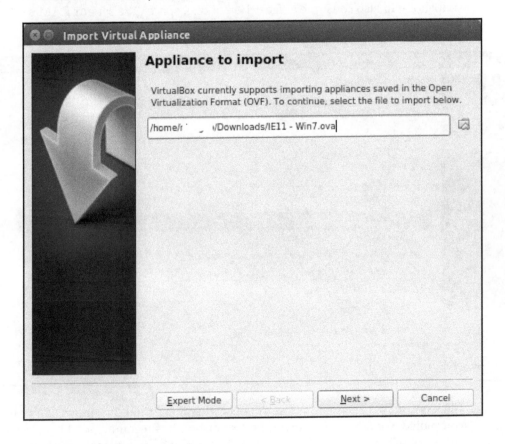

4. Before continuing, the settings can be changed. The default RAM is set to 4096 MB. The more RAM allocated and the higher the number of CPU cores set, the better performance will be noticed when running or debugging. However, the more RAM added, the same amount of disk space gets consumed when storing snapshots of the image. This means that if we allocated 1 GB of RAM, creating a snapshot will also consume at least 1GB of disk space. We set our RAM to 2048 MB, which would be a reasonable amount for us to work on:

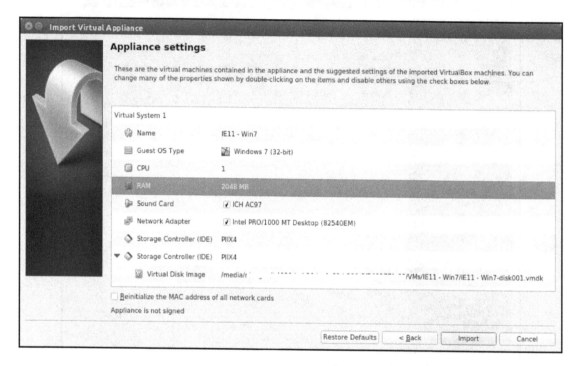

5. Click on **Import** and it should start generating the virtual disk image. Once it has completed, we need to create our first snapshot. It is recommended to create a snapshot in a powered-off state, since the amount of disk space consumed is minimal. Look for the **SnapShots** tab, then click on **Take**. Fill out the **Snapshot Name** and **Snapshot Description** fields, then click on the **OK** button. This quickly creates your first snapshot.

In a power-on state, the amount of RAM plus the amount of modified disk space in the virtual machine is equal to the total disk space that a snapshot will consume.

6. Click on **Start** to begin running the Windows 7 image. You should end up with the following window. In case it asks for a password, the default password is Passw0rd!:

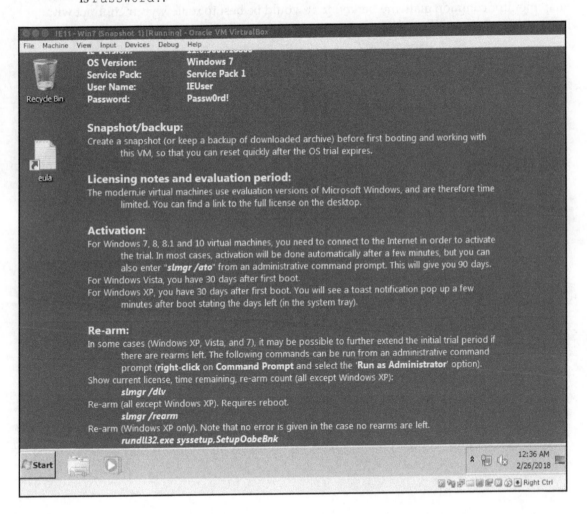

At this point, the network setup is set to NAT. This means that any network resources required by the virtual machine will use the host computer's IP address. The IP address of the virtual machine is taken from the VirtualBox's virtual DHCP service. Remember that any network communication in the virtual machine makes use of the host computer's IP address.

Since we can't prevent a certain malware from sending out information to the web in order to return information back to our virtual machine, it is important to note that some ISPs may monitor common malware behavior. It would be best to review your contract with them and make a call if needed.

Most of our reverse engineering deals with malware and, as of the time of writing, attackers usually target Windows systems. Our setup uses Microsoft Windows 7 32-bit. Feel free to use other versions. We recommend installing the 32-bit version of Microsoft Windows, as it will be easier to track virtual and physical addresses later on during low-level debugging.

Samples

We will be building our own programs to validate and understand how the low-level code behaves and what it looks like. The following list outlines the software we will be using to build our programs:

- Dev C++ (http://www.bloodshed.net/devcpp.htm)
- Visual Studio C++ (https://www.visualstudio.com/downloads/)
- MASM32 (http://www.masm32.com/)

If you are interested in malware, the samples can be obtained from the following sites:

- https://github.com/PacktPublishing/Mastering-Reverse-Engineering
- https://github.com/ytisf/theZoo

Summary

Reverse engineering has been around for years and has been a useful technique to understand how things work. In the software industry, reverse engineering helps validate and fix code flow and structures. The information from such tasks can improve the security of various aspects of software, network infrastructure, and human awareness. As a core skill requirement for the anti-malware industry, reverse engineering helps create detection and remediation information; the same information that is used to build safeguards for an institution's servers. It is also used by authorities and forensic experts to hunt down syndicates.

There are basic steps that help build reverse engineering information. Once an analyst has approval from the original author to carry out reverse engineering, they can begin with static analysis, dynamic analysis, and then low-level analysis. This is then followed by reporting the overview and details about the software.

When doing analysis, various types of tools are used, including static analysis tools, disassemblers, decompilers, debuggers, and system monitoring tools. When doing reverse engineering on malware, it is best to use these tools in an environment that has limited or no access to the network you use for personal purposes or work. This should prevent your infrastructure from being compromised. Malware should be handled properly, and we listed a couple of ways to prevent accidental double-clicks.

Malware analysis nonetheless requires the internet to get further information on how the malware works and what it does. There may be some legal issues that require you to consult the laws of your country and the policies of your local ISP, to ensure that you are not violating any of them.

The core requirement for the setup of an analysis lab is that the target operating system can be reverted back to its unmodified state.

Malware samples can be obtained from the following link: `https://github.com/PacktPublishing/Mastering-Reverse-Engineering/tree/master/tools`. These samples will be used throughout this book.

Now that we have our basic setup, let's embark on our journey through reverse engineering.

Identification and Extraction of Hidden Components

2

Today, the most common use for reverse engineering is in targeting malware. Like any other software, malware has its installation process. The difference is that it does not ask for the user's permission to install. Malware does not even install in the `Program files` folder where other legitimate applications are installed. Rather, it tends to install its malware file in folders that are not commonly entered by the user, making it hidden from being noticed. However, some malware shows up noticed and generates copies of itself in almost all noticeable folders such as the desktop. Its purpose is to get its copies executed by users, be it by accidental double-click or by curiosity. This is what we usually call malware persistence.

Persistence is when malware consistently runs in the background. In this chapter, we will be pointing out general techniques used by malware to become persistent. We will also explain common locations where malware files are stored. Major behaviors of malware and some tools that are capable of identifying how the malware installs itself in the system will also be shown. Understanding how malware is delivered will definitely help a reverse engineer explain how the attacker was able to compromise the system.

In this chapter we will learn about the following:

- The basics of the operating system environment
- Typical malware behavior:
    - Malware delivery
    - Malware persistence
    - Malware payload
- Tools used to identify hidden components

Technical requirements

The discussions will use the Windows environment. We will be using the virtual machine setup we created in the previous *chapter*. In addition, you'll need to download and install this software: the SysInternals suite (`https://docs.microsoft.com/en-us/sysinternals/downloads/sysinternals-suite`).

The operating system environment

Doing reverse engineering requires the analyst to understand where the software being reversed is being run. The major parts that software requires in order to work in an operating system are the memory and the filesystem. In Windows operating systems, besides the memory and the filesystem, Microsoft introduced the registry system, which is actually stored in protected files called registry hives.

The filesystem

The filesystem is where data is stored directly to the physical disk drive. These filesystems manage how files and directories are stored in the disk. Various disk filesystems have their own variation of efficiently reading and writing data.

There are different disk filesystems such as `FAT`, `NTFS`, `ex2`, `ex3`, `XFS`, and `APFS`. Common filesystems used by Windows are `FAT32` and `NTFS`. Stored in the filesystem is information about the directory paths and files. It includes the filename, size of the file, date stamps, and permissions.

The following screenshot shows the information stored in the filesystem about `bfsvc.exe`:

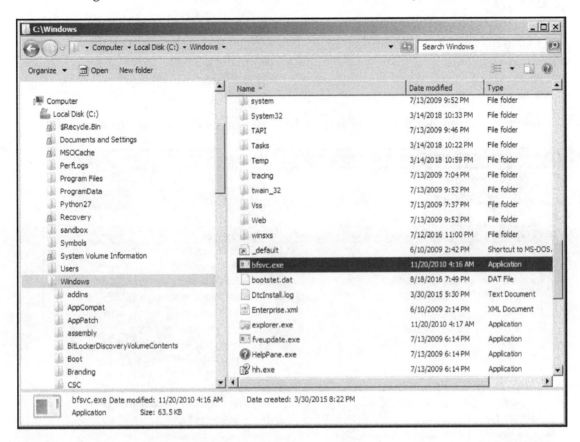

In previous MacOS X versions, file information and data are stored in resource forks. Resource forks are actually deprecated but backward compatibility still exists on recent versions of MacOS. A file has two forks stored in the filesystem, the data fork and the resource fork. The data fork contains unstructured data, while the resource fork contains structured data. The resource fork contains information such as the executable machine code, icons, shape of an alert box, string used in the file, and so forth. For instance, if you wanted to back up a Mac application by simply moving it to a Windows hard drive then moving it back, the Mac application will no longer open. While transferring, only the file gets transferred but the resource fork gets stripped out in the process. Simple copy tools don't respect the forks. Instead, Mac developers developed tools to synchronize files to and from external disks.

Memory

When a Windows executable file executes, the system allocates a memory space, reads the executable file from the disk, writes it at predefined sections in the allocated memory, then allows the code to execute from there. This block of memory is called a process block and is linked to other process blocks. Basically, every program that executes consumes a memory space as a process.

The following screenshot shows a Windows Task Manager's view of the list of processes:

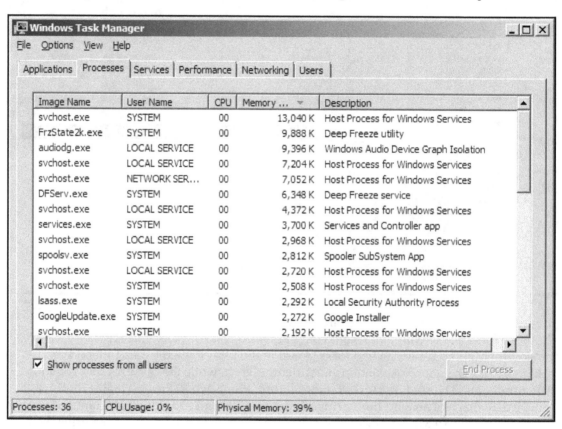

The registry system

In Windows, the registry is a common database that contains system-wide configuration and application settings. Examples of stored information in the registry are as follows:

- Associated programs that execute specific files:
    - DOCX files are associated with Microsoft Word
    - PDF files are associated with Adobe Reader
- Associated icons to specific files and folders
- Software settings:
    - Uninstall configuration
    - Update sites
    - Ports used
    - Product IDs
- User and group profiles
- Printer setup:
    - Default printer
    - Driver names
- Designated drivers for specific services

The registry is stored in hive files. The list of hive files is also found in the registry itself, as can be seen in the following screenshot:

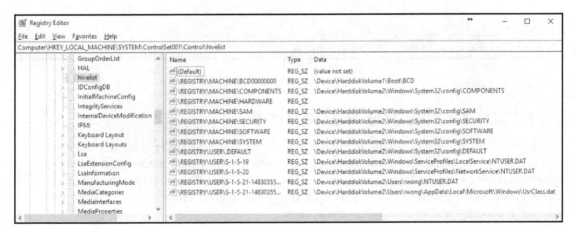

Writing and reading information from the registry requires using Windows registry APIs. The registry can be viewed visually using the Registry Editor. Entries in the right pane of the Registry Editor are the registry keys. On the left pane, the registry values are found under the **Name** column, as can be seen in the following screenshot:

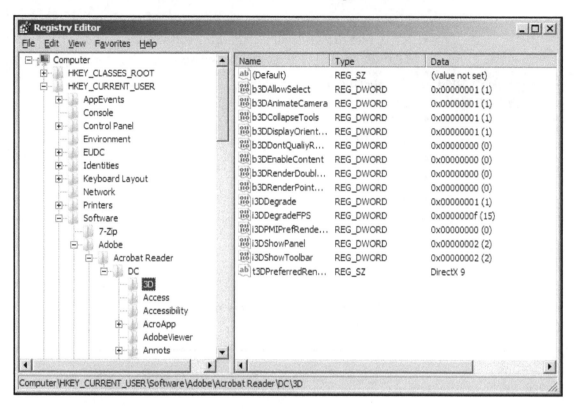

Typical malware behavior

Malware is simply defined as malicious software. You'd expect bad things to happen to your system environment once malware has entered. Once typical malware enters the system, it does two basic things: installs itself and does its evil work. With the intent of forcing itself to be installed in the system malware does not need to notify the user at all. Instead, it directly makes changes to the system.

Persistence

One of the changes malware makes in the system is to make itself resident. Malware persistence means that the malware will still be running in background and, as much as possible, all the time. For example, malware gets executed after every boot-up of the system, or malware gets executed at a certain time of the day. The most common way for malware to achieve persistence is to drop a copy of itself in some folder in the system and make an entry in the registry.

The following view of the registry editor shows a registry entry by the `GlobeImposter` ransomware:

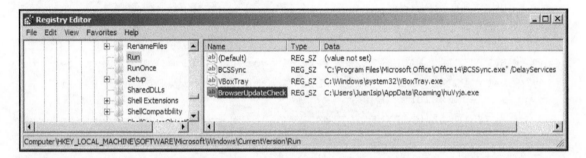

Any entries made under the registry key `HKEY_LOCAL_MACHINE\SOFTWARE\Microsoft\Windows\CurrentVersion\Run` are expected to run every time Windows starts. In this case, the `GlobeImposter` ransomware's executable file stored in `C:\Users\JuanIsip\AppData\Roaming\huVyja.exe` becomes persistent. `BrowserUpdateCheck` is the registry value, while the path is the registry data. What matters under this registry key are the paths, regardless of the registry value name.

There are several areas in the registry that can trigger the execution of a malware executable file.

Run keys

Entering a file path in the registry data under these registry keys will trigger execution when Windows starts, as can be seen in the following registry path for the Windows 64-bit versions

- `HKEY_LOCAL_MACHINE\Software\Microsoft\Windows\CurrentVersion\Run`
- `HKEY_LOCAL_MACHINE\Software\Microsoft\Windows\CurrentVersion\RunOnce`
- `HKEY_LOCAL_MACHINE\Software\Microsoft\Windows\CurrentVersion\RunOnceEx`
- `HKEY_LOCAL_MACHINE\Software\Microsoft\Windows\CurrentVersion\RunServices`
- `HKEY_LOCAL_MACHINE\Software\Microsoft\Windows\N\RunServicesOnce`
- `HKEY_LOCAL_MACHINE\Software\Microsoft\Windows\CurrentVersion\Policies\Explorer\Run`
- `HKEY_LOCAL_MACHINE\SOFTWARE\Wow6432Node\Windows\CurrentVersion\Run`

Programs that are listed under these registry keys will trigger execution when the current user logs in, as can be seen in the following registry path:

- `HKEY_CURRENT_USER\Software\Microsoft\Windows\CurrentVersion\Run`
- `HKEY_CURRENT_USER\Software\Microsoft\Windows\CurrentVersion\RunOnce`
- `HKEY_CURRENT_USER\Software\Microsoft\Windows\CurrentVersion\RunOnceEx`
- `HKEY_LOCAL_MACHINE\Software\Microsoft\Windows\CurrentVersion\RunServices`
- `HKEY_LOCAL_MACHINE\Software\Microsoft\Windows\CurrentVersion\RunServicesOnce`
- `HKEY_CURRENT_USER\Software\Microsoft\Windows NT\CurrentVersion\Windows\Run`

The keys names containing `Once` will have the listed programs that run only once. The malware may still persist if it keeps on placing its own file path under the `RunOnce`, `RunOnceEx` or `RunServicesOnce` keys.

Load and Run values

The following registry values, under their respective registry key, will trigger execution when any user logs in:

- HKEY_CURRENT_USER\Software\Microsoft\Windows NT\CurrentVersion\Windows
    - Load = <file path>
    - Run = <file path>

BootExecute value

- HKEY_LOCAL_MACHINE\SYSTEM\ControlSetXXX\Control\Session Manager
    - XXX in ControlSetXXX is a three digit number usually ControlSet001, ControlSet002, or ControlSet003.
    - BootExecute = <file path>
        - The default value of BootExecute is autocheck autochk *

Winlogon key

- HKEY_LOCAL_MACHINE\SOFTWARE\Microsoft\Windows NT\CurrentVersion\Winlogon
    - Activities under this registry key are executed during Windows logon
    - UserInit = <file path>
        - The default value of Userinit is C:\Windows\system32\userinit.exe
    - Notify = <dll file path>
        - Notify is not set by default. It is expected to be a dynamic link library file
    - Shell = <exe file path>
        - The default value of Shell is explorer.exe
- HKEY_CURRENT_USER\SOFTWARE\Microsoft\Windows NT\CurrentVersion\Winlogon
    - Shell = <exe file path>
        - The default value of Shell is explorer.exe

Policy scripts keys

- `HKEY_LOCAL_MACHINE\Software\Microsoft\Windows\CurrentVersion\Group Policy\Scripts\Shutdown\0\N`
    - where `N` is a number starting from `0`. Multiple scripts or executables can be run during the shutdown sequence
    - `Script = [file path of executable file or script]`
- `HKEY_LOCAL_MACHINE\Software\Microsoft\Windows\CurrentVersion\Group Policy\Scripts\Startup\0\N`
    - This is where `N` is a number starting from `0`. Multiple scripts or executables can be run during the startup sequence.
    - `Script = [file path of executable file or script]`
- `HKEY_CURRENT_USER\Software\Microsoft\Windows\CurrentVersion\Group Policy\Scripts\Logon\0\N`
    - This is where `N` is a number starting from `0`. Multiple scripts or executables can be run when a user logs off.
    - `Script = [file path of executable file or script]`
- `HKEY_CURRENT_USER\Software\Microsoft\Windows\CurrentVersion\Group Policy\Scripts\Logoff\0\N`
    - where N is a number starting from `0`. Multiple scripts or executables can be run when a user logs off
    - `Script = [file path of executable file or script]`

AppInit_DLLs values

- `HKEY_LOCAL_MACHINE\SOFTWARE\Microsoft\Windows NT\CurrentVersion\Windows`
    - `AppInit_DLLs = [a list of DLLs]`
        - The list of DLLs are delimited by a comma or space
    - `LoadAppInit_DLLs = [1 or 0]`
        - Here, `1` means enabled, and `0` means disabled

Services keys

- HKEY_LOCAL_MACHINE\SYSTEM\CurrentControlSet\Services\[Service Name]
    - This is where ServiceName is the name of the service
    - ImagePath = [sys/dll file path]
    - Loads a system file (.sys) or a library file (.dll), which is the driver executable
    - The service triggers depending on the value of the start:
        - 0 (SERVICE_BOOT_START triggers when OS is being loaded)
        - 1 (SERVICE_SYSTEM_START triggers when OS is being initialized)
        - 2 (SERVICE_AUTO_START triggers when service manager starts.)
        - 3 (SERVICE_DEMAND_START triggers when it is manually started)
        - 4 (SERVICE_DISABLED. The service is disabled from triggering)

File associations

- HKEY_CLASSES_ROOT or in HKEY_LOCAL_MACHINE\SOFTWARE\Classes\[File type or extension name]\shell\open\command
    - The entry in the (Default) registry value executes files that are described by [File type or extension name].
    - The following code shows the associated entry for executable files or .EXE files:
        - <show image of exefile entry in HKEY_LOCAL_MACHINE\SOFTWARE\Classes\exefile\shell\open\command>

- The (Default) value contains "%1" %*. %1 pertains to the executable being run as is, while %* pertains to the command-line arguments. Persistence is implemented by malware by appending its own executable. For example, the (Default) value is set to malware.exe "%1" %*. As a result, malware.exe runs and uses %1 (the executable being run) and %* as its arguments. malware.exe is then responsible for running %1 with its %*.

Startup values

The startup registry value contains the path to a folder which contains files that are executed after the user has logged in. The default folder location is at %APPDATA%\Microsoft\Windows\Start Menu\Programs\Startup.

- HKEY_CURRENT_USER\Software\Microsoft\Windows\CurrentVersion\Explorer\Shell Folders
    - Startup = [startup folder path]
- HKEY_CURRENT_USER\Software\Microsoft\Windows\CurrentVersion\Explorer\User Shell Folders
    - Startup = [startup folder path]
- HKEY_LOCAL_MACHINE\SOFTWARE\Microsoft\Windows\CurrentVersion\Explorer\User Shell Folders
    - Common Startup = [startup folder path]
- HKEY_LOCAL_MACHINE\SOFTWARE\Microsoft\Windows\CurrentVersion\Explorer\Shell Folders
    - Common Startup = [startup folder path]

The Image File Execution Options key

File paths set in the debugger of the `Image File Execution Options` key is run when the process is to be debugged or is run with the `CreateProcess` API:

- `HKEY_LOCAL_MACHINE\Software\Microsoft\Windows NT\CurrentVersion\Image File Execution Options\[Process Name]`
    - `Debugger = [executable file]`
    - `[Process Name]` pertains to the filename of the running executable
    - This persistence only triggers when there is a need for `[Process Name]` to invoke a debugger

Browser Helper Objects key

- `HKEY_LOCAL_MACHINE\Software\Microsoft\Windows\CurrentVersion\Explorer\Browser Helper Objects\[CLSID]`
    - Having the `CLSID` as a subkey simply means that it is installed and enabled as an Internet Explorer BHO
    - The `CLSID` is registered under the `HKEY_CLASSES_ROOT\CLSID\[CLSID]\InprocServer32` key
        - The `(Default)` value points to the DLL file associated with the BHO
    - The DLL file is loaded every time Internet Explorer is opened

Besides registry entries, an executable can also be triggered by schedule using the task scheduler or `cron` jobs. An executable or a script can be triggered even at certain conditions. Take, for example, the following screenshot of a Windows Task scheduler:

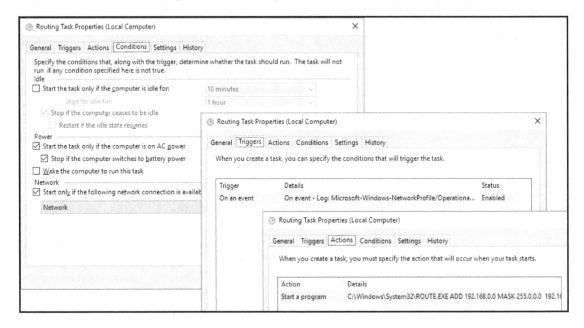

There are many more ways in which malware gets persistence other than those which have been listed previously. These are the challenges that a reverse engineer learns as they encounter new techniques.

Malware delivery

In the software security industry, the activity of an attacker to spread and compromise a system is called a malware campaign. There are various ways that malware gets into a system. The most common way that these malware executable files are delivered is through an email attachment sent to its target user(s). As communication technology changes, the logistics that these campaigns implement adapt to whatever technology there is. This includes looking for vulnerabilities in the target system and penetrating it with exploits.

Email

Malware sent as an email delivery would require the recipient to open the attached file. The email is crafted in such a way that the recipient becomes curious about opening the attachment. These unsolicited emails that are spread to many addresses are called email spam. They usually contain a subject and a message body that uses social engineering to get the recipient's attention and eventually have them execute the malware. An example of this can be seen in the following screenshot:

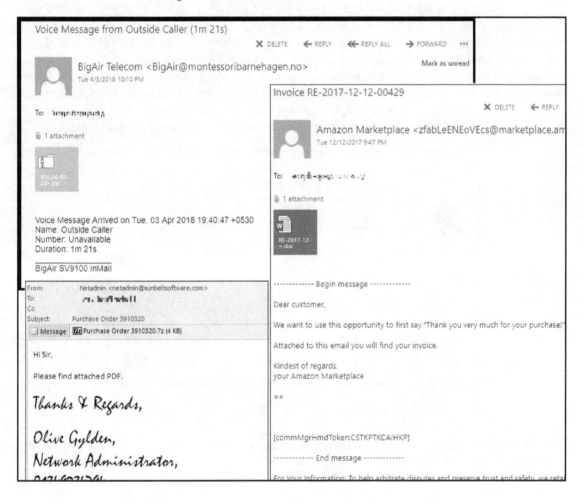

Activities that deceive a person or a group of people to do an activity is called *social engineering*. With poor security awareness, users may fall into this famous proverbial trap: *curiosity killed the cat*.

Instant messenger

Besides email, there is what we call SPIM or Instant Messaging Spam. This is spam sent to instant messaging such as Facebook, Skype, and Yahoo Messenger applications. This also includes public or private messages spimmed using Twitter, Facebook, and other social networking services. The messages usually contain a link to a compromised site containing malware or spyware. Some services that support file transfers are abused by malware spim. Today, these social networking services have implemented back-end security to mitigate SPIM. However, at the time of writing, there are still a few incidents of malware spreading through instant messaging. An example of this can be seen in the following screenshot:

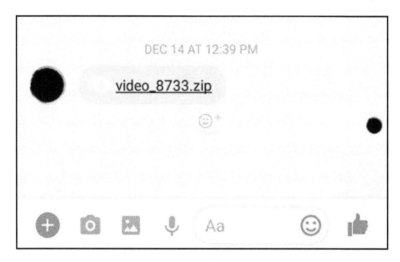

Image from John Patrick Lita from CSPCert.ph

The previous screenshot is a private message from Facebook's instant messenger containing a ZIP file that actually contains a malware file.

The computer network

It is a necessity today that a computer has to be connected to a network so users can access resources from each other. With each computer linked to another whether it is LAN (Local Area Network) or WAN (Wide Area Network), file sharing protocols are also open for attackers to abuse. Malware can attempt to drop copies of itself to file shares. However, the malware depends on the user at the remote end running the malware file from the file share. These kinds of malware are called network worms.

To list down the shared folders in Windows, you can use the `net share` command, as can be seen in the following screenshot:

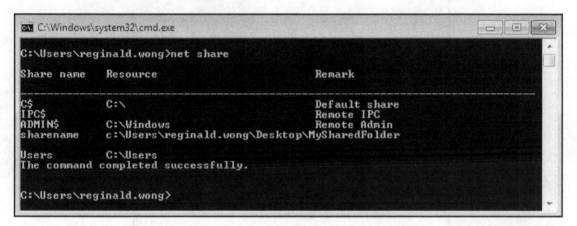

As an analyst, we can make recommendations on what to do with these shared folders. We can say that these shares either be removed, if not used. We can also have these folders reviewed for the permissions of who can access it and what type of permissions (like read and write permissions) certain users can have. That way, we are helping secure the network from getting infested by network worms.

Media storage

Network administrators are very restrictive when it comes to using thumb drives. The primary reason is that external storage devices, such as USB thumb drives, CDs, DVDs, external hard drives, and even smartphones are all media in which malware can store itself. Once a storage device gets mounted to a computer, it serves like a regular drive. Malware can simply drop copies of itself to these storage drives. Similar to network worms, these are worms that depend on the user to run the malware. But with the Windows Autorun feature turned on, malware may execute once the drive is mounted, as can be seen in the following screenshot:

The previous image is the default dialog encountered when inserting a CD drive containing setup software.

The `autorun.inf` file in the root of a drive contains information on which file to automatically execute. This is used by software installers stored in CDs so that, when the disk is inserted, it automatically runs the setup program. This is abused by malware by doing these steps:

1. Dropping a copy of its malware file in removable drives
2. Along with its dropped copy, it generates an `autorun.inf` file that points to the dropped executable file, as can be seen in the following example:

```
[autorun]
open=VBoxWindowsAdditions.exe
icon=VBoxWindowsAdditions.exe
label=VirtualBox Guest Additions
```

The `autorun.inf` for the VirtualBox setup autoplay dialog shown previously contains the text as shown in the previous screenshot. The `open` property contains the executable to be run.

Exploits and compromised websites

Exploits are also categorized under malware. Exploits are crafted to compromise specific vulnerabilities of software or network services. These are usually in the form of binary data. Exploits take advantage of vulnerability, thereby causing the target software or service to behave in such a manner that the attacker intends it should behave. Usually, the attacker intends to gain control over the target system or simply take it down.

Once an attacker identifies vulnerabilities on its target, an exploit is crafted containing code that would download malware that can give the attacker more access. This concept was used to develop exploit kits. Exploit kits are a set of known vulnerability scanners and known exploits packaged as a toolkit.

The following diagram gives an example:

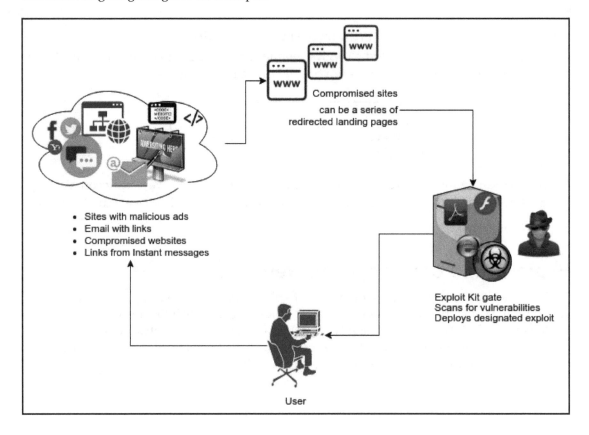

In a malware campaign, social engineering is used to lure users to visit links that are actually compromised. Usually, the compromised sites were manually hacked and have been injected with a hidden script that redirects to another website. The malicious links are spammed to email messages, instant messaging, and social networking sites. Visiting legitimate sites that are compromised with malicious advertisements also counts as bait. These sites include software or media piracy sites, the dark web, or even pornographic sites. Once the user clicks the link, typically, the site redirects to another compromised site, and to another, until it reaches the exploit kit landing gate page. From the user's internet browser, the exploit kit gate gathers information on the machine, such as software versions, and then determines whether or not the software is known to be vulnerable. It then delivers all exploits applicable to the vulnerable software. The exploits typically contain code that will download and execute malware. As a result, the unaware user gets a compromised system.

Software piracy

Hacking tools, pirated software, serial generating tools, and pirated media files are just some of the distributed software where malware or adware may be included. For example, the setup file of the installer of pirated software may be downloading malware and installing it in the background without asking the user for permission.

Malware file properties

The initial behavior of common malware is to drop a copy of itself, drop its malware component embedded in it, or download its malware component. It creates the dropped files which are usually found in these folders:

- The Windows System folder: `C:\Windows\System32`
- The Windows folder: `C:\Windows`
- The user profile folder: `C:\Users\[username]`
- The Appdata folder: `C:\Users\[username]\AppData\Roaming`
- The recycle bin folder: `C:\$Recycle.Bin`
- The desktop folder: `C:\Users\[username]\Desktop`
- The temporary folder: `C:\Users\[username]\AppData\Local\Temp`

As part of its social engineering, another cheap technique is to change the icon of a malware file to something that would lure the user to open it, for example, folder icons, Microsoft Office icons, or Adobe PDF icons. It also uses file names that are deceiving, such as the words *INVOICE, New Folder, Scandal, Expose, Pamela, Confidential,* and so on. The following screenshot gives examples of actual malware that mimics known documents:

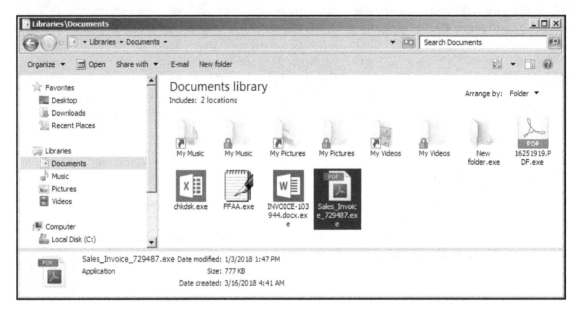

Notice that highlighting the fake PDF file shows that it is actually an application.

Payload – the evil within

The attacker develops malware for a purpose. This is typically to cause harm to the target, maybe because of hate, for fun, for monetary or, probably, political reasons. Here are some typical malware payloads that were seen in the wild:

- Encrypting files for ransom
- Deleting all files
- Formatting drives
- Gaining full access to the system and the network

- Stealing accounts and passwords
- Stealing documents, images, and videos
- Changing specific configuration and settings
- Turning the computer into a proxy server
- Installing `cryptocoin` miners
- Continuously opening websites - ad or porn sites
- Installing more malware
- Installing adware

One of the conclusions that a reverse engineer includes in the report is the payload. This determines what malware actually does to the machine other than getting installed.

Tools

Identifying the registry entry, files dropped, and running processes that are related to the malware requires tools. There are existing tools that we can use to extract these objects. There are two analysis events we should consider: analysis after the malware has been executed and analysis before the malware executes. Since our aim for this chapter is to extract components, we will discuss the tools that can help us find suspected files. Analysis tools that are used after we have extracted our suspected malware will be discussed in further chapters.

When a system has already been compromised, the analyst would need to use tools that can identify suspected files. Each suspected file will be analysed further. To start off, we can identify it based on persistence.

1. List down all processes and their respective file information
2. From the list of known registry persistence paths, look for entries containing the file paths
3. Extract the suspected files

The above steps may require pre-existing tools from Microsoft Windows, such as:

- The Registry Editor (regedit/regedt32) to search the registry
- You can also use the command line for accessing the registry reg.exe, as seen in the following screenshot:

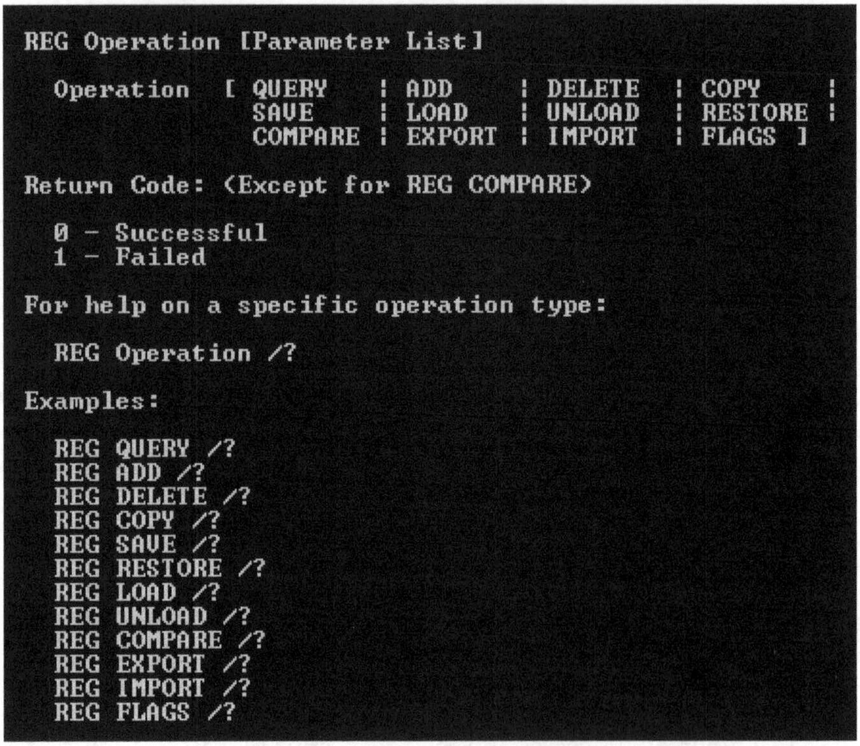

```
REG Operation [Parameter List]

    Operation  [ QUERY    : ADD      : DELETE   : COPY     :
                 SAVE      : LOAD     : UNLOAD   : RESTORE  :
                 COMPARE   : EXPORT   : IMPORT   : FLAGS ]

Return Code: <Except for REG COMPARE>

  0 - Successful
  1 - Failed

For help on a specific operation type:

  REG Operation /?

Examples:

  REG QUERY /?
  REG ADD /?
  REG DELETE /?
  REG COPY /?
  REG SAVE /?
  REG RESTORE /?
  REG LOAD /?
  REG UNLOAD /?
  REG COMPARE /?
  REG EXPORT /?
  REG IMPORT /?
  REG FLAGS /?
```

- Task manager (taskmgr) to list down the processes
- Windows Explorer (explorer) or Command prompt (cmd) to traverse directories and retrieve the files.

However, there are also third-party tools that we can use that can help us list down suspected files. Here are a few we will briefly discuss:

- Autoruns
- Process explorer

Autoruns

The startup list we saw earlier in this chapter, covers registry entries, schedule jobs, and file location. The bottom line is that this tool covers all of those, including other areas we have not discussed, such as Microsoft Office add-ons, codecs, and printer monitors, as can be seen in the following screenshot:

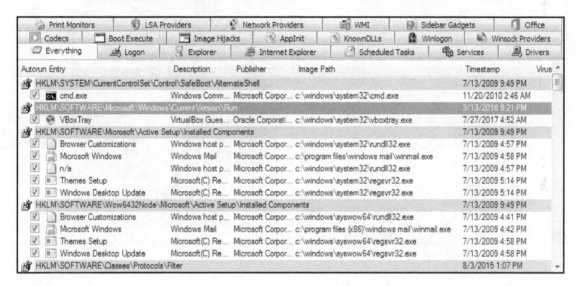

There are 32- and 64-bit versions of the autoruns tool. The screenshot above shows all possible triggers for an executable which was based on the research of the SysInternals' authors Mark Russinovich and Bryce Cogswell. The screenshot also categorizes each autorun entry, shows the description of each entry, and indicates the file path related to the entry.

As for reverse engineers, the identification of suspected files can be determined by having knowledge of what files are common to the startup prior to the system getting compromised. Continuous practice and experience will make the reverse engineer easily identify which are good or suspected executable files.

The Process explorer

In essence, the `Process` explorer tool is similar to the Task Manager, as demonstrated in the following screenshot:

Process	CPU	Private Bytes	Working Set	PID	Description	Company Name
System Idle Process	97.03	0 K	24 K	0		
System	0.03	33,008 K	7,224 K	4		
Interrupts	0.38	0 K	0 K	n/a	Hardware Interrupts and DPCs	
smss.exe		428 K	1,084 K	268	Windows Session Manager	Microsoft Corporation
csrss.exe	< 0.01	2,856 K	4,664 K	340	Client Server Runtime Process	Microsoft Corporation
wininit.exe		1,456 K	4,272 K	380	Windows Start-Up Application	Microsoft Corporation
services.exe		4,700 K	8,660 K	484	Services and Controller app	Microsoft Corporation
svchost.exe		4,188 K	9,012 K	604	Host Process for Windows S...	Microsoft Corporation
WmiPrvSE.exe		2,592 K	6,240 K	2296	WMI Provider Host	Microsoft Corporation
WmiPrvSE.exe		3,636 K	7,016 K	2424	WMI Provider Host	Microsoft Corporation
VBoxService.exe		3,280 K	5,960 K	664	VirtualBox Guest Additions S...	Oracle Corporation
svchost.exe		3,596 K	7,216 K	728	Host Process for Windows S...	Microsoft Corporation
svchost.exe	0.06	14,852 K	20,408 K	800	Host Process for Windows S...	Microsoft Corporation
svchost.exe	< 0.01	6,656 K	16,784 K	868	Host Process for Windows S...	Microsoft Corporation
dwm.exe		1,740 K	5,760 K	1396	Desktop Window Manager	Microsoft Corporation
svchost.exe	0.01	19,356 K	32,804 K	908	Host Process for Windows S...	Microsoft Corporation
svchost.exe	< 0.01	8,812 K	15,752 K	112	Host Process for Windows S...	Microsoft Corporation
svchost.exe	< 0.01	11,776 K	14,036 K	316	Host Process for Windows S...	Microsoft Corporation
spoolsv.exe		6,192 K	11,540 K	1072	Spooler SubSystem App	Microsoft Corporation
svchost.exe		13,168 K	15,380 K	1100	Host Process for Windows S...	Microsoft Corporation
armsvc.exe	< 0.01	1,152 K	3,752 K	1208	Adobe Acrobat Update Servi...	Adobe Systems Incorporated
taskhost.exe		3,760 K	7,672 K	1300	Host Process for Windows T...	Microsoft Corporation
svchost.exe	0.03	7,168 K	14,096 K	1384	Host Process for Windows S...	Microsoft Corporation
SearchIndexer.exe		20,572 K	19,084 K	932	Microsoft Windows Search I...	Microsoft Corporation
wmpnetwk.exe	< 0.01	11,276 K	11,504 K	1244	Windows Media Player Netw...	Microsoft Corporation
svchost.exe	0.81	10,508 K	14,152 K	2324	Host Process for Windows S...	Microsoft Corporation
taskhost.exe		6,368 K	12,676 K	2936	Host Process for Windows T...	Microsoft Corporation
lsass.exe		4,044 K	10,796 K	500	Local Security Authority Proc...	Microsoft Corporation

CPU Usage: 2.97%   Commit Charge: 14.85%   Processes: 35   Physical Usage: 27.37%

The advantage of this tool is that it can show more information about the process itself, such as how it was run, including the parameters used, and even its autostart location, as can be seen in the following example:

In addition, the process explorer has tools to send it VirusTotal identification, shows a list of strings identified from its image and the threads associated with it. From a reverser's point of view, the highly used information here is the command-line usage, and autostart location. VirusTotal is an online service that scans a submitted file or URL using multiple security software, as demonstrated in the following screenshot:

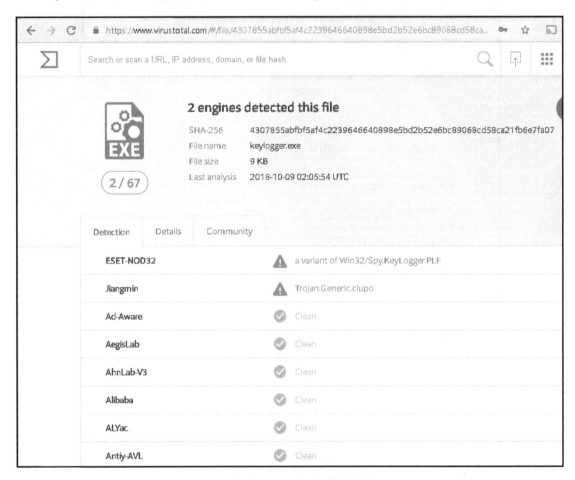

The results are not conclusive, but it gives the submitter an idea about the file's credibility of being legit software or malware.

Summary

In the first chapter, we learned about reverse engineering and its importance when analyzing malware. To begin with our reverse engineering adventures, we have to learn the system we are analyzing. We discussed the three main areas in the Windows operating system environment: memory, disk, and the registry. In this chapter, we aimed to find malware from a compromised Windows system by extracting suspected files. To do that, we listed common startup areas in the system that we can search into. These areas include the registry, task schedules, and startup folder.

We learned that typical malware behaves by installing itself and runnng code that harms the system. Malware installs itself basically for persistence which results in the malware file triggering most of the time the system is online. We then listed a few behaviors as to why malware was called malicious. This malicious code consisted of anything to do with crime entailing monetary or political gain, such as ransom and backdoor access.

We ended this chapter by listing tools we can use to easily identify the suspected files. We first introduced pre-existing Windows tools such as the Registry editor, Task Manager and the Task Scheduler. We followed these with two more tools from SysInternals: autoruns and Process explorer. With these tools at hand, we should be able to list down our suspected files. However, as with any other tasks, we will be able to master identification faster with practice and experience.

Further reading

- https://msdn.microsoft.com/en-us/library/windows/desktop/ms724871(v=vs.85).aspx
- https://medium.com/@johnpaticklita/cryptomalware-spreads-on-facebook-79a299590116

The Low-Level Language

3

The main piece of knowledge required in advance for any reverse engineer is assembly language. Understanding assembly language is like learning the ABCs of reversing. It may look hard at first, but eventually it will become like a muscle memory. Assembly language is the language that is used to communicate with the machine. The source code of a program can be understood by humans but not by the machine. The source code has to be compiled down to its assembly language code form for the machine to understand it.

But, as humans, what if the source code is not available? Our only way to understand what a program does is to read its assembly codes. In a way, what we are building here is a way to turn an assembly language code back to the source code. That would be why this is called reversing.

We will provide a brief introduction to assembly language, focusing on the x86 Intel architecture. So, why x86? There are a lot of architectures out there, such as 8080, ARM, MIPS, PowerPC, and SPARC, but we are focusing on Intel x86 as it is the most popular and widely used architecture today.

In this chapter, we will get to learn the basics of assembly language. We will start by reviewing binary numbers, followed by using assembly language instructions to implement binary arithmetic, we will then learn how to compile our own low-level program, and, finally, how to debug a program.

This chapter has been divided into sections. We will learn about the following:

- Binary numbers, bases, and the ASCII table
- x86 architecture
- Assembly language instructions
- Tools used to edit and compile an assembly-language source code
- Debugging tools
- Exceptions and error handling
- Windows APIs
- High-level language constructs

We will include instructions to set up and develop your assembly language code. This also comes with exercises that may help to inspire you to develop programs using assembly language.

Technical requirements

It is best, but not required, that the reader has some background knowledge of any programming language. Having a programming background will help the reader to understand assembly language more quickly. There are references given at the end of this chapter that the reader can use for further programming development and research not provided in this book.

Some tools that we will use here include the following:

- Binary editors, such as HxD Editor or HIEW (Hacker's View)
- Text editors, such as Notepad++

Binary numbers

Computers were designed to electronically process and store data using signals. A signal is like an on/off switch, where both the "on" and "off" positions can be denoted by the numbers "1" and "0" respectively. These two numbers are what we call binary numbers. The next section will discuss how binary numbers are used and how this relates to other number bases.

Bases

The place value of a digit in a number determines its value at that position. In the standard decimal numbers, the value of a place is ten times the value of the place on its right. The decimal number system is also called base-10, which is composed of digits from 0 to 9.

Let's say that position 1 is at the right-most digit of the whole number, as follows:

```
2018
Place value at position 1 is 1 multiplied by 8 represents 8.
Place value at position 2 is 10 multiplied by 1 represents 10.
Place value at position 3 is 100 multiplied by 0 represents 0.
Place value at position 4 is 1000 multiplied by 2 represents 2000.
```

The sum of all represented numbers is the actual value. Following this concept will help us to read or convert into other number bases.

In base-2 numbers, the value of a place is 2 times the value of the place on its right. Base-2 uses only 2 digits, composed of 0 and 1. In this book, we will append a small b to denote that the number is of base-2 format. Base-2 numbers are also called binary numbers. Each digit in a binary string is called a bit. Consider the following as an example:

```
11010b
Place value at position 1 is 1 multiplied by 0 represents 0.
Place value at position 2 is 2 multiplied by 1 represents 2.
Place value at position 3 is 4 multiplied by 0 represents 0.
Place value at position 4 is 8 multiplied by 1 represents 8.
Place value at position 5 is 16 multiplied by 1 represents 16.

The equivalent decimal value of 11010b is 26.
```

In base-16 numbers, the value of a place is 16 times the value of the place on its right. It is composed of digits 0 to 9 and letters A to F where A is equivalent to 10, B is 11, C is 12, D is 13, E is 14, and F is 15. We will denote base-16 numbers, also known as hexadecimal numbers, with the letter h. In this book, hexadecimal numbers with an odd number of digits will be prefixed with 0 (zero). Hexadecimal numbers can also instead be prefixed with "0x" (zero and a lowercase x). The 0x is a standard used on various programming languages denoting that the number next to it is of hexadecimal format:

```
BEEFh
Place value at position 1 is 1 multiplied by 0Fh (15) represents 15.are
Place value at position 2 is 16 multiplied by 0Eh (14) represents 224.
Place value at position 3 is 256 multiplied by 0Eh (14) represents 3584.
Place value at position 4 is 4096 multiplied by 0Bh (11) represents 45056.

The equivalent decimal value of BEEFh is 48879.
```

Converting between bases

We have already converted hexadecimal and binary numbers into decimal, or base-10. Converting base-10 into other bases simply requires division of the base being converted into, while taking note of the remainders.

The following is an example for base-2

```
87 to base-2

87 divided by 2 is 43 remainder 1.
```

```
43 divided by 2 is 21 remainder 1.
21 divided by 2 is 10 remainder 1.
10 divided by 2 is 5 remainder 0.
5 divided by 2 is 2 remainder 1.
2 divided by 2 is 1 remainder 0.
1 divided by 2 is 0 remainder 1.
and nothing more to divide since we're down to 0.

base-2 has digits 0 and 1.
Writing the remainders backward results to 1010111b.
```

The following is an example for base-16:

```
34512 to base-16

34512 divided by 16 is 2157 remainder 0.
2157 divided by 16 is 134 remainder 13 (0Dh)
134 divided by 16 is 8 remainder 6.
6 divided by 16 is 0 remainder 6.

base-16 has digits from 0 to 9 and A to F.
Writing the remainders backward results to 66D0h.
```

Converting from hexadecimal into binary simply requires knowing how many binary digits there are in a hexadecimal digit. The highest digit for a hexadecimal number is 0Fh (15) and is equivalent to 1111b. Take note that there are 4 binary digits in a hexadecimal digit. An example conversion is shown here:

```
ABCDh
 0Ah = 1010b
 0Bh = 1011b
 0Ch = 1100b
 0Dh = 1101b

Just combine the equivalent binary number.
ABCDh = 1010101111001101b
```

Split the binary number into four digits each when converting from binary into hexadecimal, as shown here:

```
1010010111010111b
 1010b = 10 (0Ah)
 0101b = 5
 1101b = 13 (0Dh)
 0111b = 7

1010010111010111b = A5D7h
```

So, why the use of base-2 and base-16 in computers, rather than our daily base-10 usage? Well, for base-2, there are two states: an on and an off signal. A state can easily be read and transmitted electronically. Base-16 compresses the representation of the binary equivalent of a decimal number. Take 10 for instance: this number is represented as `1010b` and consumes 4 bits. To maximize the information that can be stored in 4 bits, we can represent numbers from 0 to 15 instead.

A 4-bit value is also called a nibble. It is half of a byte. Bytes can represent alphabets, numbers, and characters. This representation of characters is mapped in the ASCII table. The ASCII table has three sections: control, printable, and extended characters. There are 255 (`FFh`) ASCII characters. Lists of printable characters that can be typed on the keyboard and some of the extended characters with keyboard format can be found at `https://github.com/PacktPublishing/Mastering-Reverse-Engineering/tree/master/ch3`.

Though not directly visible from the English language keyboard, symbols can still be displayed by using the character's equivalent code.

Binary arithmetic

Since a byte is the common unit used in computers, let's play with it. We can start with basic arithmetical functions: addition, subtraction, multiplication, and division. The pencil-and-paper method is still a strong method for doing binary math. Binary arithmetic is similar to doing arithmetic in decimal numbers. The difference is that there are only two numbers used, 1 and 0.

Addition is carried out as follows:

```
    1b                10101b
+  1b            +    1111b
  10b               100100b
```

An example of subtraction is as follows:

```
  10b               1101b
-  1b             -  111b
   1b                110b
```

Multiplication is carried out as follows:

```
   101b            1b x 1b = 1b
x   10b            1b x 0b = 0b
   000
   101
  1010b
```

Division in binary works as follows:

```
        1010b                      1000b
10b |  10100b             11b |  11010b
       -10                        -11
       010                        0010
      -10                        -000
        00                         10b  (remainder)
       -0
        0
```

Signed numbers

Binary numbers can be structured as signed or unsigned. For signed numbers or integers, the most significant bit dictates what sign the number is in. This requires a defined size of the binary such as BYTE, WORD, DWORD, and QWORD. A BYTE has a size of 8 bits. A WORD has 16 bits while a DWORD (double WORD) has 32 bits. A QWORD (quad WORD) has 64 bits. Basically, the size doubles as it progresses.

In our example, let's use a BYTE. Identifying a positive binary number is easy. In positive numbers, the most significant bit, or 8th bit in a byte, is 0. The rest of the bits from 0 to the 7th bit is the actual value. For a negative binary number, the most significant bit is set to 1. However, the value set from 0 to the 7th bit is then calculated for a two's complement value:

```
01011011b = +91
11011011b = -37
10100101b = -91
00100101b = +37
```

The "2's complement" of a value is calculated in two steps:

1. Reverse 1s and 0s, so that 1 becomes 0 and 0 becomes 1, for example, 1010b becomes 0101b. This step is called the one's complement.
2. Add 1 to the result of the previous step, for example, 0101b + 1b = 0110b.

To write down the binary equivalent of -63, assuming it is a BYTE, we only take bits 0 to 7:

1. Convert into binary using the previous procedure:

   ```
   63 = 0111111b
   ```

288127481842

2. Do "1's complement" as follows:

```
0111111b -> 1000000b
```

3. Add 1 to the preceding outcome to get the "2's complement" result:

```
1000000b + 1 = 1000001b
```

4. Since this is a negative number, set the most significant bit to 1:

```
11000001b = -63
```

Here's how to write the decimal of a negative binary number:

1. Take note that the significant bit is 1, and so a negative sign:

```
10111011b
```

2. Take the "1's complement," then add 1:

```
  01000100b
+        1b
  01000101b
```

3. Convert the result to decimal, and place the – sign at the beginning, since this is a negative number:

```
- 01000101b = -69
```

x86

Like any other programming language, assembly language has its own variables, syntax, operations, and functions. Every line of code is processes a small amount of data. In other words, every byte is read or written per line of code.

Registers

In programming, processing data requires variables. You can simply think of registers as variables in assembly language. However, not all registers are treated as plain variables, but rather, each register has a designated purpose. The registers are categorized as being one of the following:

- General purpose registers
- Segment registers
- Flag registers
- Instruction pointers

In x86 architecture, each general purpose register has its designated purpose and is stored at WORD size, or 16 bits, as follows:

- Accumulator (AX)
- Counter (CX)
- Data (DX)
- Base (BX)
- Stack pointer (SP)
- Base pointer (BP)
- Source index (SI)
- Destination index (DI)

For registers AX, BX, CX, and DX, the least and most significant bytes can be accessed by smaller registers. For AX, the lower 8 bits can be read using the AL register, while the upper 8 bits can be read using the AH register, as shown here:

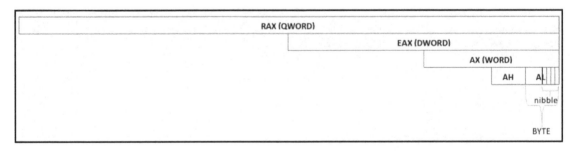

When running code, the system needs to identify where the code is at. The Instruction Pointer (IP) register is the one that contains the memory address where the next assembly instruction to be executed is stored.

System states and logical results of executed code are stored in the **FLAGS register**. Every bit of the FLAGS register has its own purpose, with some of the definitions given in the following table:

Offset	Abbreviation	Description
0	CF	Carry flag. This flag is set when an addition operation requires a bit to be carried. It is also set when a bit needs to be borrowed in a subtraction operation.
1		Reserved
2	PF	Parity flag. This flag indicates if the number of set bits is odd or even from the last instruction operation.
3		Reserved
4	AF	Adjust flag. This is used in Binary-Coded Decimals (BCD). This flag is set when a carry happens from the low to high nibble or when a borrow happens from the high to low nibble of a byte.
6	ZF	Zero flag. This flag is set when the result of the last instruction operation is zero.
7	SF	Sign flag. This flag is set when the result of the last instruction operation is a negative number.
8	TF	Trap flag. This is used when debugging. This flag is set when breakpoints are encountered. Setting the trap flag can cause an exception on every instruction, enabling debugging tools to control step-by-step debugging.
9	IF	Interrupt flag. If this flag is set, the processor responds to interrupts. Interrupts are instances where errors, external events, or exceptions are triggered from hardware or software.
10	DF	Direction flag. When set, data is read from memory backwards.
11	OF	Overflow flag. It is set if an arithmetic operation results in a value larger than what the register can contain.
12 to 13	IOPL	Input/output privilege level. The IOPL shows the ability of the program to access IO ports.
14	NT	Nested task flag. This controls the chaining of interrupt tasks or processes. If set, then it is linked to the chain.
15		Reserved
16	RF	Resume flag. It temporarily disables debug exceptions so the next instruction being debugged can be interrupted without a debug exception.
17	VM	Virtual mode. Sets the program to run in compatibility with 8086 processors.
18	AC	Alignment check. This flag is set when data written on a memory reference, such as the stack, is a non-word (for 4 byte boundaries) or non-doubleword (for 8 byte boundaries). However, this flag was more useful before the 486-architecture days.
19	VIF	Virtual interrupt flag. Similar to the interrupt flag, but works when in virtual mode.

20	VIP	Virtual interrupt pending flag. Indicates that triggered interrupts are waiting to be processed. Works in Virtual mode.
21	ID	Identification flag. Indicates if the CPUID instruction can be used. The CPUID can determine the type of processor and other processor info.
22		Reserved
23 to 31		Reserved
32 to 63		Reserved

All of these flags have a purpose, but the flags that are mostly monitored and used are the carry, sign, zero, overflow, and parity flags.

All these registers have an "extended" mode for 32-bits. It can accessed with a prefixed "E" (EAX, EBX, ECX, EDX, ESP, EIP, and EFLAGS). The same goes with 64-bit mode, which can be accessed with a prefixed "R" (RAX, RBX, RCX, RDX, RSP, and RIP).

The memory is divided into sections such as the code segment, stack segment, data segment, and other sections. The segment registers are used to identify the starting location of these sections, as follows:

- Stack segment (SS)
- Code segment (CS)
- Data segment (DS)
- Extra segment (ES)
- F segment (FS)
- G segment (GS)

When a program loads, the operating system maps the executable file to the memory. The executable file contains information to which data maps respective segments. The code segment contains the executable code. The data segment contains the data bytes, such as constants, strings, and global variables. The stack segment is allocated to contain runtime function variables and other processed data. The extra segment is similar to the data segment, but this space is commonly used to move data between variables. Some 16-bit operating systems, such as DOS, make use of the SS, CS, DS, and ES since there are only 64 kilobytes allocated per segment. However, in modern operating systems (32-bit systems and higher) these four segments are set in the same memory space, while FS and GS point to process and thread information respectively.

Memory addressing

The start of a piece of data, a series of bytes, stored in the memory can be located using its memory address. Every byte stored in the memory is assigned a memory address that identifies its location. When a program is executed by a user, the executable file is read, then mapped by the system to an allocated memory address. The executable file contains information on how it maps it, so that all executable code is in the code section, all initialized data is in the data section, and uninitialized data is in the BSS section. Code instructions found in the code section are able to access data in the data section using memory addresses, which can be hard-coded. Data can also be a list of addresses pointing to another set of data.

Endianness

When reading or writing data to memory, we use the registers or memory to process them as BYTE, WORD, DWORD, or even QWORD. Depending on the platform or program, data is read in little-endian or big-endian form.

In little-endian, a chunk of data read into a DWORD is reversed. Let's take the following piece of data as an example:

```
AA BB CC DD
```

When the data on a file or memory looks like this, in little-endian format, it will be read as DDCCBBAAh in a DWORD value. This endianness is common to Windows applications.

In the big-endian system, the same chunk of data will be read as AABBCCDDh. The advantage of using the big-endian form arises when reading streaming data such as file, serial, and network streams.

The advantage of reading in little-endian is that the address you read it from remains fixed, regardless of whether it is read as BYTE, WORD, or DWORD. For example, consider the following:

```
Address         Byte
0x00000000      AA
0x00000001      00
0x00000002      00
0x00000003      00
```

In the preceding example, we attempt to read the data from address the 0x00000000 address. When read as BYTE, it will be AAh. When read as a WORD, it will be AAh. When read as a DWORD, it will be AAh.

But when in big endian, when read as a BYTE, it will be AAh. When read as a WORD, it will be AA00h. When read as a DWORD, it will be AA000000h.

There are actually a lot more advantages over the other. Either of these can be used by an application depending on its purpose. In x86 assembly, the little-endian format is the standard.

Basic instructions

Assembly language is made up of direct lines of code that follow this syntax:

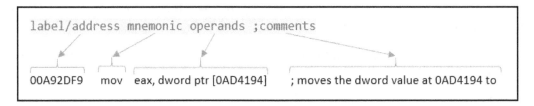

The label is used to define the location of the instruction line. It is generally used during development of an assembly code without prior knowledge of the address where the code will be placed in the memory. Some debuggers are able to support having the user label addresses with a readable name. A mnemonic is a human readable instruction, such as MOV, ADD and SUB. Every mnemonic is represented by a byte number or a couple of bytes called an opcode. The operands are the instruction's arguments. This is normally read as destination, source. In the instruction shown above, the eax register is the destination and the doubleword data stored at address 0x0AD4194. Finally, we can add comments to every instruction line of our program.

 In assembly language, code comments are denoted by a semicolon (;)

Opcode bytes

Every instruction has an equivalent opcode (operation code) byte:

```
Address      Opcode            Instructions
00A92D7C     B8 00000080       MOV EAX,80000000h
00A92D81     B9 02000000       MOV ECX,2
00A92D86     F7E1              MUL ECX
```

In the preceding code, the MOV instruction is equivalent to the B8 opcode byte. The MOV instruction at the 00A92D81 address is equivalent to B9. The difference between the two MOV instructions is the register into which the DWORD value is moved. There are a total of 5 bytes consumed in MOV EAX, 80000000h. It consists of the opcode byte, B8, and the operand value, 80000000h. The same number of bytes is also used in MOV ECX, 2, and MUL ECX uses 2 bytes.

MOV EAX, 80000000h is located at 00A92D7ch. Add 5 bytes (becomes 00A92D81) and we get to the address of the next instruction. Viewing the code in the memory would look like this:

```
Address      Bytes
00A92D7C     B8 00 00 00 80 B9 02 00 00 00 F7 E1
```

A dump of memory is usually shown in memory dumpers in paragraphs or 16 bytes per line and address aligned to 10h.

Assembly language instructions can be categorized as follows:

- Copying and accessing data instructions (for example, MOV, LEA, and MOVB)
- Arithmetic instructions (for example, ADD, SUB, MUL, and DIV)
- Binary logic instructions (for example, XOR, NOT, SHR, and ROL)
- Flow control (for example, JMP, CALL, CMP, and INT)

Copying data

The MOV instruction is used to move data. With this, data is moved either to or from a register or a memory address.

mov eax, 0xaabbccdd places the 0xaabbccdd value in the eax register.

mov eax, edx places the data value from theedx register to the eax register.

Let's take the following memory entries as an example:

```
Address   Bytes
00000060: 60 61 62 63 64 65 66 67 68 69 6A 6B 6C 6D 6E 6F
00000070: 70 71 72 73 74 75 76 77 78 79 7A 7B 7C 7D 7E 7F
00000080: 80 81 82 83 84 85 86 87 88 89 8A 8B 8C 8D 8E 8F
00000090: 90 91 92 93 94 95 96 97 98 99 9A 9B 9C 9D 9E 9F
```

Reading data may require using directives to help the assembler. We use `byte ptr`, `word ptr`, or `dword ptr`:

```
; the following lines reads from memory
mov al, byte ptr [00000071]        ; al = 71h
mov cx, word ptr [00000071]        ; cx = 7271h
mov edx, dword ptr [00000071]      ; edx = 74737271h

; the following lines writes to memory
mov eax, 011223344h
mov byte ptr [00000080], al        ; writes the value in al to address
00000080
mov word ptr [00000081], ax        ; writes the value in ax to address
00000081
mov dword ptr [00000083], eax      ; writes the value in eax to address
00000083
```

The memory will look like this afterward:

```
00000060: 60 61 62 63 64 65 66 67 68 69 6A 6B 6C 6D 6E 6F
00000070: 70 71 72 73 74 75 76 77 78 79 7A 7B 7C 7D 7E 7F
00000080: 44 44 33 44 33 22 11 87 88 89 8A 8B 8C 8D 8E 8F
00000090: 90 91 92 93 94 95 96 97 98 99 9A 9B 9C 9D 9E 9F
```

MOV and LEA

MOV is used to read the value at a given address, while LEA (Load Effective Address) is used to get the address instead:

```
mov eax, dword ptr [00000060]             ; stores 63626160h to eax
mov eax, dword ptr [00000060]             ; stores 00000060h to eax
```

So, how is the LEA instruction helpful if you can calculate the address by yourself? Let's take the following C code as an example:

```
struct Test {
    int x;
    int y;
} test[10];
```

```
int value;
int *p;

// some code here that fills up the test[] array

for (int i=0; i<10, i++) {
    value = test[i].y;
    p = &test[i].y;
}
```

The C code starts with defining test[10], an array of struct Test, which contains two integers, x and y. The for-loop statement takes the value of y and the pointer address of y in a struct test element.

Let's say the base of the test array is in EBX, the for-loop counter, i, is in ECX, the integers are DWORD values, and so struct Test will contain two DWORD values. Knowing that a DWORD has 4 bytes, the equivalent of value = test[i].y; in assembly language will look like mov edx, [ebx+ecx*8+4]. Then, the equivalent of p = &test[i].y; in assembly language will look like lea esi, [ebx+ecx*8+4]. Indeed, without using LEA, the address can still be calculated with arithmetic instructions. However, calculating for the address could be done much more easily using LEA:

```
; using MUL and ADD
mov ecx, 1111h
mov ebx, 2222h
mov eax, 2              ; eax = 2
mul ecx                 ; eax = 2222h
add eax, ebx            ; eax = 4444h
add eax, 1              ; eax = 4445h

; using LEA
mov ecx, 1111h
mov ebx, 2222h
lea eax, [ecx*2+ebx+1]  ; eax = 4445h
```

The preceding code shows that the six lines of code can be optimized to three lines using the LEA instruction.

Arithmetic operations

x86 instructions are based on the CISC architecture, where arithmetical instructions such as ADD, SUB, MUL, and DIV have a more low-level set of operations behind them. Arithmetical instructions work with the help of a set of flags that indicates certain conditions to be met during the operation.

Addition and subtraction

In addition (ADD) and subtraction (SUB), the OF, SF, and CF flags are affected. Let's see some examples of usage as instruction.

`add eax, ecx` adds whatever value is in the `ecx` register to the value in `eax`. The results of adding `eax` and `ecx` goes into `eax`.

Let's take the following example to see how it sets the OF, SF and CF flags:

```
mov ecx, 0x0fffffff
mov ebx, 0x0fffffff
add ecx, ebx
```

The registers are DWORDs. The `ecx` and `ebx` registers were set with `0x0fffffff` (268,435,455), adding these results to `0x1ffffffe` (536,870,910). SF was not set, since the result did not touch the most significant bit (MSB). CF was not set because the result is still within the capacity of a DWORD. Assuming that both were signed numbers, the result is still within the capacity of a signed DWORD number:

```
mov ecx, 0x7fffffff
mov ebx, 0x7fffffff
add ecx, ebx
```

The result in `ecx` becomes `0xfffffffe` (−2). `CF = 0; SF = 1; OF = 1`. Assuming that both `ecx` and `ebx` were unsigned, the CF flag will not be set. Assuming that both `ecx` and `ebx` were signed numbers and both are positive numbers, the OF flag will be set. And since the most significant bit becomes 1, the SF flag is also set.

Now, how about adding two negative numbers? Let's consider the following example:

```
mov ecx, 0x80000000
mov ebx, 0x80000000
add ecx, ebx
```

Basically, we're adding both `ecx` and `ebx`, containing `0x80000000` (-2,147,483,648), the result of which becomes zero (0). `CF = 1; SF = 0; OF = 1`. The SF flag was not set since the MSB of the result is 0. Adding both MSB of ecx and ebx will definitely exceed the capacity of a DWORD value. At the signed number perspective, the OF flag is also set, since adding both negative values exceeds the signed DWORD capacity.

Let's try the borrow concept in this next example:

```
mov ecx, 0x7fffffff
mov edx, 0x80000000
sub ecx, edx
```

What happens here is that we are subtracting `0x80000000` (-2,147,483,648) from `0x7fffffff` (2,147,483,647). In fact, what we are expecting is the sum of 2,147,483,648 and 2,147,483,647. The result in `ecx` becomes `0xffffffff` (-1). CF = 1; SF = 1; OF = 1. Remember that we are doing a subtraction operation, thereby causing CF to be set, due to borrowing. The same goes for the OF flag.

Increment and decrement instructions

The INC instruction simply adds 1, while DEC subtracts 1. The following code results in `eax` becoming zero (0):

```
mov eax, 0xffffffff
inc eax
```

The following code results in `eax` becoming `0xffffffff`:

```
mov eax, 0
dec eax
```

Multiplication and division instructions

MUL is used for multiplication and DIV for division. In multiplication, we expect that multiplying values would exceed the capacity of the register value. Hence the product is stored in AX, `DX:AX` or `EDX:EAX` (long or `QWORD`):

```
mov eax, 0x80000000
mov ecx, 2
mul ecx
```

The product stored in eax is zero (0), and `edx` now contains `0x00000001`. SF =0; CF = 1; and OF = 1.

For division, the dividend is placed in AX, `DX:AX`, or `EDX:EAX`, and after the division operation, the quotient is placed in AL, AX, or EAX. The remainder is stored in AH, DX, or EDX.

Other signed operations

NEG

This operation does a two's complement.

Consider the following as an example: NEG EAX or NEG dword ptr [00403000].

If EAX were 01h, it becomes FFFFFFFFh (-1).

MOVSX

This moves a BYTE to WORD or WORD to DWORD, including the sign. It is a more flexible instruction than CBW, CWDE, CWD, since it accommodates operands.

Consider the following as an example: MOVSX EAX, BX.

If BX were FFFFh (-1) and the sign flag is set, EAX will be FFFFFFFFh (-1).

CBW

Similar to MOVSX, it converts a BYTE into WORD, including the sign. The affected register is AL and AX. This is an instruction without any operands and is similar to MOVSX. The effect turns the byte AL extend to its word counterpart, AX. Such conversion is dentoed with a "->" sign. For example, AL -> AX means we are extending the 8-bit number to a 16-bit without compromising the stored value.

If AL were FFh (-1), AX will be FFFFh (-1).

CWDE

This is similar to CBW, but converts a WORD into DWORD. It affects AX->EAX.

CWD

This is similar to CBW, but converts a WORD into DWORD. It affects AX-> DX:AX.

IMUL/IDIV

This performs MUL and DIV, but accepts operands from other registers or memory.

Bitwise algebra

Boolean algebra or bitwise operations are necessary in low-level programming since it can perform simple calculations by changing the bits of a number. It is commonly used in cryptography's obfuscation and decoding.

NOT

This operation reverses the bits.

Consider the following as an example: NOT AL

If AL equals 1010101b (55h), it becomes 10101010b (AAh).

AND

This operation sets bit to 1 if both are 1s, otherwise it sets bit to 0.

Consider the following as an example: AND AL, AH

If AL equals 10111010b (BAh) and AH equals 11101101b (EDh), AL becomes 10101000b (A8h).

OR

This operation sets bit to 0 if both are 0s, else it sets bit to 1.

Consider the following as an example: OR AL, AH

If AL equals 10111010b (BAh) and AH equals 11101100b (ECh), AL becomes 11111110b (FEh).

XOR

This operation sets bit to 0 if both bits are equal, else it sets bit to 1.

Consider the following as an example: XOR EAX, EAX

XOR-ing the same value will become 0. Thus EAX becomes 0:

```
XOR AH, AL
```

If AH were 100010b (22h) and AL were 1101011b (6Bh), AH becomes 1001001b (49h).

SHL/SAL

This operation shifts bits to the left.

Consider the following as an example: `SHL AL, 3`

If `AL` were `11011101b` (DDh), shifting it to the left by 3 makes AL equal to `11101000b` (E8h).

SHR/SAR

This operation shifts bits to the right.

Consider the following as an example: `SHR AL, 3`

If `AL` were `11011101b` (DDh), shifting it to the right by 3 makes AL equal to `011011b` (1Bh).

ROL

This operation rotates bits to the left.

Consider the following as an example: `ROL AL, 3`

if `AL` were `11011101b` (DDh), rotating it to the left by 3 makes AL equal to `11101110b` (EEh).

ROR

This operation rotates bits to the right.

Consider the following as an example: `ROR AL, 3`

If `AL` were `11011101b` (DDh), rotating it to the right by 3 makes AL equal to `10111011b` (BBh).

Control flow

The beauty of a program is that we can carry out a number of different behaviors based on condition and state. For example, we can make a certain task repeat until a counter reaches a defined maximum. In C programming, the program's flow is controlled by instructions such as the `if-then-else` and `for-loop` statements. The following are common instructions used in assembly language, in conjunction with program control flow. The affected register in this is the index pointer IP/EIP, which holds the current address where the next instruction to execute is located.

```
JMP
```

Short for jump, this means that the operand is an address that it will go to. It sets the EIP to the next instruction line. There are two main variations for the address: direct and indirect.

A `JMP` using a direct address would literally jump to the given address. Consider as an example: `JMP    00401000`. This will set the `EIP` to `00401000h`.

A `JMP` using an indirect address would jump to an address that can only be known when the jump is executed. The address has to be retrieved or calculated somehow prior to the `JMP` instruction. Here are some examples:

```
jmp    eax
jmp    dword ptr [00403000]
jmp    dword ptr [eax+edx]
jmp    dowrd ptr [eax]
jmp    dword ptr [ebx*4+eax]
```

CALL and RET

Similar to `JMP`, this goes to the address stated in the operand, but stores the address of the next instruction to the stack after the CALL instruction. The address is stored in the stack and will be used by the `RET` instruction later to point `EIP` back to it. For example, consider the following:

```
Address                 Instruction
00401000                CALL 00401100
00401005                MOV ECX, EAX
00401007
...
00401100                MOV EAX, F00BF00B
00401105                RET
```

When the CALL happens at the address `00401000`, the top of the stack will contain the value `00401005h`, which will be the return address. The code passes it to the instruction at the address `00401100`, where `EAX` is set to `F00bF00Bh`. Then the `RET` instruction retrieves the return address from the top of the stack and sets the EIP. A subroutine or procedure is the term used for the lines of instructions from the call.

The `RET` instruction can optionally have an operand. The operand is the number of stack `DWORD`s it will release before retrieving the return address. This is useful when the stack is used within the subroutine as it serves as a cleanup of the used stack.

Conditional jumps

These are jumps that depend on the flags and the counter register:

Instruction	Flags	Description
JZ / JE	ZF = 1	Jump if zero/Jump if equal
JNZ / JNE	ZF = 0	Jump if not zero/Jump if not equal
JS	SF = 1	Jump if sign
JNS	SF = 0	Jump if not sign
JC / JB / JNAE	CF = 1	Jump if carry/Jump if below/Jump if not above or equal
JNC / JNB / JAE	CF = 0	Jump if not carry/jump if not below/Jump if above or equal
JO	OF = 1	Jump if overflow
JNO	OF = 0	Jump if not overflow
JA / JNBE	CF = 0 and ZF = 0	Jump if above/Jump if not below or equal
JNA / JBE	CF = 1 or ZF = 1	Jump if not above/Jump if below or equal
JG / JNLE	ZF = 0 and SF = OF	Jump if greater/Jump if not less or equal
JNG / JLE	ZF = 1 or SF != OF	Jump if not greater/Jump if less or equal
JL / JNGE	SF != OF	Jump if less/Jump if not greater or equal
JNL / JGE	SF = OF	Jump if not less/Jump if greater or equal
JP / JPE	PF = 1	Jump if parity/Jump if parity is even
JNP / JPO	PF = 0	Jump if not parity/Jump if parity is odd
JCXZ	CX = 0	Jump if CX is zero.
JECXZ	ECX = 0	Jump if ECX is zero.
LOOP	ECX > 0	Jump if ECX is not zero. Decrements ECX.
LOOPE	ECX > 0 and ZF = 1	Jump if ECX is not zero and zero flag is set. Decrements ECX.
LOOPNE	ECX > 0 and ZF = 0	Jump if ECX is not zero and zero flag is not set. Decrements ECX.

Flagging instructions

Besides the arithmetic, bit-wise operations, interrupts, and return values from functions, these instructions are also able to set flags.

CMP performs a SUB instruction on the first and second operands, but does not modify the registers or the immediate value. It only affects the flags.

TEST performs an AND instruction on the first and second operands, but does not modify the registers or the immediate value. It only affects the flags.

Stack manipulation

The stack is a memory space where data is temporarily stored. Adding and removing data in the stack is in a first-in-last-out method. Subroutines compiled from programs in C initially allocate space in the stack, called a stack frame, for its uninitialized variables. The address of the top of the stack is stored in the ESP register:

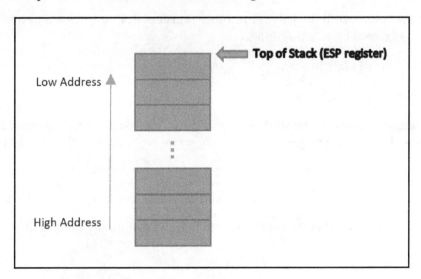

The stack is controlled by two common instructions: PUSH and POP.

PUSH decreases the top-of-stack address by a DWORD size, for a 32-bit address space, then stores the value from its operand.

Consider the following as an example: PUSH 1

If the top of the stack, stored in ESP, is at address 002FFFFCh, then the ESP becomes 002FFFF8h and stores 1 at the new ESP address.

POP retrieves the value from the top of the stack (ESP) then stores it to the register or memory space indicated in the operand. Then ESP is increased by a DWORD size.

Consider the following as an example: POP EAX

If the address of the top of the stack, stored in ESP, is at address 002FFFF8h, and the stored DWORD value at the top of the stack is 0xDEADBEEF, then 0xDEADBEEF will be stored in EAX, while ESP becomes 002FFFFCh.

PUSHA/PUSHAD both push all the general purpose registers to the stack in this order (for 32-bit builds): EAX, ECX, EDX, EBX, EBP, ESP, EBP, ESI, and EDI. PUSHA is intended for 16-bit operands, while PUSHAD is for 32-bit operands. However, both may be synonymous to each other, adapting to the current operand size.

POPA/POPAD both pop all the general purpose registers from the stack and retrieved in a reverse order as stored by PUSHA/PUSHAD.

PUSHF pushes the EFLAGS to stack.

POPF pops the EFLAGS from stack.

ENTER is commonly used at the start of a subroutine. It is used to create a stack frame for the subroutine. Internally, ENTER 8,0 may roughly be equivalent to the following:

```
push ebp                    ; save the current value of ebp
mov ebp, esp                ; stores current stack to ebp
add esp, 8                  ; create a stack frame with a size of 8 bytes
```

LEAVE is used to reverse what the ENTER instruction did eventually destroying the stack frame created.

Tools – builder and debugger

Before we proceed with more instructions, it would be best to try actually programming with assembly language. The tools we will need are a text editor, the assembly code builder, and the debugger.

Popular assemblers

All programming languages need to be built to become an executable on the system platform that the program was built for. Unless you want to enter each opcode byte in a binary file, developers have made tools to convert that source code to an executable that contains code that the machine can understand. Let's take a look at some of the most popular assembly language builders today.

MASM

Also known as Microsoft Macro Assembler, MASM has been around for more than 30 years. It is maintained by Microsoft and is part of the Visual Studio product. It was developed for compiling x86 source code to executable code.

Compiling takes two steps: compiling the source into an object file, then linking all necessary modules required by the object file into a single executable.

```
Administrator: C:\Windows\system32\cmd.exe

c:\masm32>bin\ml.exe /c /coff hello.asm
Microsoft (R) Macro Assembler Version 6.14.8444
Copyright (C) Microsoft Corp 1981-1997.  All rights reserved.

 Assembling: hello.asm

***********
ASCII build
***********


c:\masm32>bin\link.exe /SUBSYSTEM:CONSOLE hello.obj
Microsoft (R) Incremental Linker Version 5.12.8078
Copyright (C) Microsoft Corp 1992-1998. All rights reserved.


c:\masm32>dir hello.*
 Volume in drive C is Windows 7
 Volume Serial Number is 3C9E-098B

 Directory of c:\masm32

12/13/2003  06:57 PM               902 hello.asm
05/11/2018  03:03 AM             2,560 hello.exe
05/11/2018  03:03 AM               549 hello.obj
               3 File(s)          4,011 bytes
               0 Dir(s)  27,621,662,720 bytes free

c:\masm32>hello.exe
Hello world
c:\masm32>_
```

The MASM package comes along with a text editor that has the menu containing the compiler and linker to build the source as an executable. This comes very handy as there is no need to go to the command line to run the compiler and linker to build the executable. A simple "Console Build All" command on the following source generates an executable that can be run in the command terminal:

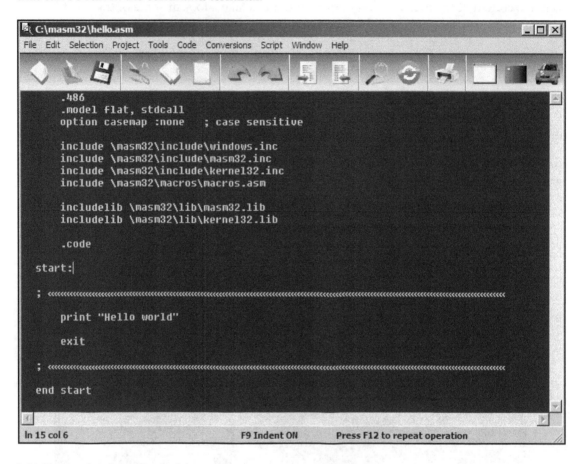

MASM can be downloaded from http://www.masm32.com/.

NASM

NASM is the abbreviation of **Netwide Assembler**. NASM is very similar to MASM with slight differences between its syntax, directives, and variable declaration. A great thing about NASM is that sectioning of code and data is easily identified:

```
1
2   SECTION .text
3       global main
4       main:
5           push message
6           call printf
7           call exit
8
9   SECTION .data
10      extern exit, printf
11      message dd 'Hello World!', 0
12
```

Both MASM and NASM also require compiling and linking to build the executable:

```
C:\MinGW\bin>nasm -f win32 --prefix _ hello.asm

C:\MinGW\bin>gcc -o hello hello.obj

C:\MinGW\bin>dir hello*
 Volume in drive C has no label.
 Volume Serial Number is 04D9-E554

 Directory of C:\MinGW\bin

05/11/2018  10:46 PM                220 hello.asm
05/11/2018  10:56 PM             27,931 hello.exe
05/11/2018  10:55 PM                381 hello.obj
               3 File(s)         28,532 bytes
               0 Dir(s)  10,933,223,424 bytes free

C:\MinGW\bin>hello.exe
Hello World!
C:\MinGW\bin>
```

However, unlike MASM, the installer package does not have its own editor. NASM is very popular in the Linux community due to its development as opensource software. The package contains only the compiler for the object file; you'll have to download a GCC compiler to generate the executable.

The official website for downloading NASM is at `https://www.nasm.us/`. For Windows, MinGW (`http://www.mingw.org/`) can be used to generate the executable.

FASM

FASM, or Flat Assembler, is similar MASM and NASM. Like MASM, it has its own source editor. Like NASM, the sections are easily identifiable and configured, and the software comes in flavors for both Windows and Linux:

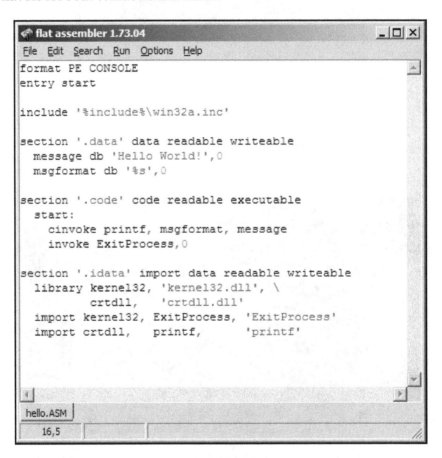

FASM can be downloaded from `http://flatassembler.net/`.

In our assembly language programming, we will use FASM, since we can use its editor in both Windows and Linux.

x86 Debuggers

Debuggers are program developers' tools for tracing through their code. These tools are used to validate that the program follows the expected behavior. With a debugger, we can trace our code line per line. We get to see every instruction in action as it make changes to the registers and data stored in the memory. In reversing, debuggers are used to analyze programs at its low-level. With what we learned about assembly language, the target compiled program, and a debugger, we are able to do reverse engineering.

Besides the tools introduced in this book, there are a lot of tools available in the internet that may have more or less features. The point is that reverse engineering rely on the tools and we need to keep ourselves updated with the latest tool. Feel free to download other tools that you want to explore and see which one makes your reversing feel more comfortable.

WinDbg

Developed by Microsoft to perform debugging on Microsoft Windows, `WinDbg` is a powerful tool that can debug in user and kernel mode. It can load memory dumps and crash dumps caused by errors flagged by Windows itself. In kernel mode, it can be used to remotely debug a device driver or a Windows operating system. It can load symbol files linked to the program that aid the developer or analyst in identifying the proper library function format and other information.

`WinDbg` has a graphical user interface, and by default, shows a command box where you can type in and enter commands. You can add a set of information windows and dock them. It can show the disassembly, registers and flags, the stack (using the memory dump window), and a memory dump of whichever address entered:

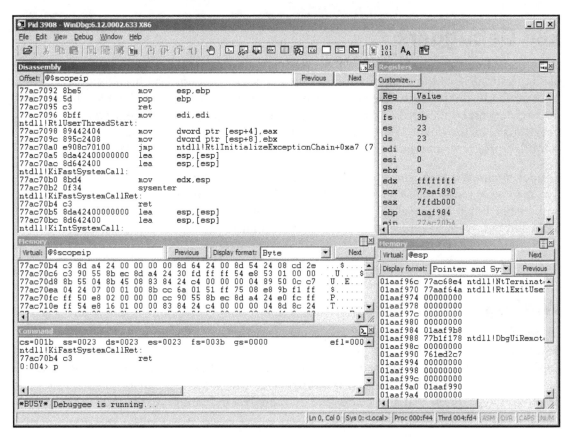

`Windbg` **can be downloaded from** `https://docs.microsoft.com/en-us/windows-hardware/drivers/debugger/`.

Ollydebug

This is the most popular debugger on the x86 32-bit Windows platform due to its lightweight package file size. Its default interface shows the important information needed by a reverse engineer: a disassembly view where tracing happens; registers and flags panes; and the stack and memory views.

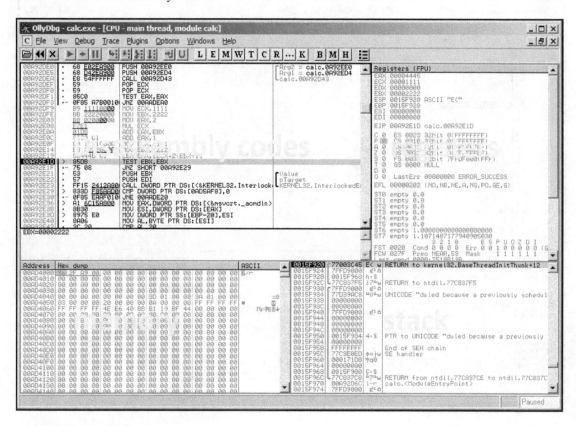

OllyDebug can be downloaded from http://www.ollydbg.de/.

x64dbg

This debugger is most recommended as the developers keep this up-to-date, working with the community. It also supports both 64- and 32-bit Windows platforms with a lot of useful plugins available. It has a similar interface as Ollydebug.

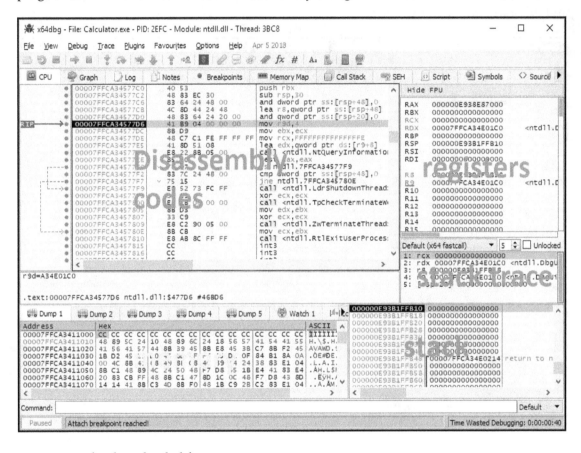

x64dbg can be downloaded from `https://x64dbg.com/`.

Hello World

We are going to use FASM for building our first assembly language program. And we will debug the executable using x64dbg.

Installation of FASM

Using our Windows setup, download FASM from `http://flatassembler.net/`, then `extract FASM into a folder of your choice:`

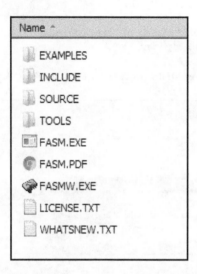

Run `FASMW.EXE` to bring up the FASM GUI.

It works!

In your text editor, write down the following code, or you can simply do a Git clone of the data at `https://github.com/PacktPublishing/Mastering-Reverse-Engineering/blob/master/ch3/fasmhello.asm`.

```
format PE CONSOLE
entry start

include '%include%\win32a.inc'

section '.data' data readable writeable
  message db 'Hello World!',0
  msgformat db '%s',0

section '.code' code readable executable
  start:
    push message
    push msgformat
    call [printf]
```

```
        push 0
        call [ExitProcess]

    section '.idata' import data readable writeable
        library kernel32, 'kernel32.dll', \
                msvcrt, 'msvcrt.dll'
        import kernel32, ExitProcess, 'ExitProcess'
        import msvcrt, printf, 'printf'
```

Save it by clicking on **File->Save as**..., then click on **Run->Compile**:

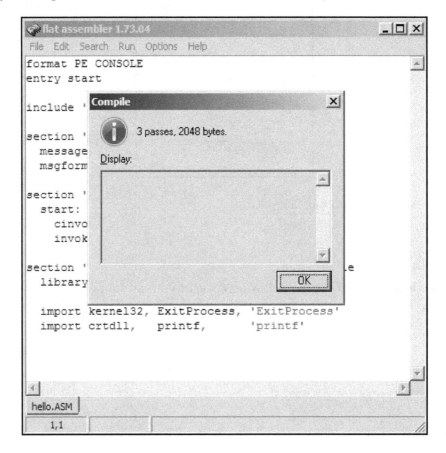

The executable file will be located where the source was saved:

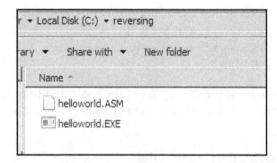

If "Hello World!" did not show up, one thing to note is that this is a console program. You'll have to open up a command terminal and run the executable from there:

```
C:\reversing>dir
 Volume in drive C has no label.
 Volume Serial Number is 04D9-E554

 Directory of C:\reversing

05/12/2018  07:50 PM    <DIR>          .
05/12/2018  07:50 PM    <DIR>          ..
05/12/2018  07:50 PM               501 helloworld.ASM
05/12/2018  07:50 PM             2,048 helloworld.EXE
               2 File(s)          2,549 bytes
               2 Dir(s)  10,827,882,496 bytes free

C:\reversing>helloworld.EXE
Hello World!
C:\reversing>
```

Dealing with common errors when building

Write Failed Error – This means that the builder or compiler is not able to write to the output file. It is possible that the executable file it was going to build to is still running. Try looking for the program that was run previously and terminate it. You can also terminate it from the process list or Task Manager.

Unexpected Characters – Check for the syntax at the indicated line. Sometimes the included files also need to be updated because of changing syntax on recent versions of the builder.

Invalid argument – Check for the syntax at the indicated line. There might be missing parameters of a definition or a declaration.

Illegal instruction – Check for the syntax at the indicated line. If you are sure that the instruction is valid, it might be that the builder version doesn't match where the instruction was valid. While updating the builder to the most recent version, also update the source to comply with the recent version.

Dissecting the program

Now that we have built our program and got it working, let's discuss what the program contains and is intended for.

A program is mainly structured with a code section and a data section. The code section, as its name states, is where program codes are placed. On the other hand, the data section is where the data, such as text strings, used by the program code is located. There are requirements before a program can be compiled. These requirements define how the program will be built. For example, we can tell the compiler to build this program as a Windows executable, instead of a Linux executable. We can also tell the compiler which line in the code should the program start running. An example of a program structure is given here:

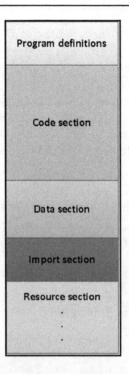

We can also define the external library functions that the program will be using. This list is described under a separate sections called the Import section. There are various sections that can be supported by a compiler. An example of these extended sections include the resource section, which contains data such as icons and images.

With the a basic picture of a what a program is structured, let see how our program was written. The first line, `format PE CONSOLE`, indicates that the program will be compiled as a Windows PE executable file and built to run on the console, better known in Windows as Command Prompt.

The next line, `entry start`, means that the program will start running code located at the `start` label. The name of the label can be changed as desired by the programmer. The next line, `include '%include%\win32a.inc'`, will add declarations from the FASM library file `win32a.inc`. The declared functions expected are for calling the `printf` and `ExitProcess` API functions discussed in the `idata` section.

There are three sections built in this program: the data, code, and idata sections. The section names here are labeled as `.data`, `.code`, and `.idata`. The permissions for each section are also indicated as either `readable`, `writeable`, and `executable`. The data section is where integers and text strings are placed and listed using the define byte (db) instruction. The code section is where lines of instruction code are executed. The idata section is where imported API functions are declared.

On the next line, we see that the data section is defined as a `writeable` section:

```
section '.data' data readable writeable
```

The program's `.data` section contains two constant variables, message and msgformat. Both text strings are ASCIIZ (ASCII-Zero) strings, which means that they are terminated with a zero (0) byte. These variables are defined with the db instruction:

```
message db 'Hello World!',0
msgformat db '%s',0
```

The next line defines the code section. It is defined with read and execute permissions:

```
section '.code' code readable executable
```

It is in the `.code` section where the start: label is and where our code is. Label names are prefixed with a colon character.

In C programming, printf is a function commonly used to print out messages to the console using the C syntax, as follows:

```
int printf ( const char * format, ... );
```

The first parameter is the message containing format specifiers. The second parameter contains the actual data that fills up the format specifiers. In assembly language perspective, the printf function is an API function that is in the msvcrt library. An API function is set up by placing the arguments in the memory stack space before calling a function. If your program is built in C, a function that requires 3 parameters (for example, myfunction(arg1, arg2, arg3)) will have the following as an equivalent in assembly language:

```
push <arg3>
push <arg2>
push <arg1>
call myfunction
```

For a 32-bit address space, the `push` instruction is used to write a DWORD (32 bits) of data on the top of the stack. The address of the top of the stack is stored in the ESP register. When a `push` instruction is executed, the ESP decreases by 4. If the argument is a text string or a data buffer, the address is push-ed to the stack. If the argument is a number value, the value is directly push-ed to the stack.

Following the same API calling structure, with two arguments, our program called `printf` in this manner:

```
push message
push msgformat
call [printf]
```

In the data section, the addresses, labeled as `message` and `msgformat`, are pushed to the stack as a setup before calling the `printf` function. Addresses are usually placed in square brackets, `[]`. As discussed previously, the value at the address is used instead. The `printf` is actually a label that is the local address in the program declared in the `.idata` section. `[printf]` then means that we are using the address of the `printf` API function from the `msvcrt` library. Thus, `call [printf]` will execute the `printf` function from the `msvcrt` library.

The same goes for `ExitProcess`. `ExitProcess` is a `kernel32` function that terminates the running process. It requires a single parameter, which is the exit code. An exit code of 0 means that the program will terminate without any errors:

```
push 0
call [ExitProcess]
```

In C syntax, this code is equivalent to `ExitProcess(0)`, which terminates the program with a success result defined with zero.

The program's `.idata` section contains external functions and is set with read and write permissions:

```
section '.idata' import data readable writeable
```

In the following code snippet, there are two portions. The first part indicates which library files the functions are located in. The `library` command is used to set the libraries required, and uses the syntax `library <library name>, <library file>`. A backslash, `\`, is placed to indicate that the next line is a continuation of the current line:

```
library kernel32, 'kernel32.dll', \
        msvcrt, 'msvcrt.dll'
```

Once the libraries are declared, specific API functions are indicated using the `import` command. The syntax is `import <library name>, <function name>, <function name in library file>`. Two external API functions are imported here, *kernel32*'s *ExitProcess* and *msvcrt*'s *printf*:

```
import kernel32, ExitProcess, 'ExitProcess'
import msvcrt, printf, 'printf'
```

A annotated version of the program can be found at `https://github.com/PacktPublishing/Mastering-Reverse-Engineering/blob/master/ch3/FASM%20commented.txt`

The library of API functions can be found in the MSDN library (`https://msdn.microsoft.com/en-us/library`), which also has an offline version packaged in the Visual Studio installer. It contains detailed information about what the API function is for and how to use it. The online version looks like the following:

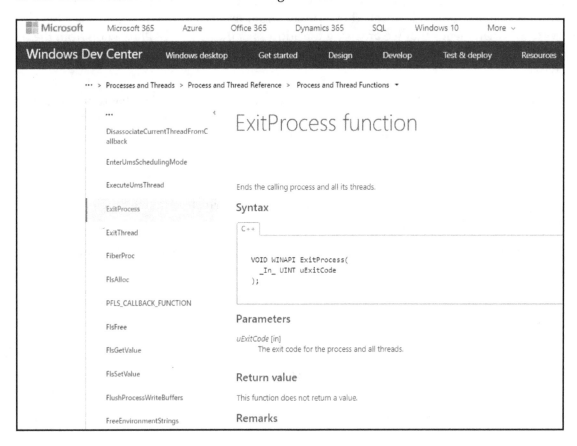

After Hello

We encountered an external call to the `printf` and `ExitProcess` API functions. These specific functions were developed for Windows as a means of communication between the user-mode and the kernel-mode. Generally, for most operating systems, the kernel is responsible for literally displaying the output on the monitor, writing files to the disk, reading keyboard strokes, transmitting data to USB ports, sending data to the printer, transmitting data to the network wire, and so forth. In essence, everything that has something to do with hardware has to go through the kernel. Our program, however, is in the user-mode, and we use the APIs to tell the kernel to do stuff for us.

Calling APIs

Calling APIs within our program just requires us to define the library file where the API function is, and the API name itself. As we did with our Hello World program, we import the API function by setting it up in the import section:

```
section '.idata' import data readable writeable      ; import section has
read and write permissions
   library kernel32, 'kernel32.dll', \                ; functions came from
kernel32 and msvcrt dlls
          msvcrt, 'msvcrt.dll'
   import kernel32, ExitProcess, 'ExitProcess'        ; program will use
ExitProcess and printf functions
   import msvcrt, printf, 'printf'
```

And then we call the APIs with a CALL instruction, as follows:

```
        call [printf]
        call [ExitProcess]
```

Common Windows API libraries

KERNEL32 contains base functions of Windows that are responsible for file I/O operations and memory management, including processes and threads management. Some functions are helpers for calling more native APIs in the NTDLL library.

USER32 contains functions that deal with the display and graphical interface, such as program windows, menu, and icons. It also contains functions that controls window messages.

ADVAPI32 contains functions that has to do with the Windows registry.

MSVCRT contains standard C library functions from Microsoft Visual C++ runtime, such as printf, scanf, malloc, strlen, fopen, and getch.

WS2_32, **WININET**, **URLMON**, and **NETAPI32** are libraries that contain functions that have to do with networking and internet communication.

Short list of common API functions

The API functions can be categorized based on their purposes. A complete list can be found at the MSDN Library, but the most common ones are listed here:

Purpose	API functions
Console output	KERNEL32!GetStdHandle, MSVCRT!printf
File handling	KERNEL32!ReadFile, KERNEL32!WriteFile, KERNEL32!CreateFile
Memory management	KERNEL32!VirtualAlloc, KERNEL32!VirtualProtect, MSVCRT!malloc
Process and threads	KERNEL32!ExitProcess, KERNEL32!CreateProcess, KERNEL32!CreateThread, SHELL32!ShellExecute
Window management	USER32!MessageBoxA, USER32!CreateWindowExA, USER32!RegisterWindowMessageW
Strings	MSVCRT!strlen, MSVCRT!printf
Network communication	WININET!InternetAttemptConnect, WS2_32!socket, WS2_32!connect, URLMON!URLDownloadToFile
Cryptography	CryptDecrypt, CryptEncrypt
Registry	RegDeleteKey, RegCreateKey, RegQueryValueExW, RegSetValueExW

Debugging

At certain points, our program may produce unpredictable errors or invalid output. In that case, we need to trace what went wrong, by debugging each line of code. But before that, there are some general debug commands we need to know.

Single-stepping a program means debugging per line of code. There are two modes to single step: step into and step over. During debugging, when the line being debugged is a CALL instruction, single-step debugging continues in the subroutine when a **step into** mode is used. The **step over** mode, however doesn't enter the subroutine, but rather lets the subroutine finish up running and the single step continues on the line after the CALL instruction. See the following comparison:

Step into	Step over

`CALL 00401000 ; <-- STEP INTO`
`SUBROUTINE`
`    MOV  EBX, EAX`
`    ...`
`00401000:`
`    MOV EAX, 37173 ; <- DEBUG POINTER`
`GOES HERE`
`    RET`
	`CALL 00401000 ; <-- STEP OVER`
	`SUBROUTINE`
	`    MOV  EBX, EAX ; <- DEBUG POINTER`
	`GOES HERE`
	`    ...`
	`00401000:`
	`    MOV EAX, 37173`
	`    RET`

A **run** or **continue** makes the debugger execute instructions continuously until the program terminates, encounters an error, or until it encounters a manually set breakpoint.

Placing a **breakpoint** is a way to enable to the debugger to interrupt a code that was set to freely run. For example, if I placed a breakpoint at address 0040200A in the following code, and let the debugger automatically run every instruction starting from 00402000, the debugger stops at address 0040200A and leaves the user to continue doing single steps or run:

```
00402000   push 0040100D
00402005   push 0040100D
0040200A   call dword ptr [printf]   ; <-- breakpoint set here
00402010   push 0
00402012   call dword ptr [ExitProcess]
```

Let's debug our Hello World program.

Download x64dbg from https://x64dbg.com/.

It is a ZIP archive that you will have to extract. And once extracted, open the x96dbg.exe from the release folder. This will show the launcher dialog where you get to select x32dbg (for 32-bit debugging) and x64dbg (for 64-bit debugging) as your debugger:

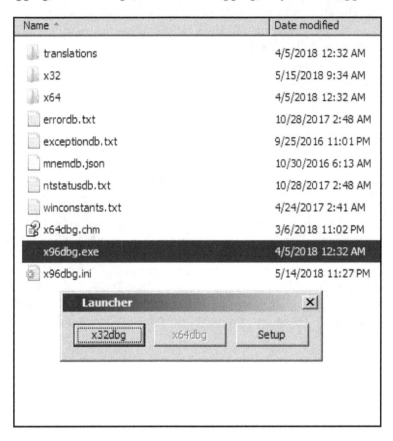

The Hello World program we developed is a 32-bit program, thus, select x32dbg. Then click on File->Open, then browse and open the helloworld.exe program. Opening it will show you where the EIP is at in the disassembly window as follows:

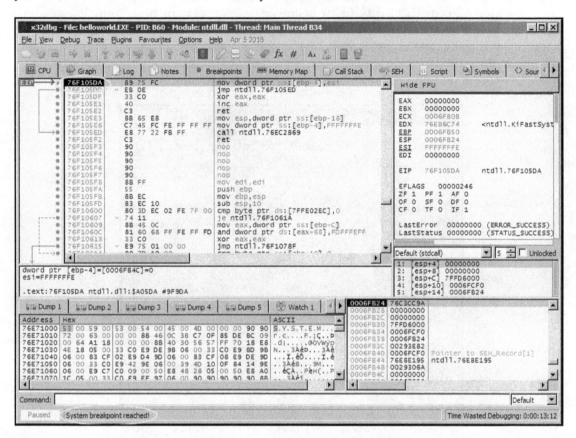

At the bottom of the window, it says: "**System breakpoint reached!**" EIP is at a high-memory region address and the window title also indicates "Module: ntdll.dll - Thread: Main Thread." All of this suggests that we are not yet in the helloworld program, but rather still in the ntdll.dll code that loads up the helloworld program to memory, initializes it and then starts to run it. If you go to Options->Preferences, and in the Events table of the Settings window, by default, the System Breakpoint* is checked. This causes the debugger to pause in the ntdll.dll before we even reach our helloworld code. Uncheck the System Breakpoint*, click on Save, then exit the debugger, as shown here:

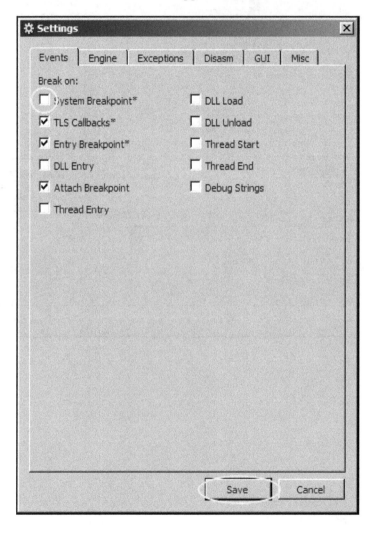

Now that we have removed the System Breakpoint, repeat loading the helloworld program. The EIP should now be in the helloworld code:

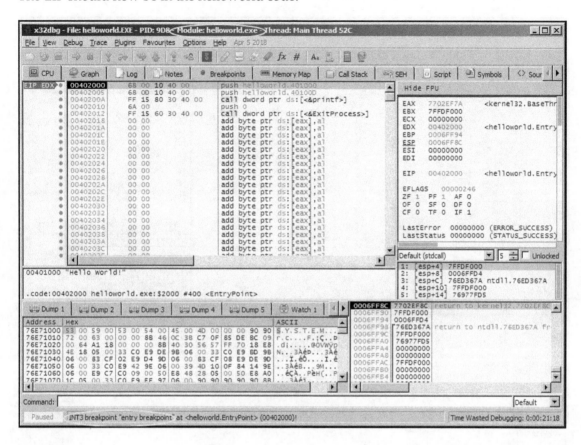

Click on the Debug menu. You should see that there are keyboard keys assigned to Step into, Step over, Run and more debugging options:

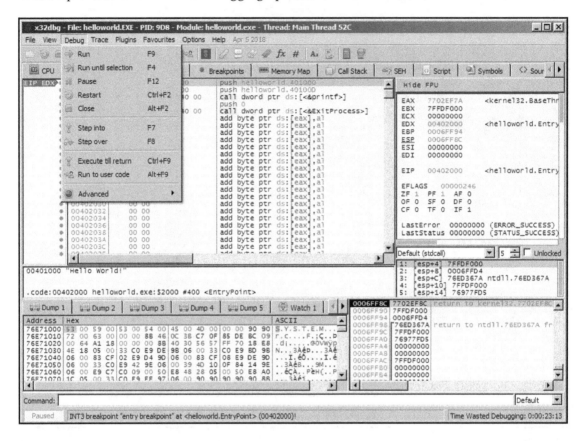

The stack frame window is located at the lower right pane. Take note of the information there, then press *F7* or *F8* to do a single step. The PUSH helloworld.401000 instruction just placed the address of "Hello World" text string at the top of the stack. At the upper right pane where the registers and flags are, all changes have their text colored red. With the stack moving its address, ESP should change. And since we are now on the next line of instruction code, EIP should have also changed.

Do another single step to push the address of "%s" to the stack. You should now be in address 0040200A. At this point, doing a step over will execute the printf function and be at address 00402010. Out of curiosity, let's do a step into instead. This leads us in the msvcrt library, where the printf function is:

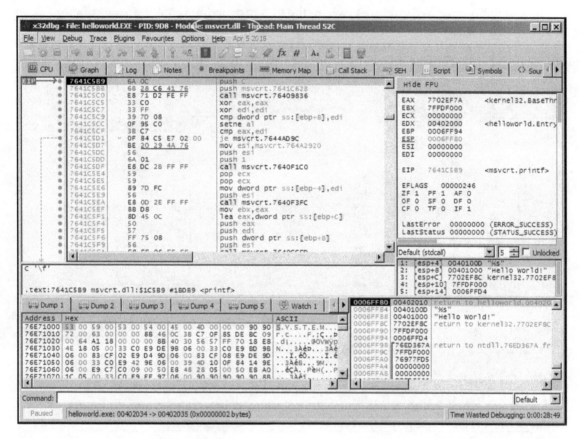

To get back to our `helloworld` program, we can do a "Run to user code," which has a mapped key of *Alt + F9* or an "Execute till return" *Ctrl + F9*. The user code pertains to our hello world program. Doing a "Run to user code" will bring us to address `00402010`, which is the instruction after the `printf` call. Doing an "Execute till return" will bring us to the address where the `RET` instruction is. Let's do an "Execute till return" instead:

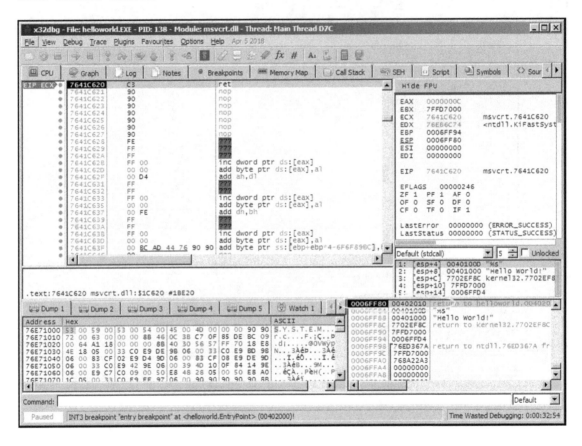

Now take a look at the stack. As discussed previously about the `CALL-RET` instructions, a `CALL` stores the address of the next instruction at the top of the stack. At this point, the address stored at the top of the stack is `00402010`. Make a single step and we should be back in our `hello world` program.

Just continue doing step overs. The last two instructions should terminate the program and the debugging will stop.

Summary

Assembly language is a low-level language that uses instructions to communicate directly with the computer system. Logic used in computers is based on an on-and-off concept, from which binary 1s and 0s were derived. We have learned how to read and write binary from various number bases, and how to do arithmetic and bitwise computations.

We introduced popular assemblers and debuggers that we can use to build and validate our program. Then, we used FASM to code and build our Win32 low-level hello world program that uses APIs to communicate with the kernel. We validated our built executable program using x64dbg to debug it. Debugging our hello world program is a good start for us to get introduced to the world of reverse engineering.

Practice makes perfect. We have a listed a few suggested programs that can be developed using assembly language.

Knowing the lowest level of a code is a good start for our reverse engineering journey. As you finish up this book, assembly language will feel somewhat like a walk in the park.

Further reading

Intel's documentation contains the complete list of x86 instructions and describes the syntax and use of each instruction in assembly language. You can get these documents from http://www.intel.com/products/processor/manuals/.

4

Static and Dynamic Reversing

Like a patient in a hospital, a file needs to undergo some triage to determine the right allocation of resources. The result of the file assessment will tell us what tools need to be used, what kind of reversing steps need to be taken, and what resources will be used. The steps involved in carrying out reversing are categorized into static and dynamic analysis.

In this chapter, we will introduce the methods and tools used in assessing a file. We will be focusing on a 32-bit Windows operating system for our examples. This will be followed by an examination of tools we can use for static and dynamic analysis. This chapter can help you to generate a checklist that will serve as a guide for you to retrieve all information on a file in the least amount of time.

In this chapter, you will do the following:

- Gain an understanding of Target assessment
- Perform static analysis
- Perform dynamic analysis

Assessment and static analysis

A file needs to undergo an initial assessment in order for us to determine what tools and analysis methods will be required. This process also helps us to create a strategy for analyzing the file. Doing such an assessment requires carrying out a light static analysis. Here are some ideas for assessment that may serve as our guide:

- Where did it originate from:
    - One of the purposes of reverse engineering is to help network administrators prevent similar malware from infiltrating the network. Knowing where a file came from would be helpful in securing the channel used to transmit it. For example, if the file being analyzed was determined to have been an email attachment, network administrators should secure the email server.

- Existing information:
    - Searching the internet for already existing information can be very helpful. There might be existing analyses that has been done on the file. We would be able to determine what behaviors to expect, which will help hasten the analysis.

- Viewing the file and extracting its text strings:
    - Using tools to view the file help us to determine the type of file. Extracting readable text from the file also gives us hints of what messages, functions, and modules it will use when opened or executed.

- File information:
    - What is the file type?
    - Header and type analysis

Static analysis

Static analysis will help us make notes of what we will do during dynamic analysis. With knowledge of the x86 assembly language, we should be able to understand a disassembled Win32 PE file and its branches. Doing so, we would be able to prepare the right tools to read, open, and debug the file based on its file type, and also understand the file's structure based on its file format.

We begin static analysis by determining the file type, then move on to understanding the file format. We can extract text strings that might help us instantly identify useful information, such as the API function used, which library modules it will use, what high level language the file was compiled from, registry keys it will try to access, and websites or IP addresses it might try to connect to.

File types and header analysis

The type of file is the most important piece of information that sets off the whole analysis. If the file type is a Windows executable, a preset of PE tools will be prepared. If the file type is a Word document, the sandbox environment we are going to use will have to be installed with Microsoft Office and analysis tools that can read the OLE file format. If the given target for analysis is a website, we may need to prepare browser tools that can read HTML and debug Java scripts or Visual Basic scripts.

Extracting useful information from file

It would be fun to manually parse each piece of information about a file using file viewing tools, such as HxD (https://mh-nexus.de/en/hxd/). But, since searching for documentation about the file would take some time, there are existing tools that were developed for reverse engineers. These tools, readily available on the internet, can easily extract and display file information, and have features that can identify what type of file it is. This extracted information helps us determine what type of file we are dealing with.

PEid and TrID

PEid and TrID are the tools that are able to detect the type of file, the compiler used, the encrypting tool, and the packer and protector used. Compressed executables are better known as packers. Some examples of these packers are UPX, PECompact, and Aspack. Protectors, on the other hand, are somewhat like packers, but rather more advanced in the sense that the original compiled code would be protected from being reversed easily. Examples of protectors include Themida, AsProtect, and Enigma Protector.

Protector software is usually commercial software. Neither tool is updated anymore but both still work very well. Here's a screenshot of PEiD's main interface:

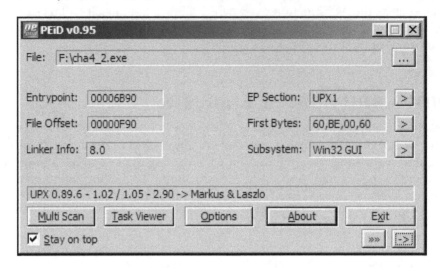

Here's a screenshot of how `TrID` can be used in a Linux Terminal:

```
> /opt/trid/trid cha4_1.exe

TrID/32 - File Identifier v2.24 - (C) 2003-16 By M.Pontello
Definitions found:  10241
Analyzing...

Collecting data from file: cha4_1.exe
 61.7% (.EXE) Win64 Executable (generic) (27625/18/4)
 14.7% (.DLL) Win32 Dynamic Link Library (generic) (6578/25/2)
 10.0% (.EXE) Win32 Executable (generic) (4508/7/1)
  4.5% (.EXE) OS/2 Executable (generic) (2029/13)
  4.4% (.EXE) Generic Win/DOS Executable (2002/3)
>
```

At the time of writing, these tools could be downloaded at the following links:
PEid is available from `http://www.softpedia.com/get/Programming/Packers-Crypters-Protectors/PEiD-updated.shtml`.
TriD is available at `http://mark0.net/soft-trid-e.html`.

python-magic

This is a Python module that is able to detect the file type. However, unlike PEiD and TrID, it also detects compilers and packers:

```
>>> import magic
>>> magic.from_file("cha4_1.exe")
'PE32 executable (GUI) Intel 80386, for MS Windows'
>>> magic.from_file("cha4_2.exe")
'PE32 executable (GUI) Intel 80386, for MS Windows, UPX compressed'
>>>
```

It can be downloaded at `https://pypi.org/project/python-magic/`.

file

Linux has a built-in command known as **file**. **file** is based on the `libmagic` library, and is able to determine file types of various file formats:

```
> file cha4_2.exe
cha4_2.exe: PE32 executable (GUI) Intel 80386, for MS Windows, UPX compressed
>
```

MASTIFF

MASTIFF is an static analyzer framework. It works on Linux and Mac. As a framework, the static analysis is based on plugins from the MASTIFF author and from the community.

These plugins include the following:

trid : This is used for identifying file types.
ssdeep : `ssdeep` is a fuzzy hash calculator. A fuzzy hash, or context triggered piecewise hashes (`CTPH`), can be used to identify nearly identical files. This is useful for identifying variants of a malware family.
pdftools : A plugin by Didier Stevens. This extracts information about PDF files.
exiftool : This shows info, from image files.
pefile : This shows information about PE files.
disitool : This is another Python script from Didier Stevens. This is used to extract digital signatures from signed executables.
pyOLEscanner : This is a tool used to extract information from OLE file types, such as Word documents and Excel spreadsheets.

An example of MASTIFF at work can be seen in the following screenshot:

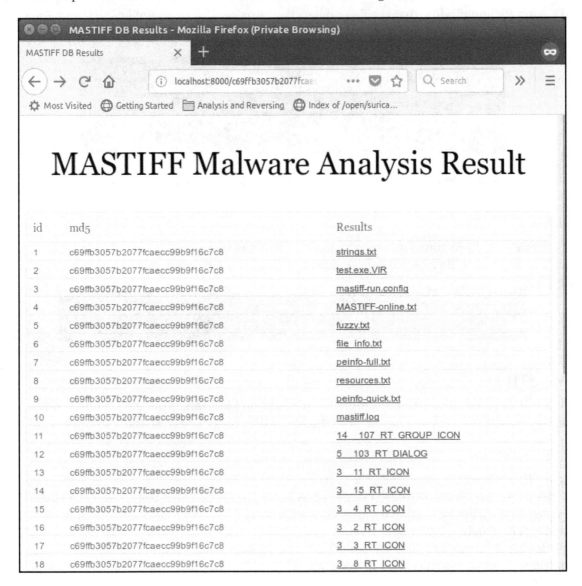

MASTIFF can be downloaded from `https://github.com/KoreLogicSecurity/mastiff`.

Other information

As part of static information gathering, a file is given its own unique hash. These hashes are used to identify a file from a database of file information. Hash information generally helps analysts share information about the file, without transmitting the file itself.

Here is an example of MASTIFF's `file_info` result on a test file:

```
File Name      /opt/mastiff/tests/test.exe
Size           89600
Time Analyzed  1528088801.84

Algorithm    Hash
----------   --------------------------------------------------------------
MD5          c69ffb3057b2077fcaecc99b9f16c7c8
SHA1         669c502ece05bd09dba947e408d3c023fa1889a0
SHA256       51d1b49ff13190d1e06ed97f1cd652ff10e6dd58cd7d5a187b801771db28676d
Fuzzy Hash   768:FDmEaj3Lq/PrBcZhuYQ2LvDejdUxJy+6F8JC6ROZU9QZU96Oz:FKEOL+V24MbDejdw44ROzP+
```

PE executables

PE executables are programs that work on Windows. Executable files have the `.exe` extension. Dynamic link libraries uses the same PE file format and use the `.dll` file extension. Windows device driver programs, also in PE file format, use the `.sys` extension. There are also other extensions that use the PE file format, such as screensavers (`.scr`).

The PE file format has a header, which is divided into the MZ header, along with its DOS stub and the PE header, followed by the data directories and section tables, as shown here:

The file format follows the original MSDOS EXE format, but was extended for Windows using the PE header. If a Windows program were run in an MSDOS environment, it would display this message: This program cannot be run in DOS mode.

The code that displays this message is part of the DOS stub.

The PE header's section table contains all the information about where code and data are located in the file, and how it will be mapped into the memory when it gets loaded as a process. The PE header contains the address where the program begins to execute code—a location known as the entry point—and will be set in the EIP register.

The data directories contain addresses of tables that, in turn, contain information such as the import table. The import table contains the libraries and APIs that will be used by the program. The table follows a structure that points to a set of addresses, pointing, in turn, to the names of libraries and their respective export functions:

The `peinfo` module used in MASTIFF is able to display the imported libraries and functions, as shown here:

```
----------Imported symbols----------

[IMAGE_IMPORT_DESCRIPTOR]
0x7BB4      0x0    OriginalFirstThunk:        0x96D8
0x7BB4      0x0    Characteristics:           0x96D8
0x7BB8      0x4    TimeDateStamp:             0x0        [Thu Jan  1 00:00:00 1970 UTC]
0x7BBC      0x8    ForwarderChain:            0x0
0x7BC0      0xC    Name:                      0x96EE
0x7BC4      0x10   FirstThunk:                0x80E8

USER32.dll.MessageBoxW Hint[511]

[IMAGE_IMPORT_DESCRIPTOR]
0x7BC8      0x0    OriginalFirstThunk:        0x95F0
0x7BC8      0x0    Characteristics:           0x95F0
0x7BCC      0x4    TimeDateStamp:             0x0        [Thu Jan  1 00:00:00 1970 UTC]
0x7BD0      0x8    ForwarderChain:            0x0
0x7BD4      0xC    Name:                      0x9B10
0x7BD8      0x10   FirstThunk:                0x8000

KERNEL32.dll.InterlockedDecrement Hint[700]
KERNEL32.dll.LCMapStringW Hint[739]
KERNEL32.dll.LCMapStringA Hint[737]
KERNEL32.dll.GetStringTypeW Hint[576]
KERNEL32.dll.MultiByteToWideChar Hint[794]
KERNEL32.dll.GetStringTypeA Hint[573]
KERNEL32.dll.GetStartupInfoW Hint[570]
KERNEL32.dll.TerminateProcess Hint[1069]
KERNEL32.dll.GetCurrentProcess Hint[425]
KERNEL32.dll.UnhandledExceptionFilter Hint[1086]
KERNEL32.dll.SetUnhandledExceptionFilter Hint[1045]
KERNEL32.dll.IsDebuggerPresent Hint[721]
KERNEL32.dll.GetModuleHandleW Hint[505]
KERNEL32.dll.Sleep Hint[1057]
KERNEL32.dll.GetProcAddress Hint[544]
KERNEL32.dll.ExitProcess Hint[260]
KERNEL32.dll.WriteFile Hint[1165]
KERNEL32.dll.GetStdHandle Hint[571]
KERNEL32.dll.GetModuleFileNameA Hint[500]
KERNEL32.dll.GetModuleFileNameW Hint[501]
KERNEL32.dll.FreeEnvironmentStringsW Hint[331]
KERNEL32.dll.GetEnvironmentStringsW Hint[449]
KERNEL32.dll.GetCommandLineW Hint[368]
KERNEL32.dll.SetHandleCount Hint[1000]
KERNEL32.dll.GetFileType Hint[471]
KERNEL32.dll.GetStartupInfoA Hint[569]
KERNEL32.dll.DeleteCriticalSection Hint[190]
KERNEL32.dll.TlsGetValue Hint[1076]
KERNEL32.dll.TlsAlloc Hint[1074]
```

HxD and HIEW are popular binary editors used in this chapter; HxD, being the more popular, is free, and can easily be used to make binary edits to a file. More information and a download link can be found at https://mh-nexus.de/en/hxd/. If you try using HxD, you'll see something similar to this screenshot:

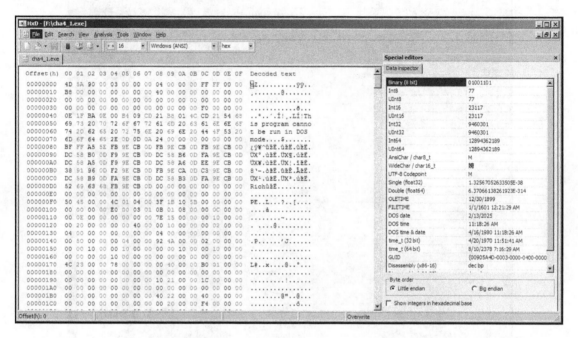

Another useful hex-editing tool is HIEW (Hacker's View). The demo and free versions are able to parse through a PE header. This tool can also show exports and imported API functions:

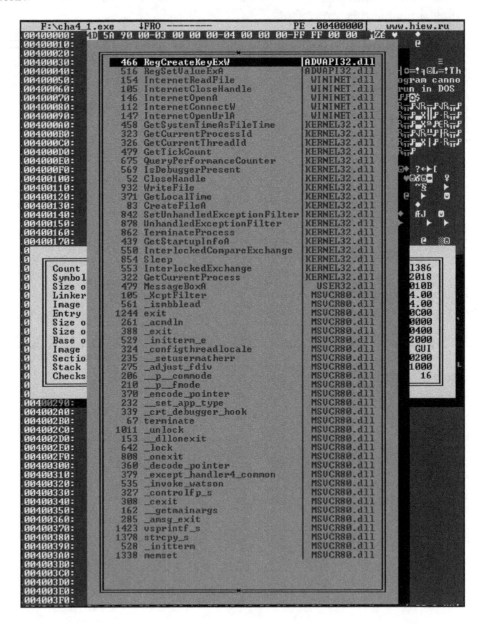

The statically imported modules, libraries, and functions are hints on what we can expect the program to access. Consider, for example, that if the PE file imports the KERNEL32.DLL library, then we should expect the file to contain core APIs that may access files, processes, and threads, or dynamically load other libraries and import functions. Here are some of the more common libraries that we should take note of:

- ADVAPI32.DLL : This library contains functions that will access the registry.
- MSVCRXX.DLL (where XX is a version number. Examples are the libraries MSVCRT.DLL and MSVCR80.DLL) – This contains Microsoft Visual C runtime functions. This tells us straight away that the program was compiled using Visual C.
- WININET.DLL : This library contains functions that accesses the internet.
- USER32.DLL : This contains window-control functions related to anything displayed on the monitor, such as dialog boxes, showing message boxes, and positioning window boxes where they should be.
- NTDLL.DLL : This library contains native functions that directly interact with the kernel system. KERNEL32.DLL and libraries like USER32.DLL, WININET.DLL, and ADVAPI32.DLL have functions that are used to forward information to the native functions to perform actual system-level operations.

Deadlisting

Deadlisting is an analysis method where we get to analyze a file's disassembled or decompiled code, and map out the flow of events that will happen when it executes. The resulting illustrated flow will serve as a guide for dynamic analysis.

IDA (Interactive Disassembler)

We previously introduced the IDA tool to show the disassembly of a given file. It has a graph-view feature that shows an overview of blocks of code and the branching of conditional flow. In deadlisting, we try to describe each block of code and what possible results it will give. This gives us an idea of what the program does.

Decompilers

Some high-level programs are compiled using p-code, such as C# and Visual Basic (p-code version). On the contrary, a decompiler attempts to recreate the high-level source code based on the p-code. A high-level syntax usually has an equivalent block of p-code that can by identified by the decompiler.

Programs compiled using the C language are laid to a file in plain assembly language. But since it is still a high-level language, some blocks of code can be identified back to their C syntax. The paid version of IDA Pro has an expensive, but very useful plugin, called Hex-Rays, that can identify these blocks of code and recreate the C source code.

ILSpy – C# Decompiler

A popular tool used to decompile a C# program is ILSpy. Some decompilers will leave the analyst with just the source being statically analyzed as is. But, in ILSpy, it is possible to save the decompiled source as a Visual Studio project. This enables the analyst to compile and debug it for dynamic analysis.

Dynamic analysis

Dynamic analysis is a type of analysis that requires live execution of the code. In static analysis, the farthest we can go is with deadlisting. If, for example, we encounter a code that decrypts or decompresses to a huge amount of data, and if we want to see the contents of the decoded data, then the fastest option would be to do dynamic analysis. We can run a debug session and let that area of code run for us. Both static analysis and dynamic analysis work hand in hand. Static analysis helps us identify points in the code where we need a deeper understanding and some actual interaction with the system. By following static analysis with dynamic analysis, we can also see actual data, such as file handles, randomly generated numbers, network socket and packet data, and API function results.

There are existing tools that can carry out an automated analysis, which runs the program in a sandbox environment. These tools either log the changes during runtime, or in between snapshots:

- Cuckoo (open source) – This tool is deployed locally. It requires a host and sandbox client(s). The host serves as a web console to which files are submitted for analysis. The files are executed in the sandbox, and all activities are logged and then sent back to the host server. The report can be viewed from the web console.

- RegShot (free) - This tool is used to take a snapshot of the registry and file system before and after running a program. The difference between the snapshots enables the analyst to determine what changes happened. The changes may include changes made by the operating system, and it is up to the analyst to identify which changes were caused by the program.
- Sandboxie (freemium) - This tool is used in the environment where the program will be run. It is claimed that internally, it uses isolation technology. In essence, the isolation technology allocates disk space, to which disk writes will only happen at the time the program is executed by Sandboxie. This enables Sandboxie to determine changes by looking only at the isolated space. A download link and some more information about Sandboxie can be found at `https://www.sandboxie.com/HowItWorks`.
- Malwr (free) - This is a free online service that uses Cuckoo. Files can be submitted at `https://malwr.com/`.
- ThreatAnalyzer (paid) - Originally known as CWSandbox, this is the most popular sandboxing technology used in the security industry for automating the extraction of information from a piece of running malware. The technology has improved a lot, especially with its reporting. In addition, it reports descriptive behaviors found, including a cloud query about the submitted file. It can cater to customized rules and flexible Python plugins to bring up behaviors seen by the analyst.
- Payload Security's Hybrid Analysis (free) - One of the most popular free online services, like Malwr, with report contents similar to that of ThreatAnalyzer.

Submitting files to online services reduce the need to set up a host-sandbox environment. However, some would still prefer to set up their own, to avoid having files shared to the community or an online service.

For malware analysis, it is advisable to do automated analysis and network information gathering at the time the file was received. Sites from which malware retrieve further data might not be available if authorities act fast enough to take such sites down.

Memory regions and the mapping of a process

In dynamic analysis, it is important to know what the memory looks like when a program gets loaded and then executed.

Since Windows and Linux are capable of multitasking, every process has its own **Virtual Address Space (VAS)**. For a 32-bit operating system, the VAS has a size of 4 GB. Each VAS is mapped to the physical memory using its respective page table and is managed by the operating system's kernel. So how do multiple VASes fit in the physical memory? The operating system manages this using paging. The paging has a list of used and unused memory, including privilege flags. If the physical memory is not enough, then paging can use disk space as an form of extended physical memory. A process and its module dependencies don't use up the whole 4 GB of space, and only these virtually allocated memory segments are listed as used in the page tables and mapped in the physical memory.

A VAS is divided into two regions: user space and kernel space, with the kernel space located in the higher address region. The division of virtual space differs between Windows and Linux:

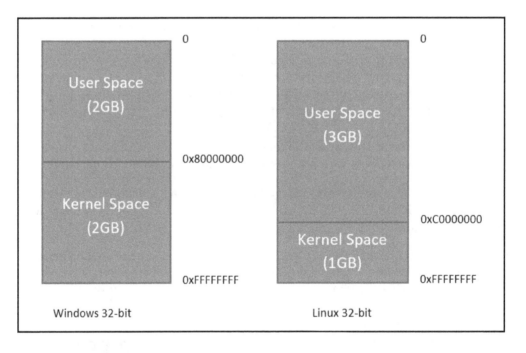

Every VAS has a kernel space listed in the page tables as a space that has exclusive privileges. Generally, these privileges are called kernel mode and user mode. These are specifically identified as protection rings. The kernel has a privilege of ring 0, while the applications that we use are run on ring 3 privilege. Device drivers are in the ring 1 or ring 2 layers, and are also identified as having kernel-mode privileges. If user-mode programs try to directly access the kernel space in kernel mode, a page fault is triggered.

Once a VAS is enabled, the user space is initially allocated for the stack, heap, the program, and the dynamic libraries. Further allocations are caused by the program at runtime by requesting memory using APIs, such as `malloc` and `VirtualAlloc`:

M Memory map

Address	Size	Owner	Section	Contains	Type		Access	Initial access
00010000	00010000			Heap	Map	00041004	RW	RW
00020000	00010000			Heap	Map	00041004	RW	RW
0006D000	00001000				Priv	00021104	RW Gua:	RW Guarded
0006E000	00002000			Stack of main thread	Priv	00021004	RW	RW
00070000	00004000				Map	00041002	R	R
00080000	00001000				Priv	00021004	RW	RW
00090000	00067000				Map	00041002	R	R
001B0000	00004000			Default heap	Priv	00021004	RW	RW
00390000	00003000			Heap	Priv	00021004	RW	RW
00400000	00001000	jbtest		PE header	Img	01001002	R	RWE CopyOnWr
00401000	00001000	jbtest	.data	Data	Img	01001008	RW Cop:	RWE CopyOnWr
00402000	00001000	jbtest	.code	Code	Img	01001020	R E	RWE CopyOnWr
00403000	00001000	jbtest	.idata	Imports	Img	01001004	RW	RWE CopyOnWr
75330000	00001000	KERNELBASE		PE header	Img	01001002	R	RWE CopyOnWr
75331000	00044000	KERNELBASE	.text	Code, imports, exports	Img	01001020	R E	RWE CopyOnWr
75375000	00002000	KERNELBASE	.data	Data	Img	01001004	RW	RWE CopyOnWr
75377000	00001000	KERNELBASE	.rsrc	Resources	Img	01001002	R	RWE CopyOnWr
75378000	00003000	KERNELBASE	.reloc	Relocations	Img	01001002	R	RWE CopyOnWr
755D0000	00001000	msvcrt		PE header	Img	01001002	R	RWE CopyOnWr
755D1000	0009F000	msvcrt	.text	Code, imports, exports	Img	01001020	R E	RWE CopyOnWr
75670000	00007000	msvcrt	.data	Data	Img	01001008	RW Cop:	RWE CopyOnWr
75677000	00001000	msvcrt	.rsrc	Resources	Img	01001002	R	RWE CopyOnWr
75678000	00004000	msvcrt	.reloc	Relocations	Img	01001002	R	RWE CopyOnWr
76350000	00001000	kernel32		PE header	Img	01001002	R	RWE CopyOnWr
76351000	000C6000	kernel32	.text	Code, imports, exports	Img	01001020	R E	RWE CopyOnWr
76417000	00001000	kernel32	.data	Data	Img	01001004	RW	RWE CopyOnWr
76418000	00001000	kernel32	.rsrc	Resources	Img	01001002	R	RWE CopyOnWr
76419000	0000C000	kernel32	.reloc	Relocations	Img	01001002	R	RWE CopyOnWr
771E0000	00001000	ntdll		PE header	Img	01001002	R	RWE CopyOnWr
771E1000	000D7000	ntdll	.text,RT	Code, exports	Img	01001020	R E	RWE CopyOnWr
772B8000	0000A000	ntdll	.data	Data	Img	01001008	RW Cop:	RWE CopyOnWr
772C2000	0005B000	ntdll	.rsrc	Resources	Img	01001002	R	RWE CopyOnWr
7731D000	00005000	ntdll	.reloc	Relocations	Img	01001002	R	RWE CopyOnWr
77440000	00001000			PE header	Img	01001002	R	RWE CopyOnWr
7F6F0000	00005000				Map	00041002	R	R
7FFB0000	00023000			Code pages	Map	00041002	R	R
7FFD3000	00001000			Process Environment Block	Priv	00021004	RW	RW
7FFDF000	00001000			Data block of main thread	Priv	00021004	RW	RW
7FFE0000	00001000			User Shared Data	Priv	00021002	R	R
80000000	7FFF0000			Kernel memory	Kern	00000000		

The preceding screenshot is a mapped view when `jbtest.exe` had just been loaded in 32-bit Windows. Here is a more descriptive standard layout of a program in a virtual allocated space under Windows:

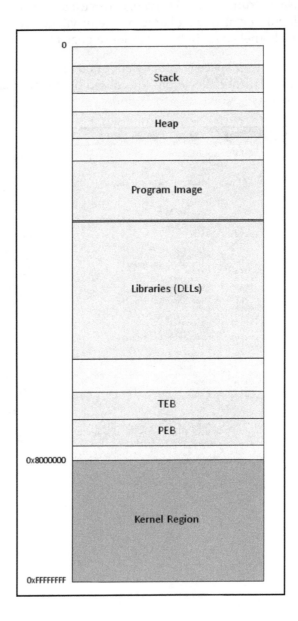

Process and thread monitoring

Monitoring the processes and threads, especially those that were created by the file we are analyzing, tells us that there are more behaviors occurring than is obvious. A process can create multiple threads, which tells us that it might be doing several behaviors at the same time. A created process tells us that a new program was just executed.

In Windows, the termination, creation, and opening of a process can be monitored by third-party tools such as Process Monitor. Though there are built-in tools, such as Task Manager, that can show information about processes, some third-party tools can give more detail about the processes and the threads tied to it.

Network traffic

The communicated data between a server and a client computer can only be seen during dynamic analysis. The packet captured during transmission will help the analyst understand what the program is sending to a server and how it will respond to any such data received.

Popular tools, such as Wireshark and Fiddler, are used to capture packets of data and store them as `pcap` files. In Linux, the `tcpdump` tool is commonly used to do the same thing.

Monitoring system changes

For Windows, there are three aspects we need to monitor: memory, disk, and registry. File monitoring tools look at created, modified, or deleted files and directories. On the other hand, registry monitoring tools look at created, updated, or deleted registry keys, values, and data. We can use tools such as `FileMon` and `RegMon` to do this job.

Post-execution differences

Comparing differences between snapshots taken before and after running the executable shows all the system changes that happened. For this type of analysis, any events that happened in between are not identified. This is useful for finding out how a software installer installed a program. And as a result, the difference comes in handy, especially when manually uninstalling a piece of software. The tool used here is RegShot.

Debugging

Deadlisting gives us most of the information we need, including the program's branching flow. Now, we have an opportunity to validate the path that the program will follow when doing debugging. We get to see the data that are temporarily stored in the registers and memory. And instead of manually trying to understand a decryption code, debugging it would easily show the resulting decrypted data.

Tools used for debugging in Windows include the following:

- `OllyDebug`
- `x86dbg`
- `IDA Pro`

Tools used for debugging Linux include the following:

- `gdb`
- `radare2`

Try it yourself

To try out the tools we have learned about, let's try doing some static analysis on `ch4_2.exe`. To help out, here's a list of what we need to find:

- File information:
    - file type
    - imported DLLs and APIs
    - text strings
    - file hash
- What the file does

Jumping right into getting file information, we will use TrID (`http://mark0.net/soft-trid-e.html`) to identify the file type. Execute the following line:

```
trid cha4_2.exe
```

The TrID result tells us that we have here a Windows 32-bit executable file that is UPX packed:

```
D:\Home\Packt\Mastering-Reverse-Engineering\ch4>trid cha4_2.exe

TrID/32 - File Identifier v2.24 - (C) 2003-16 By M.Pontello
Definitions found:  8131
Analyzing...

Collecting data from file: cha4_2.exe
 39.3% (.EXE) UPX compressed Win32 Executable (27066/9/6)
 38.6% (.EXE) Win32 EXE Yoda's Crypter (26569/9/4)
  9.5% (.DLL) Win32 Dynamic Link Library (generic) (6578/25/2)
  6.5% (.EXE) Win32 Executable (generic) (4508/7/1)
  2.9% (.EXE) Generic Win/DOS Executable (2002/3)
```

Knowing that this is a UPX packed file, we can try the UPX (https://upx.github.io/) tool's decompress feature to help us restore the file back to its original form before it was packed. A packed file is a compressed executable file that decompresses and then executes the program during runtime. The primary purpose of a packed file is to reduce the file size of executables while retaining the program's original behavior. We will be discussing more about packers in *Chapter 10*, *Packing and Encryption*, of this book. For now, let's just unpack this file with the UPX tool using the -d parameter:

```
upx -d cha4_2.exe
```

This results to the file being expanded back to its original form:

```
D:\Home\Packt\Mastering-Reverse-Engineering\ch4>upx -d cha4_2.exe
                  Ultimate Packer for eXecutables
                  Copyright (C) 1996 - 2013
UPX 3.91w       Markus Oberhumer, Laszlo Molnar & John Reiser   Sep 30th 2013

        File size        Ratio      Format      Name
   --------------------   --------   ---------   -----------
        7680 <-    5632   73.33%     win32/pe    cha4_2.exe

Unpacked 1 file.
```

And if we use `TrID` this time, we should get a different result:

```
D:\Home\Packt\Mastering-Reverse-Engineering\ch4>trid cha4_2.exe

TrID/32 - File Identifier v2.24 - (C) 2003-16 By M.Pontello
Definitions found:  8131
Analyzing...

Collecting data from file: cha4_2.exe
 64.6% (.EXE) Win64 Executable (generic) (27625/18/4)
 15.4% (.DLL) Win32 Dynamic Link Library (generic) (6578/25/2)
 10.5% (.EXE) Win32 Executable (generic) (4508/7/1)
  4.6% (.EXE) Generic Win/DOS Executable (2002/3)
  4.6% (.EXE) DOS Executable Generic (2000/1)
```

It is still a Windows executable file, so we can use CFF Explorer to check for more information:

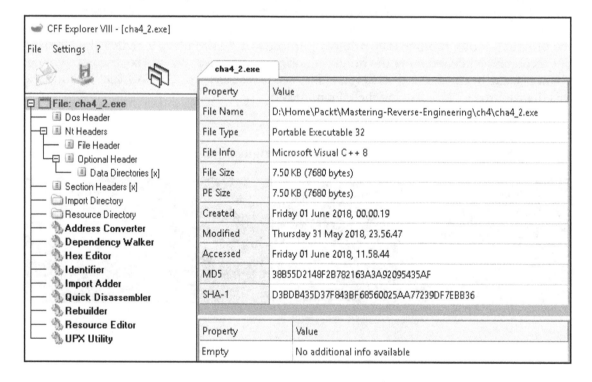

On the left pane, if we select Import Directory, we should see a list of imported library files and API functions it will use, as shown here:

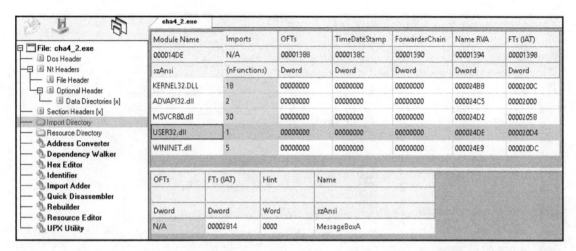

Clicking on USER32.dll, we see that the MessageBoxA API is going to be used by the program.

Using the bintext (`http://b2b-download.mcafee.com/products/tools/foundstone/bintext303.zip`) tool, we can see a list of text strings found in the file:

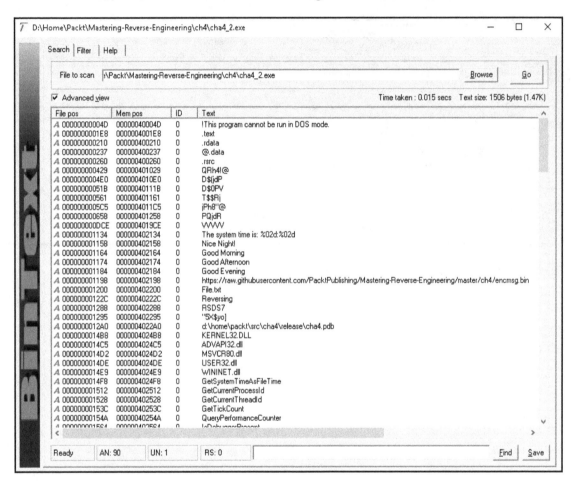

These appear to be the notable text strings, which suggest that the program checks for the time and displays various greetings. It will probably retrieve a file from the internet. It may do something about the `File.txt` file. But all these are just educated guesses, which makes good practice for reversing, as it helps use to build an overview of the relationship between each aspect of our analysis:

```
000000001134 000000402134 0 The system time is: %02d:%02d
000000001158 000000402158 0 Nice Night!
000000001164 000000402164 0 Good Morning
000000001174 000000402174 0 Good Afternoon
000000001184 000000402184 0 Good Evening
000000001198 000000402198 0
https://raw.githubusercontent.com/PacktPublishing/Mastering-Reverse-Enginee
ring/master/ch4/encmsg.bin
000000001200 000000402200 0 File.txt
00000000122C 00000040222C 0 Reversing
```

The hash (MD5, SHA1, SHA256) of a file will help as a reference to every file we analyze. There are a lot of file hash-generating tools available in the internet. To generate the hashes of this file, we chose a tool called HashMyFiles. This is a tool compiled for Windows OS and can be added to the context menu (right-click) of the Windows Explorer:

Filename	MD5	SHA1	CRC32	SHA-256
cha4_2.exe	38b55d2148f2b782163a3a92095435af	d3bdb435d37f843bf68560025aa77239df7eb	0bfe57ff	810c0ac30aa69248a41c175813ede941

It can display the file's CRC, MD5, SHA1, SHA-256, SHA-512, and SHA-384, as follows:

```
MD5: 38b55d2148f2b782163a3a92095435af
SHA1: d3bdb435d37f843bf68560025aa77239df7ebb36
CRC: 0bfe57ff
SHA256: 810c0ac30aa69248a41c175813ede941c79f27ddce68a91054a741460246e0ae
SHA512:
a870b7b9d6cc4d86799d6db56bc6f8ad811fb6298737e26a52a706b33be6fe7a8993f9acdbe
7fe1308f9dbf61aa1dd7a95015bab72b5c6af7b7359850036890e
SHA384:
b0425bb66c1d327d7819f13647dc50cf2214bf00e5fb89de63bcb442535860e13516de870cb
f07237cf04d739ba6ae72
```

Usually, we only take either MD5, SHA1, or SHA256.

We should not forget the file size and the creation time using a simple file property check:

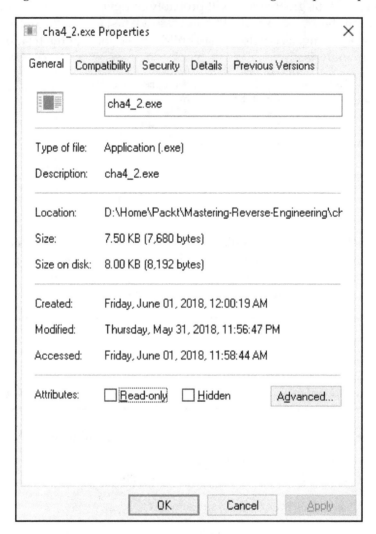

The **Modified date** is more relevant in terms of when the file was actually compiled. The **Created date** is when the file was written or copied to the directory where it is now. That means that the first time the file was built, both the **Created** and **Modified** dates were the same.

To statically analyze the file's behavior, we will be using a disassembly tool known as IDA Pro. A freeware version of IDA Pro can be found at `https://www.hex-rays.com/products/ida/support/download_freeware.shtml`. But, if you can afford the luxury of its paid version, which we highly recommend, please do purchase it. We find the features and supported architectures of the paid version way better. But for this book, we will be using every available tool that does not require purchasing.

There are currently two known free versions of IDA Pro. We have made backups of the tool available at `https://github.com/PacktPublishing/Mastering-Reverse-Engineering/tree/master/tools/Disassembler%20Tools`. And since we are dealing with a 32-bit Windows executable file, select the 32-bit version.

Once IDA Pro is installed, open up `cha4_2.exe` inside. Wait for the auto-analysis to complete and it will redirct the disassembly to the `WinMain` function:

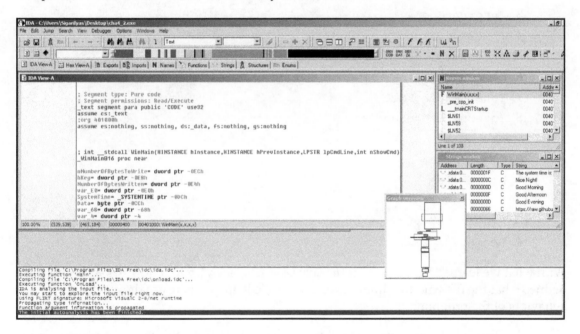

Scrolling down will show more disassembly code that we learned in *Chapter 3, The Low-Level Language*. For deadlisting behaviors, we usually look for instructions that call APIs. The very first API we encounter is a call to GetSystemTime:

```
lea      eax, [esp+0ECh+SystemTime]
push     eax                    ; lpSystemTime
call     ds:GetLocalTime
movzx    ecx, [esp+0ECh+SystemTime.wMinute]
movzx    edx, [esp+0ECh+SystemTime.wHour]
```

Following the code, we encounter these API functions in this sequence:

1. vsprintf_s
2. MessageBoxA
3. InternetOpenA
4. InternetConnectW
5. InternetOpenUrlA
6. memset
7. InternetReadFile
8. InternetCloseHandle
9. strcpy_s
10. CreateFileA
11. WriteFile
12. CloseHandle
13. RegCreateKeyExW
14. RegSetValueExA

With what we learned in *Chapter 3, The Low Level Language*, try to follow the code and deduce what the file will do without executing it. To help out, here are the expected behaviors of the program:

1. Displaying a message depending on the current system time. The messages can be one of the following:
   - Good Morning
   - Good Afternoon
   - Good Evening
   - Nice Night

2. Reading the contents of a file from the internet, decrypting the contents, and saving it to a file named `File.txt`.
3. Making a registry key, `HKEY_CURRENT_USER\Software\Packt`, and storing the same decrypted data in the `Reversing` registry value.

This may take a long time for beginners, but with continuous practice, analysis will be done at a fast pace.

Summary

Both approaches to analysis, static and dynamic, have their means to extract information and are required to properly analyze a file. Before doing dynamic analysis, it is recommended to start with static analysis first. We stick to our goal of generating an analysis report from the information we get. The analyst is not limited to using just the tools and resources outlined here to conduct an analysis—any information from the internet is useful, but validating it with your own analysis will stand as proof. Taking all items from the file, such as notable text strings, imported API functions, system changes, code flows, and possible blocks of behaviors are important, as these may be useful when building an overview of the file.

The result of the static analysis draws together the approach and resources that need to be prepared for dynamic analysis. For example, if the static analysis identified the file as a `Win32` PE file executable, then tools for analyzing PE files will need to be prepared.

As part of dynamic analysis, we discussed about **Virtual Allocated Space (VAS)** and how a program is mapped in memory along with its library dependencies. This information comes in handy when attempting reversing in further chapters.

We also introduced a few tools that we can use to engage in both static and dynamic approaches, and ended this chapter with a brief exercise on a 32-bit Windows PE executable file. In the next chapter, we will show more use of some of these tools as we reverse-engineer files.

References

The files used in this chapter can be downloaded from `https://github.com/ PacktPublishing/Mastering-Reverse-Engineering`.

5
Tools of the Trade

In the previous chapters, we used some simple reversing tools, such as PEiD, CFF Explorer, IDA Pro, and OllyDbg, which aided us in our reversing adventure. This chapter explores and introduces more tools we can use and choose from. The selection of tools depend on the analysis required. For example, if a file was identified as an ELF file type, we'd need to use tools for analyzing a Linux executable.

This chapter covers tools for Windows and Linux, categorized for static and dynamic analysis. There are a lot of tools available out there—don't limit yourself to the tools discussed in this book.

In this chapter, you will achieve the following learning outcomes:

- Setting up tools
- Understanding static and dynamic tools for Windows, and Linux
- Understanding support tools

Analysis environments

The environment setup in reverse engineering is crucial to the result. We need a sandbox environment where we can dissect and play with the file, without worrying that we may break something. And since the most popular operating systems are Microsoft Windows and Linux, let's discuss using these operating systems in a virtual environment.

Virtual machines

From the first chapter, we introduced using VirtualBox as our desktop virtualization system. The reason we chose VirtualBox was because of it being freeware. But besides VirtualBox, choosing the right sandboxing software depends on user preferences and requirements. There are pros and cons for every piece of sandboxing software, so it is worth exploring those on offer to find out which software you prefer. Here's a small list of virtualization software:

- **VMWare Workstation:** This is a commercial, and widely popular, piece of virtualization software. VMWare Workstation can be downloaded from `https://www.vmware.com`.

- **VirtualBox:** This is free and open source virtualization software. It can be downloaded from `https://www.virtualbox.org`.

- **Qemu (Quick Emulator):** This is actually not virtualization software, but rather, an emulator. Virtualization software uses virtualization features of the CPU, but uses real CPU resources to do this, while emulators simply imitate a CPU and its resources. That is, running an operating system in a virtualized environment uses the real CPU, while running an operating system in an emulated environment uses an imitated CPU. The Qemu module can be installed from Linux standard repositories. It has ports for both Windows and macOS, and can be downloaded from `https://www.qemu.org`.

- **Bochs:** An emulator that is limited to emulating the x86 CPU architecture. It is released as an open source and usually used for debugging the **Master Boot Record** (**MBR**) of small disk images. See `http://bochs.sourceforge.net` for more details.

- **Microsoft Hyper-V:** A virtualization feature of selected Microsoft Windows versions, including Windows 10. Activate it from the following menu like so:

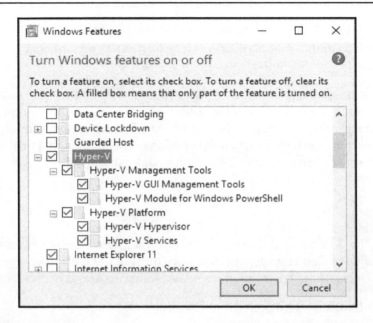

- **Parallels:** A commercial virtualization program, primarily designed to run Windows in a macOS host. More information about this piece of software can be found at `https://www.parallels.com/`.

The advantage of emulators is that other CPU architectures, such as ARM, can be emulated. Unlike virtualization software, emulators depend on the bare-metal machine's hypervisor. The drawback is possible slow performance as every emulated instruction is interpreted.

Windows

It is recommended to do analysis on a 32- or 64-bit Windows 10 system, or the most recent version on offer. At the least, Windows 7 can still be used, since it is light and has a stable environment for running executable files. As much as possible, selecting the most popular and widely used version of Windows will be the best choice. Choosing old versions such as XP may not be very helpful, unless the program we are going to reverse was solely built for Windows XP.

At the time of writing, there are two ways we can get Windows for our analysis:

- Install Windows 10 from an installer or ISO image that can be downloaded from `https://www.microsoft.com/en-us/software-download/windows10`.

- Deploy the Windows appliance used for testing old versions of Edge and Internet Explorer. The appliance can be downloaded from `https://developer.microsoft.com/en-us/microsoft-edge/tools/vms`.

These downloads do not have any license installed, and will expire within a short period. For the second option in the preceding list, after the deploying the appliance, it is best to take an initial snapshot *before* running the virtual machine. Reverting to this initial snapshot should reset the expiration back to when the appliance was deployed. Further snapshots should also be created, containing configuration updates and installed tools.

Linux

Linux can easily be downloaded due to it being open source. Popular systems are usually forked from Debian or Red Hat systems. But since most of the tools developed for analysis are built under Debian-based systems, we selected Lubuntu as our analysis environment.

 Lubuntu is a light version of Ubuntu.

However, we are not leaving Red Hat-based systems from our list. If a program was designed to run only on Red Hat-based systems, we should do our dynamic reversing and debugging on a Red Hat-based system. As noted, reverse engineering requires not only the tools fit for the target, but the environment as well.

Lubuntu can be downloaded from `https://lubuntu.net`. But, if you prefer using Ubuntu, you can download the installer from `https://www.ubuntu.com`.

Information gathering tools

Knowing what we are dealing with prepares us further. For example, if a file were identified as a Windows executable, we then prepare Windows executable tools. Information gathering tools helps us identify what the file type is and its properties. The information gathered becomes a part of the analysis profile. These tools are categorized as file type identifying, hash calculating, text string gathering, and monitoring tools.

File type information

These tools gather primary information about a file. The data gathered includes the filename, file size, file type, and file type-specific properties. The result of these tools enables the analyst to plan how to analyze the file:

- **PEiD:** A tool used to identify the file type, the packer, and compiler. It is built to run in Windows. It is not maintained, but still very useful.
- **TrID:** A command-line tool similar to PEiD. This tool has Windows and Linux versions. It can read a community-driven signature database of various file types.
- **CFF Explorer:** This tool is primarily used to read and make edits in a PE format file. It runs under Windows and has a lot of features, such as listing processes and dumping processes to a file. It can also be used to rebuild a process dump.
- **PE Explorer:** Another tool used to read and edit the structure of PE files. It can also unpack a number of executable compressed programs, such as UPX, Upack, and NSPack. PE Explorer only runs in Windows.
- **Detect-it-Easy (DiE):** Downloaded from `https://github.com/horsicq/Detect-It-Easy`, DiE is an open source tool that uses a community-driven set of algorithmic signatures to identify files. The tool has builds for Windows and Linux.
- **ExifTool:** This tool was primarily designed to read and edit the metadata of image files with an EXIF file format. It was further developed to extend features for other file formats, including PE files. ExifTool is available for Windows and Linux and can be downloaded from `https://sno.phy.queensu.ca/~phil/exiftool/`.

Hash identifying

Information gathering also includes identifying a file by its hash. Not only does the hash help validate a transferred file; it is also commonly used as a unique ID for a file analysis profile:

- **Quickhash:** This is an open source tool available for Windows, Linux, and macOS that generates the MD5, SHA1, SHA256, and SHA512 of any file. It can be downloaded from `https://quickhash-gui.org/`.

- **HashTab:** This tool runs in Windows and can be integrated as a tab in the properties information of a file. It calculates the MD5, SHA1, and a couple of hash algorithms.
- **7-zip:** This tool is actually a file archiver, but it has an extension tool that can be enabled to calculate the hash of a file in MD5, SHA1, SHA256, and so forth.

Strings

Text-string gathering tools are mainly used to quickly identify possible functions or messages used by the program. It is not always true that every text string is used by the program. Program flow still depends on conditions set in the program. However, the string locations in the file can be used as markers that the analyst can trace back:

- **SysInternals Suite's strings:** This is a command-line tool for Windows that shows the list of text strings in any type of file.
- **BinText:** This is a GUI-based Windows tool that can display the ASCII and Unicode text strings for any given file.

Monitoring tools

Without manually digging deeper into the program's algorithm, simply running the program can give plenty of information about its behavior. Monitoring tools usually work by placing sensors in common or specific system library functions, then logging the parameters used. Using monitoring tools is a fast way to produce an initial behavior analysis of a program:

- **SysInternals Suite's Procmon or Process Monitor:** Running only on Windows, this is a real-time monitoring tool that monitors processes, thread, filesystem, and registry events. It can be downloaded from `https://docs.microsoft.com/en-us/sysinternals/downloads/procmon` and is a part of the SysInternals Suite package.
- **API Monitor:** This powerful tool helps reverse engineering by monitoring API calls as the program runs. The analyst has to set which API the tool needs to hook. Once an API is hooked, all user-mode processes using the API will be logged. API Monitor can be downloaded from `http://www.rohitab.com/apimonitor`.

- **CaptureBAT:** In addition to what Process Monitor can do, this command-line tool is also capable of monitoring network traffic.

Default command-line tools

There are a couple of useful tools that are already built into the operating system we are working on. These come in handy when third party tools are not available:

- **strings:** This is a Linux command used to list the strings found in a given file.
- **md5sum:** This is a Linux command used to calculate the MD5 hash of a given file.
- **file:** This is a command line in Linux used to identify files. It uses the libmagic library.

Disassemblers

Disassemblers are tools used to look at the low-level code of a program compiled from either a high-level language, or of the same low-level language. As part of analysis, deadlisting and recognizing the blocks of code help to build up the behavior of the program. It is then be easier to identify only code blocks that need to be thoroughly debugged, without running through the whole program code:

- **IDA Pro:** A popular tool used in the software security industry to disassemble various low-level language built on the x86 and ARM architectures. It has a wide list of features. It can generate a graphical flow of code, showing code blocks and branching. It also has scripting that can be used to parse through the code and disassemble it into more meaningful information. IDA Pro has an extended plugin, called Hex-Rays, that is capable of identifying assembly codes to its equivalent C source or syntax. The free version of IDA Pro can be downloaded from https://www.hex-rays.com/products/ida/support/download_freeware.shtml.

- **Radare:** Available on Windows, Linux, and macOS, this open source tool shows the disassembled equivalent of a given program. It has a command-line interface view, but there are existing plugins that can show it using the computer's browser. Radare's source can be downloaded and built from `https://github.com/radare/radare2`. Information on how to install binaries can be found at its website, available at `https://rada.re`.
- **Capstone:** This is an open source disassembly and decompiler engine. The engine is used by many disassembly and decompiler tools, such as Snowman. Information about this tool can be found at `https://www.capstone-engine.org/`.
- **Hopper:** A disassembly tool for Linux and macOS operating systems. It has a similar interface as IDA Pro and is capable of debugging using GDB.
- **BEYE:** Also known as Binary EYE, this is a hex viewer and editing tool with the addition of a disassembly view mode. BEYE is available for Windows and Linux. It can be downloaded from `https://sourceforge.net/projects/beye/`.
- **HIEW:** Also known as Hacker's View, is similar to BEYE, but has better information output for PE files. The paid version of HIEW has more features supporting a lot of file types and machine architectures.

Debuggers

When debugging tools are used, this would mean that we are in the code-tracing phase of our analysis. Debuggers are used to step in every instruction the program is supposed to do. In the process of debugging, actual interaction and changes in memory, disk, network, and devices can be identified:

- **x86dbg:** This is a Windows user-mode debugger. It is open source and can debug 32- and 64-bit programs. It is capable of accepting plugins written by users. The source code can be downloaded from `https://github.com/x64dbg`. The builds can be downloaded from `https://x64dbg.com`.
- **IDA Pro:** Paid versions of IDA Pro are capable of debugging using the same disassembly interface. It is very useful when you want to see a graphical view of decrypted code.

- **OllyDebug:** A popular Windows debugger, due to its portability and rich features. It can accommodate plugins written by its users, adding capabilities such as unpacking a loaded executable compressed file (by reaching the original entry point) and memory dumping. Ollydebug can be downloaded from `http://www.ollydbg.de/`.

- **Immunity Debugger:** The interface of this program looks like a highly improved version of OllyDebug. It has plugin support for Python and other tools. Immunity Debugger can be downloaded from Immunity, Inc.'s site at `https://www.immunityinc.com/products/debugger/`. Older versions can be found at `https://github.com/kbandla/ImmunityDebugger/`.

- **Windbg:** A debugger developed by Microsoft. The interface is quite plain, but can be configured to show every kind of information needed by a reverser. It is capable of being set up to remotely debug device drivers, software in the kernel levels, and even a whole Microsoft operating system.

- **GDB:** Also known as GNU Debugger, GDB is originally a debugger developed for Linux and a couple of other operating systems. It is capable of debugging not only low-level languages but also used for debugging high-level languages such as C, C++, and Java. GDB can also be used in Windows. GDB uses a command-line interface, but there are existing GUI programs that use GDB for a more informative look.

- **Radare:** Radare also has a debugger packaged along with it. It can also do remote debugging by using GDB remotely. Its interface is command line-based but has an integrated visual view. Its developers also made a better visual view using the browser. Basically, compared with GDB, Radare would be much preferred. It is also primarily built for Linux, but has compiled binaries on offer for Windows and macOS.

Decompilers

Disassemblers are used to show the low-level code of a compiled high-level program. Decompilers, on the other hand, attempt to show the high-level source code of the program. These tools work by identifying blocks of low-level code that match with corresponding syntax in the high-level program. It is expected that these tools won't be able to show what the original program's source code looks like, but nonetheless, they help speed up analysis with a better view of the program's pseudo code:

- **Snowman:** This is a C and C++ decompiler. It can run as a standalone tool, or as an IDA Pro plugin. The source can be found at `https://github.com/yegord/snowman`, while its compiled binaries can be downloaded from `https://derevenets.com/`. It is available for Windows and Linux.
- **Hex-Rays:** This is also a C and C++ decompiler and runs as a plugin for IDA Pro. It is sold commercially as part of IDA Pro. Users should expect this to have a better decompiled output than Snowman.
- **dotPeek:** This is a free .NET decompiler by Jetbrains. It can be downloaded from `https://www.jetbrains.com/decompiler/`.
- **iLSpy:** This is an open source .NET decompiler. The source and pre-compiled binaries can be found at `https://github.com/icsharpcode/ILSpy`.

Network tools

The following is a list of tools that are used to monitor the network:

- **tcpdump:** This is a Linux-based tool used to capture network traffic. It can be installed from the default repositories.
- **Wireshark:** This tool is capable of monitoring network traffic. Incoming and outgoing network traffic, including packet information and data, is logged in real time. Originally named Ethereal, Wireshark is available for Windows, Linux, and macOS, and can be downloaded from `https://www.wireshark.org/`.
- **mitmproxy:** Also known as Man-In-The-Middle Proxy. As its name states, it is set up as a proxy, and thus able to control and monitor network traffic before data is either sent externally or received by internal programs.
- **inetsim:** Essentially, this tool fakes network and internet connectivity, thereby trapping any network traffic sent externally by a program. This is very useful for analyzing malware, preventing it from sending data externally, while having knowledge of where it connects to and what data it tries to send.

Editing tools

There may be instances where we need to modify the contents of a program to make it work properly, or validate a code behavior. Modifying data in a file can also change the code flow where conditional instructions may happen. Changing instructions can also work around anti-debugging tricks:

- **HxD Hex Editor:** A Windows binary file viewer and editor. You can use this to view the binary contents of a file.
- **Bless:** A Linux binary file viewer and editor.
- **Notepad++:** A Windows text editor, but can also read binary files, though reading binary files with hexadecimal digits would require a hex-editing plugin. Still, this is useful for reading and analyzing scripts, due to its wide range of supported languages, including Visual Basic and JavaScript.
- **BEYE:** A useful tool for viewing and editing any file type. BEYE is available for Windows and Linux.
- **HIEW:** The feature that makes this software worthwhile is its ability to do on-the-fly encryption using assembly language.

Attack tools

There may be cases where we need to craft our own packets to fool the program into thinking that it is receiving live data from the network. Though these tools are primarily developed to generate exploited network packets for penetration testing, these can also be used for reverse engineering:

- **Metasploit** (https://www.metasploit.com/): This is a framework with scripts that can generate exploited packets to send to the target for penetration tests. The scripts are modular and users can develop their own scripts.
- **ExploitPack** (http://exploitpack.com/): This has the same concept as Metasploit, though is maintained by a different group of researchers.

Automation tools

Developing our own programs to do analysis may sometimes be a must. For example, if the program contains a decryption algorithm, we can develop a separate program that can run the same algorithm that may be used for similar programs with the same decryption algorithm. If we wanted to identify variants of the file we were analyzing, we could automate the identification for incoming files using one of the following:

- **Python:** This scripting language is popular because of it availability across multiple platforms. It is pre-installed in Linux operating systems; compiled binaries for Windows can be downloaded from `https://www.python.org/`.
- **Yara:** A tool and language from the developers of VirusTotal. It is capable of searching the contents of files for a set of binary or text signatures. Its most common application is in searching for malware remnants in a compromised system.
- **Visual Studio:** A piece of Microsoft software for coding and building programs. It can be used by reverse engineers when decompiled programs need to be debugged graphically. For example, we can debug a decompiled C# program using Visual Studio, instead of trying to understand each p-code of disassembled C# codes.

Software forensic tools

Reverse engineering includes analyzing the post-execution of a program. This entails gathering and determining objects and events from memory and disk images. With these tools, we can analyze the suspended state of an operating system with the process of the program being analyzed still in running memory.

Here is a list of different forensic software that can be downloaded:

- Digital Forensics Framework (`https://github.com/arxsys/dff`)
- Open Computer Forensics Architecture

    `https://github.com/DNPA/OcfaArch`

    `https://github.com/DNPA/OcfaLib`

    `https://github.com/DNPA/OcfaModules`

    `https://github.com/DNPA/OcfaDocs`

    `https://github.com/DNPA/OcfaJavaLib`

- CAINE (`https://www.caine-live.net/`)
- X-Ways Forensics Disk Tools (`http://www.x-ways.net/forensics/`)
- SIFT (`https://digital-forensics.sans.org/community/downloads`)
- SleuthKit (`http://www.sleuthkit.org/`)
- LibForensics (`https://code.google.com/archive/p/libforensics/`)
- Volatility (`https://github.com/volatilityfoundation`):

In malware analysis, Volatility is one of the popular pieces of open source software used. It is able to read suspended states of virtual machines. The advantage of such tools is that malware, such as rootkits, that try to hide themselves from user domains can be extracted using memory forensic tools.

- BulkExtractor (`http://downloads.digitalcorpora.org/downloads/bulk_extractor/`)
- PlainSight (`http://www.plainsight.info/index.html`)
- Helix3 (`http://www.e-fense.com/products.php`)
- RedLine (`https://www.fireeye.com/services/freeware/redline.html`)
- Xplico (`https://www.xplico.org/`)

Automated dynamic analysis

These are tools used to automatically gather information by running the program in an enclosed sandbox.

- **Cuckoo:** This is a piece of Python-coded software deployed in Debian-based operating systems. Usually, Cuckoo is installed in the hosting Ubuntu system, and sends files to be analyzed in the VMWare or VirtualBox sandbox clients. Its development is community-driven, and as such, a lot of open source plugins are available for download.
- **ThreatAnalyzer:** Sold commercially, ThreatAnalyzer, previously known as CWSandbox, has been popular in the anti-virus community for its ability to analyze malware and return very useful information. And because users are able to develop their own rules, ThreatAnalyzer, as a backend system, can be used to determine if a submitted file contains malicious behaviors or not.
- **Joe Sandbox:** This is another commercial tool that shows meaningful information about the activities that a submitted program carries out when executed.

- **Buster Sandbox Analyzer (BSA):** The setup of BSA is different from the first three tools. This one does not require a client sandbox. It is installed in the sandbox environment. The concept of this tool is to allocate disk space where a program can run. After running, everything that happened in the space is logged and restored back afterwards. It is still recommended to use BSA in an enclosed environment.
- **Regshot:** this is a tool used to capture a snapshot of the disk and registry. After running a program, the user can take a second snapshot. The difference of the snapshots can be compared, thereby showing what changes were made in the system. Regshot should be run in an enclosed environment.

Online service sites

There are existing online services that can also aid us in our reversing.

- **VirusTotal:** This submits a file or a URL and cross-references it with a list of detections from various security programs. The result gives us an idea if the file is indeed malicious or not. It can also show us some file information, such as the SHA256, MD5, file size, and any indicators.
- **Malwr:** Files submitted here will be submitted to a backend Cuckoo system.
- **Falcon Sandbox:** This is also known as hybrid-analysis, and is an online automated analysis system developed by Payload Security. Results from Cuckoo and hybrid-analysis uncover similar behaviors, but one may show more information than the other. This may depend on how the client sandbox was set up. If, say, the .NET framework was not installed in the sandbox, submitted .NET executables will not run as expected.
- **whois.domaintools.com:** This is a site that shows the whois information about a domain or URL. This may come in handy, especially when trying to determine which country or state a program is trying to connect to.
- **robtex.com:** A similar site to whois, that shows historical info and a graphical tree of what a given site is connected to.
- **debuggex.com:** This is an online regular expressions service, where you can test your regex syntax. This can come in handy when developing scripts, or reading scripts or codes that contain regular expressions.

Submitting files or URLs to these online sites would mean that you are sharing information to their end. It would be best to ask for the permission of the owner of the file or URL before submitting.

Summary

In this chapter, we listed some of the tools used for reverse engineering. We tried to categorized the tools based on their purposes. But just as how we choose every piece of software that we use, the reverser's preferred set of tools depend on the packed features they contain, how user-friendly they are, and most importantly, whether or not they have the features required to do the job. We have covered the tools we can use for static analysis, including binary viewer and disassembly tools. We also listed useful debugging tools that we can use for Windows and Linux.

From the list, I personally recommend HIEW, x86dbg, IDA Pro, Snowman, and iLSpy for Windows analysis of PE binary executables. And on the Linux side, BEYE, Radare, GDB, and IDA Pro are great for analyzing ELF files.

We also covered some online services that can help us gain more information about sites we extracted from the analysis. We also introduced systems that can automate analysis, when we are going to deal with a lot of files. In addition, we listed a few forensic tools that we can use to analyze suspended memory.

As always, these tools have their pros and cons, and those eventually chosen will depend on the user and the type of analysis needed. The tools each have their own unique capability and comfort. For the next chapters, we will be using a mix of these tools. We may not use all of them, but we'll use what will get the analysis done.

In the next chapter, we'll learn more tools as we engage in reverse engineering on Linux platforms.

6

RE in Linux Platforms

A lot of our tools work great in Linux. In the previous chapter, we introduced a few Linux command-line tools that are already built-in by default. Linux already has Python scripting installed, as well. In this chapter, we are going to discuss a good setup for analyzing Linux files and hosting Windows sandbox clients.

We are going to learn how to reverse an ELF file by exploring the reversing tools. We will end this chapter by setting up a Windows sandbox client, running a program in it, and monitoring the network traffic coming from the sandbox.

Not all of us are fond of using Linux. Linux is an open source system. It is a technology that will stick with us. As a reverse engineer, no technology should be an obstacle, and it is never too late to learn this technology. The basics of using Linux systems can easily be found on the internet. As much as possible, this chapter tries to detail the steps required to install and execute what is needed in a way that you can follow.

In this chapter, you will look at the following

- Understanding of linux executables
- Reversing an ELF file
- Virtualization in Linux – an analysis of a Windows executable under a Linux host
- Network traffic monitoring

Setup

This chapter discusses Linux reverse engineering, so we need to have a Linux setup. For reverse engineering, it is recommended to deploy Linux on a bare-metal machine. And since most of the analysis tools that have been developed are Debian-based, let's use 32-bit Ubuntu Desktop. I chose Ubuntu because it has a strong community. Because of that, most of the issues may already have a resolution or solutions may be readily available.

Why build our setup on a bare-metal machine? It is a better host for our sandbox clients, especially when monitoring network traffic. It also has an advantage in proper handling of Windows malware, preventing compromise due to accidental malware execution.

You can go to `https://www.ubuntu.com/` to obtain an ISO for the Ubuntu installer. The site includes an installation guide. For additional help, you can visit the community forum at `https://ubuntuforums.org/`.

 "Bare-metal machines" refers to computers that execute code directly on the hardware. It is usually a term used to refer to hardware, as opposed to virtual machines.

Linux executable – hello world

To begin with, let's create a hello world program. Before anything else, we need to make sure that the tools required to build it are installed. Open a Terminal (the Terminal is Linux's version of Windows' Command Prompt) and enter the following command. This may require you to enter your super user password:

```
sudo apt install gcc
```

The C program compiler, `gcc`, is usually pre-installed in Linux.

Open any text editor and type the lines of following code, saving it as *hello.c*:

```
#include <stdio.h>
void main(void)
{
    printf ("hello world!\n");
}
```

You can use `vim` as your text editor by running `vi` from the Terminal.

To compile and run the program, use the following commands:

```
> gcc hello.c -o hello
> ./hello
hello world!
>
```

The `hello` file is our Linux executable that displays a message in the console.

Now, on to reversing this program.

dlroW olleH

As an example of good practice, the process of reversing a program first needs to start with proper identification. Let's start with `file`:

```
refun@refun:~$ file hello
hello: ELF 32-bit LSB executable, Intel 80386, version 1 (SYSV), dynamically lin
ked, interpreter /lib/ld-linux.so.2, for GNU/Linux 2.6.32, BuildID[sha1]=3a4a608
29703bd8cc8d8dcae3f0d86dd188bcb66, not stripped
refun@refun:~$
```

It is a 32-bit ELF file-type. ELF files are native executables on Linux platforms.

Next stop, let's take a quick look at text strings with the `strings` command:

```
refun@refun:~$ strings hello
/lib/ld-linux.so.2
libc.so.6
_IO_stdin_used
puts
```

This command will produce something like the following output:

```
/lib/ld-linux.so.2
libc.so.6
_IO_stdin_used
puts
__libc_start_main
__gmon_start__
GLIBC_2.0
PTRh
UWVS
t$,U
[^_]
hello world!
;*2$"(
GCC: (Ubuntu 5.4.0-6ubuntu1~16.04.10) 5.4.0 20160609
crtstuff.c
__JCR_LIST__
deregister_tm_clones
__do_global_dtors_aux
completed.7209
__do_global_dtors_aux_fini_array_entry
frame_dummy
__frame_dummy_init_array_entry
hello.c
__FRAME_END__
__JCR_END__
__init_array_end
_DYNAMIC
__init_array_start
__GNU_EH_FRAME_HDR
_GLOBAL_OFFSET_TABLE_
__libc_csu_fini
_ITM_deregisterTMCloneTable
__x86.get_pc_thunk.bx
_edata
__data_start
puts@@GLIBC_2.0
__gmon_start__
__dso_handle
_IO_stdin_used
__libc_start_main@@GLIBC_2.0
__libc_csu_init
_fp_hw
__bss_start
main
_Jv_RegisterClasses
__TMC_END__
```

```
_ITM_registerTMCloneTable
.symtab
.strtab
.shstrtab
.interp
.note.ABI-tag
.note.gnu.build-id
.gnu.hash
.dynsym
.dynstr
.gnu.version
.gnu.version_r
.rel.dyn
.rel.plt
.init
.plt.got
.text
.fini
.rodata
.eh_frame_hdr
.eh_frame
.init_array
.fini_array
.jcr
.dynamic
.got.plt
.data
.bss
.comment
```

The strings are listed in order from the start of the file. The first portion of the list contained our message and the compiler information. The first two lines also show what libraries are used by the program:

```
/lib/ld-linux.so.2
libc.so.6
```

The last portion of the list contains names of sections of the file. We only know of a few bits of text that we placed in our C code. The rest are placed there by the compiler itself, as part of its code that prepares and ends the graceful execution of our code.

Disassembly in Linux is just a command line away. Using the −d parameter of the objdump command, we should be able to show the disassembly of the executable code. You might need to pipe the output to a file using this command line:

```
objdump -d hello > disassembly.asm
```

The output file, disassembly.asm, should contain the following code:

```
hello:        file format elf32-i386


Disassembly of section .init:

080482a8 <_init>:
 80482a8:        53                          push   %ebx
 80482a9:        83 ec 08                    sub    $0x8,%esp
 80482ac:        e8 8f 00 00 00              call   8048340 <__x86.get_pc_thunk.bx>
 80482b1:        81 c3 4f 1d 00 00           add    $0x1d4f,%ebx
 80482b7:        8b 83 fc ff ff ff           mov    -0x4(%ebx),%eax
 80482bd:        85 c0                       test   %eax,%eax
 80482bf:        74 05                       je     80482c6 <_init+0x1e>
 80482c1:        e8 3a 00 00 00              call   8048300 <__libc_start_main@plt+0x
10>
 80482c6:        83 c4 08                    add    $0x8,%esp
 80482c9:        5b                          pop    %ebx
 80482ca:        c3                          ret

Disassembly of section .plt:

080482d0 <puts@plt-0x10>:
 80482d0:        ff 35 04 a0 04 08           pushl  0x804a004
 80482d6:        ff 25 08 a0 04 08           jmp    *0x804a008
 80482dc:        00 00                       add    %al,(%eax)
        ...

080482e0 <puts@plt>:
 80482e0:        ff 25 0c a0 04 08           jmp    *0x804a00c
 80482e6:        68 00 00 00 00              push   $0x0
 80482eb:        e9 e0 ff ff ff              jmp    80482d0 <_init+0x28>

080482f0 <__libc_start_main@plt>:
 80482f0:        ff 25 10 a0 04 08           jmp    *0x804a010
 80482f6:        68 08 00 00 00              push   $0x8
 80482fb:        e9 d0 ff ff ff              jmp    80482d0 <_init+0x28>

Disassembly of section .plt.got:

08048300 <.plt.got>:
 8048300:        ff 25 fc 9f 04 08           jmp    *0x8049ffc
 8048306:        66 90                       xchg   %ax,%ax

Disassembly of section .text:

08048310 <_start>:
 8048310:        31 ed                       xor    %ebp,%ebp
 8048312:        5e                          pop    %esi
 8048313:        89 e1                       mov    %esp,%ecx
 8048315:        83 e4 f0                    and    $0xfffffff0,%esp
 8048318:        50                          push   %eax
 8048319:        54                          push   %esp
```

If you notice, the disassembly syntax is different from the format of the Intel assembly language that we learned. What we see here is the AT&T disassembly syntax. To get an Intel syntax, we need to use the `-M intel` parameter, as follows:

```
objdump -M intel -d hello > disassembly.asm
```

The output should give us this disassembly result:

```
hello:       file format elf32-i386


Disassembly of section .init:

080482a8 <_init>:
 80482a8:        53                       push    ebx
 80482a9:        83 ec 08                 sub     esp,0x8
 80482ac:        e8 8f 00 00 00           call    8048340 <__x86.get_pc_thunk.bx>
 80482b1:        81 c3 4f 1d 00 00        add     ebx,0x1d4f
 80482b7:        8b 83 fc ff ff ff        mov     eax,DWORD PTR [ebx-0x4]
 80482bd:        85 c0                    test    eax,eax
 80482bf:        74 05                    je      80482c6 <_init+0x1e>
 80482c1:        e8 3a 00 00 00           call    8048300 <__libc_start_main@plt+0x
10>
 80482c6:        83 c4 08                 add     esp,0x8
 80482c9:        5b                       pop     ebx
 80482ca:        c3                       ret

Disassembly of section .plt:

080482d0 <puts@plt-0x10>:
 80482d0:        ff 35 04 a0 04 08        push    DWORD PTR ds:0x804a004
 80482d6:        ff 25 08 a0 04 08        jmp     DWORD PTR ds:0x804a008
 80482dc:        00 00                    add     BYTE PTR [eax],al
        ...

080482e0 <puts@plt>:
 80482e0:        ff 25 0c a0 04 08        jmp     DWORD PTR ds:0x804a00c
 80482e6:        68 00 00 00 00           push    0x0
 80482eb:        e9 e0 ff ff ff           jmp     80482d0 <_init+0x28>

080482f0 <__libc_start_main@plt>:
 80482f0:        ff 25 10 a0 04 08        jmp     DWORD PTR ds:0x804a010
 80482f6:        68 08 00 00 00           push    0x8
 80482fb:        e9 d0 ff ff ff           jmp     80482d0 <_init+0x28>

Disassembly of section .plt.got:
```

The result shows the disassembly code of each function. In summary, there were a total of 15 functions from executable sections:

```
Disassembly of section .init:
080482a8 <_init>:

Disassembly of section .plt:
080482d0 <puts@plt-0x10>:
080482e0 <puts@plt>:
080482f0 <__libc_start_main@plt>:

Disassembly of section .plt.got:
08048300 <.plt.got>:

Disassembly of section .text:
08048310 <_start>:
08048340 <__x86.get_pc_thunk.bx>:
08048350 <deregister_tm_clones>:
08048380 <register_tm_clones>:
080483c0 <__do_global_dtors_aux>:
080483e0 <frame_dummy>:
0804840b <main>:
08048440 <__libc_csu_init>:
080484a0 <__libc_csu_fini>:

Disassembly of section .fini:
080484a4 <_fini>:
```

The disassembly of our code is usually at the `.text` section. And, since this is a GCC-compiled program, we can skip all the initialization code and head straight to the `main` function where our code is at:

```
0804840b <main>:
 804840b:        8d 4c 24 04             lea     ecx,[esp+0x4]
 804840f:        83 e4 f0                and     esp,0xfffffff0
 8048412:        ff 71 fc                push    DWORD PTR [ecx-0x4]
 8048415:        55                      push    ebp
 8048416:        89 e5                   mov     ebp,esp
 8048418:        51                      push    ecx
 8048419:        83 ec 04                sub     esp,0x4
 804841c:        83 ec 0c                sub     esp,0xc
 804841f:        68 c0 84 04 08          push    0x80484c0
 8048424:        e8 b7 fe ff ff          call    80482e0 <puts@plt>
 8048429:        83 c4 10                add     esp,0x10
 804842c:        90                      nop
 804842d:        8b 4d fc                mov     ecx,DWORD PTR [ebp-0x4]
 8048430:        c9                      leave
 8048431:        8d 61 fc                lea     esp,[ecx-0x4]
 8048434:        c3                      ret
 8048435:        66 90                   xchg    ax,ax
 8048437:        66 90                   xchg    ax,ax
 8048439:        66 90                   xchg    ax,ax
 804843b:        66 90                   xchg    ax,ax
 804843d:        66 90                   xchg    ax,ax
 804843f:        90                      nop
```

I have highlighted the API call on puts. The puts API is also a version of printf. GCC was smart enough to choose puts over printf for the reason that the string was not interpreted as a **C-style formatting string**. A formatting string, or formatter, contains control characters, which are denoted with the % sign, such as %d for integer and %s for string. Essentially, *puts* is used for non-formatted strings, while printf is used for formatted strings.

What have we gathered so far?

Assuming we don't have any idea of the source code, this is the information we have gathered so far:

- The file is a 32-bit ELF executable.
- It was compiled using GCC.
- It has 15 executable functions, including the main() function.
- The code uses common Linux libraries: libc.so and ld-linux.so.
- Based on the disassembly code, the program is expected to simply show a message.
- The program is expected to display the message using *puts*.

Dynamic analysis

Now let's do some dynamic analysis. Remember that dynamic analysis should be done in a sandbox environment. There are a few tools that are usually pre-installed in Linux that can be used to display more detailed information. We're introducing ltrace, strace, and gdb for this reversing activity.

Here's how ltrace is used:

```
refun@refun:~$ ltrace ./hello
__libc_start_main(0x804840b, 1, 0xbfe57774, 0x8048440 <unfinished ...>
puts("hello world!"hello world!
)                              = 13
+++ exited (status 13) +++
refun@refun:~$
```

The output of ltrace shows a readable code of what the program did. ltrace logged library functions that the program called and received. It called *puts* to display a message. It also received an exit status of *13* when the program terminated.

The address *0x804840b* is also the address of the main function listed in the disassembly results.

`strace` is another tool we can use, but this logs system calls. Here's the result of running `strace` on our hello world program:

```
refun@refun:~$ strace ./hello
execve("./hello", ["./hello"], [/* 61 vars */]) = 0
brk(NULL)                               = 0x8e1b000
access("/etc/ld.so.nohwcap", F_OK)      = -1 ENOENT (No such file or directory)
mmap2(NULL, 4096, PROT_READ|PROT_WRITE, MAP_PRIVATE|MAP_ANONYMOUS, -1, 0) = 0xb7
f7f000
access("/etc/ld.so.preload", R_OK)      = -1 ENOENT (No such file or directory)
open("/etc/ld.so.cache", O_RDONLY|O_CLOEXEC) = 3
fstat64(3, {st_mode=S_IFREG|0644, st_size=86787, ...}) = 0
mmap2(NULL, 86787, PROT_READ, MAP_PRIVATE, 3, 0) = 0xb7f69000
close(3)                                = 0
access("/etc/ld.so.nohwcap", F_OK)      = -1 ENOENT (No such file or directory)
open("/lib/i386-linux-gnu/libc.so.6", O_RDONLY|O_CLOEXEC) = 3
read(3, "\177ELF\1\1\1\3\0\0\0\0\0\0\0\0\3\0\3\0\1\0\0\0320\207\1\0004\0\0\0"..
., 512) = 512
fstat64(3, {st_mode=S_IFREG|0755, st_size=1786484, ...}) = 0
mmap2(NULL, 1792540, PROT_READ|PROT_EXEC, MAP_PRIVATE|MAP_DENYWRITE, 3, 0) = 0xb
7db3000
mmap2(0xb7f63000, 12288, PROT_READ|PROT_WRITE, MAP_PRIVATE|MAP_FIXED|MAP_DENYWRI
TE, 3, 0x1af000) = 0xb7f63000
mmap2(0xb7f66000, 10780, PROT_READ|PROT_WRITE, MAP_PRIVATE|MAP_FIXED|MAP_ANONYMO
US, -1, 0) = 0xb7f66000
close(3)                                = 0
mmap2(NULL, 4096, PROT_READ|PROT_WRITE, MAP_PRIVATE|MAP_ANONYMOUS, -1, 0) = 0xb7
db2000
set_thread_area({entry_number:-1, base_addr:0xb7db2700, limit:1048575, seg_32bit
:1, contents:0, read_exec_only:0, limit_in_pages:1, seg_not_present:0, useable:1
}) = 0 (entry_number:6)
mprotect(0xb7f63000, 8192, PROT_READ)   = 0
mprotect(0x8049000, 4096, PROT_READ)    = 0
mprotect(0xb7fa8000, 4096, PROT_READ)   = 0
munmap(0xb7f69000, 86787)               = 0
fstat64(1, {st_mode=S_IFCHR|0620, st_rdev=makedev(136, 4), ...}) = 0
brk(NULL)                               = 0x8e1b000
brk(0x8e3c000)                          = 0x8e3c000
write(1, "hello world!\n", 13hello world!
)               = 13
exit_group(13)                          = ?
+++ exited with 13 +++
refun@refun:~$
```

`strace` logged every system call that happened, starting from when it was being executed by the system. `execve` is the first system call that was logged. Calling *execve* runs a program pointed to by the filename in its function argument. open and read are system calls that are used here to read files. `mmap2`, `mprotect`, and `brk` are responsible for memory activities such as allocation, permissions, and segment boundary setting.

Deep inside the code of puts, it eventually executes a write system call. *write*, in general, writes data to the object it was pointed to. Usually, it is used to write to a file. In this case, *write*'s first parameter has a value of 1. The value of 1 denotes STDOUT, which is the handle for the console output. The second parameter is the message, thus, it writes the message to STDOUT.

Going further with debugging

First, we need to install gdb by running the following command:

```
sudo apt install gdb
```

The installation should look something like this:

```
$> sudo apt install gdb
Reading package lists... Done
Building dependency tree
Reading state information... Done
The following additional packages will be installed:
  gdbserver libbabeltrace-ctf1 libbabeltrace1 libc6-dbg
Suggested packages:
  gdb-doc
The following NEW packages will be installed:
  gdb gdbserver libbabeltrace-ctf1 libbabeltrace1 libc6-dbg
0 upgraded, 5 newly installed, 0 to remove and 46 not upgraded.
Need to get 6,017 kB of archives.
After this operation, 26.6 MB of additional disk space will be used.
Do you want to continue? [Y/n] Y
Get:1 http://archive.ubuntu.com/ubuntu xenial/main i386 libbabeltrace1 i386 1.3.
2-1 [39.1 kB]
Get:2 http://archive.ubuntu.com/ubuntu xenial/main i386 libbabeltrace-ctf1 i386
1.3.2-1 [98.6 kB]
Get:3 http://archive.ubuntu.com/ubuntu xenial-updates/main i386 gdb i386 7.11.1-
0ubuntu1~16.5 [2,570 kB]
Get:4 http://archive.ubuntu.com/ubuntu xenial-updates/main i386 gdbserver i386 7
.11.1-0ubuntu1~16.5 [184 kB]
Get:5 http://archive.ubuntu.com/ubuntu xenial-updates/main i386 libc6-dbg i386 2
.23-0ubuntu10 [3,125 kB]
65% [5 libc6-dbg 781 kB/3,125 kB 25%]                          221 kB/s 10s
```

Then, use gdb to debug the `hello` program, as follows:

```
gdb ./hello
```

gdb can be controlled using commands. The commands are fully listed in online documentation, but simply entering *help* can aid us with the basics.

You can also use gdb to show the disassembly of specified functions, using the `disass` command. For example, let's see what happens if we use the `disass main` command:

```
(gdb) disass main
Dump of assembler code for function main:
   0x0804840b <+0>:    lea    0x4(%esp),%ecx
   0x0804840f <+4>:    and    $0xfffffff0,%esp
   0x08048412 <+7>:    pushl  -0x4(%ecx)
   0x08048415 <+10>:   push   %ebp
   0x08048416 <+11>:   mov    %esp,%ebp
   0x08048418 <+13>:   push   %ecx
   0x08048419 <+14>:   sub    $0x4,%esp
   0x0804841c <+17>:   sub    $0xc,%esp
   0x0804841f <+20>:   push   $0x80484c0
   0x08048424 <+25>:   call   0x80482e0 <puts@plt>
   0x08048429 <+30>:   add    $0x10,%esp
   0x0804842c <+33>:   nop
   0x0804842d <+34>:   mov    -0x4(%ebp),%ecx
   0x08048430 <+37>:   leave
   0x08048431 <+38>:   lea    -0x4(%ecx),%esp
   0x08048434 <+41>:   ret
End of assembler dump.
```

Then, again we have been given the disassembly in AT&T sytnax. To set gdb to use Intel syntax, use the following command:

```
set disassembly-flavor intel
```

This should give us the Intel assembly language syntax, as follows:

```
(gdb) disass *main
Dump of assembler code for function main:
=> 0x0804840b <+0>:      lea     ecx,[esp+0x4]
   0x0804840f <+4>:      and     esp,0xfffffff0
   0x08048412 <+7>:      push    DWORD PTR [ecx-0x4]
   0x08048415 <+10>:     push    ebp
   0x08048416 <+11>:     mov     ebp,esp
   0x08048418 <+13>:     push    ecx
   0x08048419 <+14>:     sub     esp,0x4
   0x0804841c <+17>:     sub     esp,0xc
   0x0804841f <+20>:     push    0x80484c0
   0x08048424 <+25>:     call    0x80482e0 <puts@plt>
   0x08048429 <+30>:     add     esp,0x10
   0x0804842c <+33>:     nop
   0x0804842d <+34>:     mov     ecx,DWORD PTR [ebp-0x4]
   0x08048430 <+37>:     leave
   0x08048431 <+38>:     lea     esp,[ecx-0x4]
   0x08048434 <+41>:     ret
End of assembler dump.
(gdb) 
```

To place a breakpoint at the *main* function, the command would be b *main.

Take note that the asterisk (*) specifies an address location in the program.

After placing a breakpoint, we can run the program using the run command. We should end up at the address of the main function:

```
(gdb) b *main
Breakpoint 1 at 0x804840b
(gdb) run
Starting program: /home/refun/hello

Breakpoint 1, 0x0804840b in main ()
(gdb) info registers
eax            0xb7fbcdbc        -1208234564
ecx            0x1934d2fe        422892286
edx            0xbffff0b4        -1073745740
ebx            0x0        0
esp            0xbffff08c        0xbffff08c
ebp            0x0        0x0
esi            0xb7fbb000        -1208242176
edi            0xb7fbb000        -1208242176
eip            0x804840b        0x804840b <main>
eflags         0x296        [ PF AF SF IF ]
cs             0x73        115
ss             0x7b        123
ds             0x7b        123
es             0x7b        123
fs             0x0        0
gs             0x33        51
(gdb)
```

To get the current values of the registers, enter `info registers`. Since we are in a 32-bit environment, the extended registers (that is, EAX, ECX, EDX, EBX, and EIP) are used. A 64-bit environment would show the registers with the R-prefix (that is, RAX, RCX, RDX, RBX, and RIP).

Now that we are at the main function, we can run each instruction with step into (the `stepi` command) and step over (the `nexti` command). Usually, we follow this with the `info registers` command to see what values changed.

 The abbreviated command equivalent of `stepi` and `nexti` are `si` and `ni` respectively.

Keep on entering `si` and `disass main` until you reach the line containing `call`
`0x80482e0 <puts@plt>`. You should end up with these `disass` and `info registers`
result:

```
(gdb) si
0x08048424 in main ()
(gdb) disass
Dump of assembler code for function main:
   0x0804840b <+0>:     lea     ecx,[esp+0x4]
   0x0804840f <+4>:     and     esp,0xfffffff0
   0x08048412 <+7>:     push    DWORD PTR [ecx-0x4]
   0x08048415 <+10>:    push    ebp
   0x08048416 <+11>:    mov     ebp,esp
   0x08048418 <+13>:    push    ecx
   0x08048419 <+14>:    sub     esp,0x4
   0x0804841c <+17>:    sub     esp,0xc
   0x0804841f <+20>:    push    0x80484c0
=> 0x08048424 <+25>:    call    0x80482e0 <puts@plt>
   0x08048429 <+30>:    add     esp,0x10
   0x0804842c <+33>:    nop
   0x0804842d <+34>:    mov     ecx,DWORD PTR [ebp-0x4]
   0x08048430 <+37>:    leave
   0x08048431 <+38>:    lea     esp,[ecx-0x4]
   0x08048434 <+41>:    ret
End of assembler dump.
(gdb)
```

The => found at the left side indicates where the instruction pointer is located. The registers
should look similar to this:

```
(gdb) info registers
eax            0xb7fbcdbc      -1208234564
ecx            0xbffff090      -1073745776
edx            0xbffff0b4      -1073745740
ebx            0x0     0
esp            0xbffff060      0xbffff060
ebp            0xbffff078      0xbffff078
esi            0xb7fbb000      -1208242176
edi            0xb7fbb000      -1208242176
eip            0x8048424       0x8048424 <main+25>
eflags         0x292   [ AF SF IF ]
cs             0x73    115
ss             0x7b    123
ds             0x7b    123
es             0x7b    123
fs             0x0     0
gs             0x33    51
(gdb)
```

Before the *puts* function gets called, we can inspect what values were pushed into the stack. We can view that with x/8x $esp:

```
(gdb) x/8x $esp
0xbffff060:      0x080484c0      0xbffff124      0xbffff12c      0x08048461
0xbffff070:      0xb7fbb3dc      0xbffff090      0x00000000      0xb7e21637
(gdb)
```

The x command is used to show a memory dump of the specified address. The syntax is x/FMT ADDRESS. FMT has 3 parts: the repeat count, the format letter, and the size letter. You should be able to see more information about the x command with help x. x/8x $esp shows 8 DWORD hexadecimal values from the address pointed by the esp register. Since the address space is in 32 bits, the default size letter was shown in DWORD size.

puts expects a single parameter. Thus, we are only interested in the first value pushed at the 0x080484c0 stack location. We expect that the parameter should be an address to where the message should be. So, entering the x/s command should give us the contents of the message, as follows:

```
(gdb) x/s 0x080484c0
0x80484c0:       "hello world!"
(gdb)
```

Next, we need to do a step over (ni) the call instruction line. This should display the following message:

```
(gdb) disass
Dump of assembler code for function main:
   0x0804840b <+0>:     lea     ecx,[esp+0x4]
   0x0804840f <+4>:     and     esp,0xfffffff0
   0x08048412 <+7>:     push    DWORD PTR [ecx-0x4]
   0x08048415 <+10>:    push    ebp
   0x08048416 <+11>:    mov     ebp,esp
   0x08048418 <+13>:    push    ecx
   0x08048419 <+14>:    sub     esp,0x4
   0x0804841c <+17>:    sub     esp,0xc
   0x0804841f <+20>:    push    0x80484c0
=> 0x08048424 <+25>:    call    0x80482e0 <puts@plt>
   0x08048429 <+30>:    add     esp,0x10
   0x0804842c <+33>:    nop
   0x0804842d <+34>:    mov     ecx,DWORD PTR [ebp-0x4]
   0x08048430 <+37>:    leave
   0x08048431 <+38>:    lea     esp,[ecx-0x4]
   0x08048434 <+41>:    ret
End of assembler dump.
(gdb) ni
hello world!
0x08048429 in main ()
(gdb)
```

But if you used `si`, the instruction pointer will be in the *puts* wrapper code. We can still go back to where we left off using the `until` command, abbreviated as `u`. Simply using the `until` command steps in one instruction. You'll have to indicate the address location where it will stop. It is like a temporary breakpoint. Remember to place an asterisk before the address:

```
(gdb) si
0x080482e0 in puts@plt ()
(gdb) u
0x080482e6 in puts@plt ()
(gdb) u 0x08048429
Function "0x08048429" not defined.
(gdb) u *0x08048429
hello world!
0x08048429 in main ()
```

The remaining 6 lines of code restore the values of *ebp* and *esp* right after entering the main function, then returning with *ret*. Remember that a call instruction would store the return address at the top of the stack, before actually jumping to the function address. The `ret` instruction will read the return value pointed to by the *esp* register.

The values of `esp` and `ebp`, right after entering the main function, should be restored before the *ret* instruction. Generally, a function begins by setting up its own stack frame for use with the function's local variables.

Here's a table showing the changes in the values of the `esp`, `ebp`, and `ecx` registers after the instruction at the given address.

 Note that the stack, denoted by the *esp* register, starts from a high address and goes down to lower addresses as it is used to store data.

Address	Instruction	esp	ebp	ecx	Remarks
0x0804840b	lea ecx,[esp+0x04]	0xbffff08c	0	0xbffff090	Initial values after entering main. [0xbffff08c] = 0xb7e21637 This is the return address.
0x0804840f	and esp,0xfffffff0	0xbffff080	0 .	0xbffff090	Aligns the stack in 16-byte paragraphs. In effect, this subtracts 0xc from esp.
0x08048412	push DWORD PTR [ecx-0x4]	0xbffff07c	0	0xbffff090	[0xbffff07c] = 0xb7e21637 ecx - 4 = 0xbffff08c points to the return address. The return address is now placed in two stack addresses.
0x08048415	push ebp	0xbffff078	0	0xbffff090	Begins stack frame setup. [0xbffff078] = 0
0x08048416	mov ebp,esp	0xbffff078	0xbffff078	0xbffff090	Saves esp.

0x08048418	push ecx	0xbffff074	0xbffff078	0xbffff090	Saves ecx. [0xbffff074] = 0xbffff090
0x08048419	sub esp,0x4	0xbffff070	0xbffff078	0xbffff090	Allocates 4 bytes for stack frame.
0x0804841c	sub esp,0xc	0xbffff064	0xbffff078	0xbffff090	Allocates another 12 bytes for stack frame.
0x0804841f	push 0x80484c0	0xbffff060	0xbffff078	0xbffff090	[0xbffff060] = 0x080484c0 [0x080484c0] = "hello world!"
0x08048424	call 0x80482e0 <puts@plt>	0xbffff060	0xbffff078	0xffffffff	Stack is still the same after the call.
0x08048429	add esp,0x10	0xbffff070	0xbffff078	0xffffffff	Adds 0x10 to esp reducing the stack frame.
0x0804842c	nop	0xbffff070	0xbffff078	0xffffffff	No operation
0x0804842d	mov ecx,DWORD PTR [ebp-0x4]	0xbffff070	0xbffff078	0xbffff090	Restores the value of ecx before call.
0x08048430	leave	0xbffff07c	0	0xbffff090	leave is the equivalent of mov esp, ebp pop ebp
0x08048431	lea esp,[ecx-0x4]	0xbffff08c	0	0xbffff090	ecx - 4 = 0xbffff08c [0xbffff08c] = 0xb7e21637 The address of esp is restored back.
0x08048434	ret	-	-	-	Returns to 0xb7e21637

You can either continue exploring the cleanup code after `ret`, or just make the program eventually end by using `continue` or its abbreviation, `c`, as follows:

```
(gdb) c
Continuing.
[Inferior 1 (process 12442) exited with code 015]
(gdb) 
```

A better debugger

Before moving to more Linux executable-reversing activities, let's explore more tools. gdb seems fine, but it would have been better if we were able to debug it interactively, using visual tools for debugging. In *Chapter 5*, *Tools of Trade*, we introduced the Radare, under the *Disassemblers* and *Debuggers* sections, as a tool that is capable of doing both disassembly and debugging. So, let's get a feel for using Radare.

Setup

Radare is in its second version. To install it, you'll need *git* to install from the GitHub repository, as follows:

```
git clone https://github.com/radare/radare2.git
```

The instructions for installing it are written in the README file. As of the time of writing, it is suggested that Radare2 is installed by running the sys/install.sh or sys/user.sh shell scripts from the Terminal.

Hello World in Radare2

Besides its disassembler and debugger, Radare2 is also packed with a bunch of tools . Most of these are static analysis tools.

To get the MD5 hash of the hello world binary file, we can use rabin2:

```
refun@refun:~$ ls -l hello
-rwxrwx--- 1 refun refun 7348 Jul 12 21:26 hello
refun@refun:~$ rahash2 -amd5 hello
hello: 0x00000000-0x00001cb3 md5: 799554478cf399e5f87b37fcaf1c2ae6
refun@refun:~$ rahash2 -asha256 hello
hello: 0x00000000-0x00001cb3 sha256: 90085dacc7fc863a2606f8ab77b049532bf454badef
cdd326459585bea4dfb29
refun@refun:~$ 
```

With the use of the ls command and rahash2, we are able to determine these pieces of information:

```
filesize: 7348 bytes
time stamp: July 12 21:26 of this year
md5: 799554478cf399e5f87b37fcaf1c2ae6
sha256: 90085dacc7fc863a2606f8ab77b049532bf454badefcdd326459585bea4dfb29
```

rabin2 is another tool that can extract static information from a file, such as the type of file, header information, sections, and strings.

Let's get the type of file first by using the `rabin2 -I hello` command:

```
refun@refun:~$ rabin2 -I hello
arch      x86
binsz     6107
bintype   elf
bits      32
canary    false
class     ELF32
crypto    false
endian    little
havecode  true
intrp     /lib/ld-linux.so.2
lang      c
linenum   true
lsyms     true
machine   Intel 80386
maxopsz   16
minopsz   1
nx        true
os        linux
pcalign   0
pic       false
relocs    true
relro     partial
rpath     NONE
static    false
stripped  false
subsys    linux
va        true
```

The *bintype, class, hascode,* and *os* fields indicate that the file is an executable 32-bit ELF file that runs in Linux. *arch, bits, endian,* and *machine* suggest that the file was built with an x86 code. In addition, the *lang* field indicates that the file was compiled from C language. This information will definitely help us prepare for what to expect during disassembly and debugging.

To list imported functions, we use `rabin2 -i hello`:

```
refun@refun:~$ rabin2 -i hello
[Imports]
   1 0x080482e0  GLOBAL    FUNC puts
   2 0x08048000    WEAK  NOTYPE __gmon_start__
   3 0x080482f0  GLOBAL    FUNC __libc_start_main
   2 0x08048000    WEAK  NOTYPE  gmon start
```

There are two global functions we are interested in: `puts`
and `__libc_start_main`. `puts`, as we discussed, is used to print a message.
`__libc_start_main` is a function that initializes the stack frame, sets up the registers and some data structures, sets up error handling, and then calls the `main()` function.

To get the ELF header info, use `rabin2 -H hello`:

```
refun@refun:~$ rabin2 -H hello
0x00000000   ELF MAGIC     0x464c457f
0x00000010   Type          0x0002
0x00000012   Machine       0x0003
0x00000014   Version       0x00000001
0x00000018   Entrypoint    0x08048310
0x0000001c   PhOff         0x00000034
0x00000020   ShOff         0x000017dc
```

If we are only interested with the strings we can find from the data section, use the `rabin2 -z hello` command:

```
refun@refun:~$ rabin2 -z hello
000 0x000004c0 0x080484c0  12  13 (.rodata) ascii hello world!
```

With `rabin2`, we got additional information about the file, shown here:

```
filetype: 32-bit elf file and has executable code for Linux
architecture: x86 Intel
functions: imports puts and has a main function
notable strings: hello world!
```

Let's try the `radare2` debugger itself. From the Terminal console, you can either use `radare2`'s abbreviation r2, or `radare2` itself, with the `-d <file>` as its argument:

```
refun@refun:~$ r2 -d hello
Process with PID 25143 started...
= attach 25143 25143
bin.baddr 0x08048000
Using 0x8048000
asm.bits 32
-- It's not a bug, it's a work in progress
[0xb7ee4a20]>
```

This takes you to the `radare2` console. Enclosed in square brackets, the address indicates where the current `eip` is. It is not the entry point of the hello program, but rather an address in the dynamic loader. As with `gdb`, you'll have to enter commands. To bring up help, just use **?** and it will show you a list of commands as follows:

```
[0x08048310]> ?
Usage: [.][times][cmd][~grep][@[@iter]addr!size][|>pipe] ; ...
Append '?' to any char command to get detailed help
Prefix with number to repeat command N times (f.ex: 3x)
|%var =valuealias for 'env' command
| *[?] off[=[0x]value]      pointer read/write data/values (see ?v, wx, wv)
| (macro arg0 arg1)         manage scripting macros
| .[?] [-|(m)|f|!sh|cmd]    Define macro or load r2, cparse or rlang file
| =[?] [cmd]                send/listen for remote commands (rap://, http://, <fd>
)
| <[...]                    push escaped string into the RCons.readChar buffer
| /[?]                      search for bytes, regexps, patterns, ..
| ![?] [cmd]                run given command as in system(3)
| #[?] !lang [..]           Hashbang to run an rlang script
| a[?]                      analysis commands
| b[?]                      display or change the block size
| c[?] [arg]                compare block with given data
| C[?]                      code metadata (comments, format, hints, ..)
| d[?]                      debugger commands
| e[?] [a[=b]]              list/get/set config evaluable vars
| f[?] [name][sz][at]       add flag at current address
| g[?] [arg]                generate shellcodes with r_egg
| i[?] [file]               get info about opened file from r_bin
| k[?] [sdb-query]          run sdb-query. see k? for help, 'k *', 'k **' ...
| L[?] [-] [plugin]         list, unload load r2 plugins
| m[?]                      mountpoints commands
| o[?] [file] ([offset])    open file at optional address
| p[?] [len]                print current block with format and length
| P[?]                      project management utilities
| q[?] [ret]                quit program with a return value
| r[?] [len]                resize file
| s[?] [addr]               seek to address (also for '0x', '0x1' == 's 0x1')
| S[?]                      io section manipulation information
| t[?]                      types, noreturn, signatures, C parser and more
| T[?] [-] [num|msg]        Text log utility
| u[?]                      uname/undo seek/write
| V                         visual mode (V! = panels, VV = fcngraph, VVV = callgra
ph)
| w[?] [str]                multiple write operations
| x[?] [len]                alias for 'px' (print hexadecimal)
| y[?] [len] [[[@]addr      Yank/paste bytes from/to memory
| z[?]                      zignatures management
| ?[??][expr]               Help or evaluate math expression
| ?$?                       show available '$' variables and aliases
| ?@?                       misc help for '@' (seek), '~' (grep) (see ~??)
| ?>?                       output redirection
```

We start off by using the `aaa` command. This analyzes the code for function calls, flags, references and tries to generate constructive function names:

```
[0x08048310]> aaa
[x] Analyze all flags starting with sym. and entry0 (aa)
[x] Analyze function calls (aac)
[x] Analyze len bytes of instructions for references (aar)
[x] Constructing a function name for fcn.* and sym.func.* functions (aan)
[x] Type matching analysis for all functions (afta)
[x] Use -AA or_aaaa to perform additional experimental analysis.
```

Using the `V!` command sets the console to visual mode. In this mode, we should be able to debug the program while having an interactive view of the registry and the stack. Entering `:` should show a command console. Pressing **Enter** should bring us back to visual mode. Type `V?` to show more visual mode commands. It is also best to maximize the Terminal window to get a better view of the debugger:

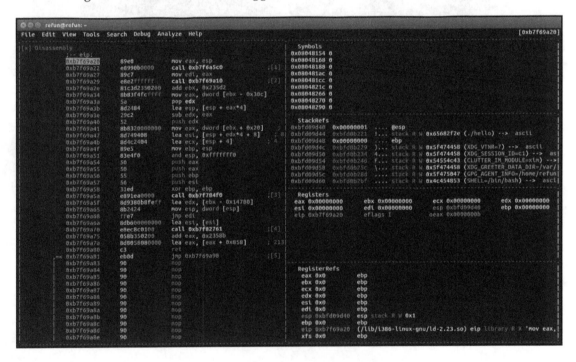

In the command console, enter `db entry0`. This should set a breakpoint at the entry point address of our program. But, since we also know that this program has a main function, you can also enter `db sym.entry` to set a breakpoint at the main function.

In visual mode, you can start the actual debugging using these keys that are available by default:

```
| F2 toggle breakpoint
| F4 run to cursor
| F7 single step
| F8 step over
| F9 continue
```

With the entry point and main function set with a breakpoint, press **F9** to run the program. We should end up in the entry point address.

 You'll need to refresh radare2's visual mode by reopening it to see the changes. To do that, just press q twice to quit visual mode. But before running V! again, you'll need to seek the current *eip* by using the s eip command.

Pressing *F9* again should bring you to the main function of our program. Remember to refresh the visual mode:

```
● ● ●  refun@refun: ~
File  Edit  View  Tools  Search  Debug  Analyze  Help                                                          [0x0804840b]
[x] Disassembly                                           Symbols
            ;-- main:                                     0x08048154 0
            ;-- eip:                                      0x08048168 0
/ (fcn) sym.main 42                                       0x08048188 0
    sym.main (int arg_4h);                                0x080481ac 0
        ; var int local_4h @ ebp-0x4                      0x080481cc 0
        ; arg int arg_4h @ esp+0x4                        0x0804821c 0
        ; DATA XREF from 0x08048327 (entry0)              0x08048268 0
   0x0804840b b   8d4c2404      lea ecx, [arg_4h]         0x08048274 0
   0x0804840f      83e4f0        and esp, 0xfffffff0
   0x08048412      ff71fc        push dword [ecx - 4]      StackRefs
   0x08048415      55            push ebp                  0xbf8eeffc  0xb7e16637  7f.. @esp (/lib/i386-linux-gnu/libc-2.23.so) library
   0x08048416      89e5          mov ebp, esp              0xbf8ef000  0x00000001  ....
   0x08048418      51            push ecx                  0xbf8ef004  0xbf8ef094  .... stack R W 0xbf8f1221 --> stack R W 0x65682f2e (|
   0x08048419      83ec04        sub esp, 4                0xbf8ef008  0xbf8ef09c  .... stack R W 0xbf8f1229 --> stack R W 0x5f474458 (|
   0x0804841c      83ec0c        sub esp, 0xc              0xbf8ef00c  0x00000000  .... ebx
   0x0804841f      68c8840408    push str.hello_world      0xbf8ef010  0x00000000  .... ebx
   0x08048424      e8b7feffff    call sym.imp.printf       0xbf8ef014  0x00000000  .... ebx
   0x08048429      83c410        add esp, 0x10             0xbf8ef018  0xb7fb0000  .... (/lib/i386-linux-gnu/libc-2.23.so) edi library R
   0x0804842c      90            nop
   0x0804842d      8b4dfc        mov ecx, dword [local_   Registers
   0x08048430      c9            leave                     eax 0xb7fb1dbc     ebx 0x00000000     ecx 0xd8ad3700     edx 0xbf8ef024
   0x08048431      8d61fc        lea esp, [ecx - 4]        esi 0xb7fb0000     edi 0xb7fb0000     esp 0xbf8eeffc     ebp 0x00000000
   0x08048434      c3            ret                       eip 0x0804840b     eflags 1PASI       oeax 0xffffffff
   0x08048435      6690          nop
   0x08048437      6690          nop
   0x08048439      6690          nop
   0x0804843b      6690          nop
   0x0804843d      6690          nop
   0x0804843f      90            nop
/ (fcn) sym._libc_csu_init 93                             RegisterRefs
    sym.__libc_csu_init (int arg_20h, int arg_2ch);        eax 0xb7fb1dbc  (unk1) eax R W 0xbf8ef09c --> stack R W 0xbf8f1229 --> s|
        ; arg int arg_20h @ esp+0x20                       ebx 0x0         ebx
        ; arg int arg_2ch @ esp+0x2c                       ecx 0xd8ad3700  ecx
        ; DATA XREF from 0x08048320 (entry0)               edx 0xbf8ef024  edx stack R W 0x0 --> ebx
   0x08048440      55            push ebp                  esi 0xb7fb0000  (/lib/i386-linux-gnu/libc-2.23.so) edi library R W 0x1b1db|
   0x08048441      57            push edi                  edi 0xb7fb0000  (/lib/i386-linux-gnu/libc-2.23.so) edi library R W 0x1b1db|
   0x08048442      56            push esi                  esp 0xbf8eeffc  esp stack R W 0xb7e16637 --> (/lib/i386-linux-gnu/libc-2.|
   0x08048443      53            push ebx                  ebp 0x0         ebx
   0x08048444      e8f7feffff    call sym.__x86.get_pc_    eip 0x0804840b  (LOAD0) (/home/refun/hello) eip sym.main program R X 'lea |
```

Press **F7** or **F8** to trace the program while seeing the stack and registers change. The letter **b** at the left of the address at line `0x0804840b` indicates that the address is set with a breakpoint.

So far, we have learned about the basic commands and keys. Feel free to explore the other commands and you'll definitely get more information and learn some easy ways to work around analyzing files.

What is the password?

So now that we know how to debug "`Unix style`", let's try the passcode program. You can download the passcode program from `https://github.com/PacktPublishing/Mastering-Reverse-Engineering/raw/master/ch6/passcode`.

Try to get some static information. Here's a list of commands you can use:

```
ls -l passcode
rahash2 -a md5,sha256 passcode
rabin2 -I passcode
rabin2 -i passcode
rabin2 -H passcode
rabin2 -z passcode
```

At this point, the information we're after is as follows:

- File size: 7,520 bytes
- MD5 hash: `b365e87a6e532d68909fb19494168bed`
- SHA256 hash:
  `68d6db63b69a7a55948e9d25065350c8e1ace9cd81e55a102bd42cc7fc527d8f`
- The type of file: ELF
    - 32-bit x86 Intel
    - Compiled C code that has notable imported functions: `printf`, `puts`, `strlen` and `__isoc99_scanf`
- Notable strings are as follows:
    - Enter password:
    - Correct password!
    - Incorrect password!

Now, for a quick dynamic analysis, let's use `ltrace ./passcode`:

```
refun@refun:~/Mastering-Reverse-Engineering-master/ch6$ ltrace ./passcode
__libc_start_main(0x804851b, 1, 0xbfd0f6e4, 0x8048620 <unfinished ...>
printf("Enter password: ")                                              = 16
__isoc99_scanf(0x80486b1, 0xbfd0f22c, 68, 4Enter password: qwerty
)                                                = 1
strlen("qwerty")                                                        = 6
puts("Incorrect password!"Incorrect password!
)                                                       = 20
+++ exited (status 0) +++
refun@refun:~/Mastering-Reverse-Engineering-master/ch6$ ltrace ./passcode
__libc_start_main(0x804851b, 1, 0xbfe12f04, 0x8048620 <unfinished ...>
printf("Enter password: ")                                              = 16
__isoc99_scanf(0x80486b1, 0xbfe12a4c, 68, 4Enter password: swordfish
)                                                = 1
strlen("swordfish")                                                     = 9
puts("Incorrect password!"Incorrect password!
)                                                       = 20
+++ exited (status 0) +++
refun@refun:~/Mastering-Reverse-Engineering-master/ch6$
```

We tried a few passwords but none returned "**Correct password!**" The file doesn't even have a hint in the list of strings for us to use. Let's try `strace`:

```
refun@refun:~/Mastering-Reverse-Engineering-master/ch6$ strace ./passcode
execve("./passcode", ["./passcode"], [/* 62 vars */]) = 0
brk(NULL)                               = 0x940f000
access("/etc/ld.so.nohwcap", F_OK)      = -1 ENOENT (No such file or directory)
mmap2(NULL, 4096, PROT_READ|PROT_WRITE, MAP_PRIVATE|MAP_ANONYMOUS, -1, 0) = 0xb7f3d000
access("/etc/ld.so.preload", R_OK)      = -1 ENOENT (No such file or directory)
open("/etc/ld.so.cache", O_RDONLY|O_CLOEXEC) = 3
fstat64(3, {st_mode=S_IFREG|0644, st_size=88173, ...}) = 0
mmap2(NULL, 88173, PROT_READ, MAP_PRIVATE, 3, 0) = 0xb7f27000
close(3)                                = 0
access("/etc/ld.so.nohwcap", F_OK)      = -1 ENOENT (No such file or directory)
open("/lib/i386-linux-gnu/libc.so.6", O_RDONLY|O_CLOEXEC) = 3
read(3, "\177ELF\1\1\1\3\0\0\0\0\0\0\0\0\3\0\3\0\1\0\0\0\320\207\1\0004\0\0\0"..., 512) = 512
fstat64(3, {st_mode=S_IFREG|0755, st_size=1786484, ...}) = 0
mmap2(NULL, 1792540, PROT_READ|PROT_EXEC, MAP_PRIVATE|MAP_DENYWRITE, 3, 0) = 0xb7d71000
mmap2(0xb7f21000, 12288, PROT_READ|PROT_WRITE, MAP_PRIVATE|MAP_FIXED|MAP_DENYWRITE, 3, 0x1af000) = 0xb7f21000
mmap2(0xb7f24000, 10780, PROT_READ|PROT_WRITE, MAP_PRIVATE|MAP_FIXED|MAP_ANONYMOUS, -1, 0) = 0xb7f24000
close(3)                                = 0
mmap2(NULL, 4096, PROT_READ|PROT_WRITE, MAP_PRIVATE|MAP_ANONYMOUS, -1, 0) = 0xb7d70000
set_thread_area({entry_number:-1, base_addr:0xb7d70700, limit:1048575, seg_32bit:1, contents:0, read_exec_only:0, limit_in_pages:1, seg_not_present
:0, useable:1}) = 0 (entry_number:6)
mprotect(0xb7f21000, 8192, PROT_READ)   = 0
mprotect(0x8049000, 4096, PROT_READ)    = 0
mprotect(0xb7f66000, 4096, PROT_READ)   = 0
munmap(0xb7f27000, 88173)               = 0
fstat64(1, {st_mode=S_IFCHR|0620, st_rdev=makedev(136, 0), ...}) = 0
brk(NULL)                               = 0x940f000
brk(0x9430000)                          = 0x9430000
fstat64(0, {st_mode=S_IFCHR|0620, st_rdev=makedev(136, 0), ...}) = 0
write(1, "Enter password: ", 16Enter password: )        = 16
read(0, asdf123
"asdf123\n", 1024)          = 8
_llseek(0, -1, 0xbf070538, SEEK_CUR)    = -1 ESPIPE (Illegal seek)
exit_group(0)                           = ?
+++ exited with 0 +++
refun@refun:~/Mastering-Reverse-Engineering-master/ch6$
```

The line with `read(0, asdf123` is where the password was manually entered. The code after this goes to the exit door. Let's do a deadlisting activity based on the disassembly, but this time, we'll use `radare2`'s graphical view. Go ahead and open up `radare2` with the `radare2 -d passcode` command. In the `radare2` console, use this sequence of commands:

```
aaa
s sym.main
VVV
```

These should open up a graphical representation of the disassembly code blocks from the *main* function. Scroll down and you should see conditional branching where the green line denotes a `true`, while the red line denotes a `false` flow. Keep scrolling down until you see the `Correct password!` text string. We'll work backwards from there:

In the 0x80485d3 block, where the Correct password! string is, we see that the message was displayed using *puts*. Going to that block is a red line from the 0x80485c7 block. In the 0x80485c7 block, the value in local_418h was compared to 0x2de (or 734 in decimal format). The value should be equal to 734 to make it go to the Correct password! block. If we were to try to decompile the C code, it would look something like this:

```
...
if (local_418h == 734)
    puts("Correct password!)
...
```

Scroll up to see where the red line came from:

By the way this graph looks, there is a loop, and to exit the loop, it would require the value at `local_414h` to be greater than or equal to the value at `local_410h`. The loop exits to the `0x80485c7` block. At the `0x8048582` block, both values at `local_418h` and `local_414h` are initialized to 0. These values are compared in the `0x80485b9` block.

Inspecting the `0x8048598` block, there are three variables of concern: `local_40ch`, `local_414h`, and `local_418h`. If we were to make a pseudo code of this block, it would look like this:

```
eax = byte at address [local_40ch + local_414h]
add eax to local_418h
increment local_414h
```

`local_414h` seem to be a pointer of the data pointed to by `local_40c`. `local_418` starts from 0, and each byte from `local_40ch` is added. Looking at an overview, a checksum algorithm seems to be happening here:

```
...
// unknown variables for now are local_40ch and local_410h
int local_418h = 0;
for (int local_414h = 0; local_414h < local_410h; local_414++)
{
    local_418h += local_40ch[local_414h];
}

if (local_418h == 734)
    puts("Correct password!)
...
```

Let's move further up and identify what `local_40ch` and `local_410h` should be:

```
; var int local_ch @ ebp-0xc
; var int local_4h @ ebp-0x4
; arg int arg_4h @ esp+0x4
; DATA XREF from 0x08048437 (entry0)
; 4
lea ecx, [arg_4h]
and esp, 0xfffffff0
push dword [ecx - 4]
push ebp
mov ebp, esp
push ecx
sub esp, 0x414
; [0x14:4]=-1
; 20
mov eax, dword gs:[0x14]
mov dword [local_ch], eax
xor eax, eax
sub esp, 0xc
; 0x80486a0
; "Enter password: "
push str.Enter_password:
call sym.imp.printf;[ga]
add esp, 0x10
sub esp, 8
lea eax, [local_40ch]
push eax
push 0x80486b1
call sym.imp.__isoc99_scanf;[gb]
add esp, 0x10
sub esp, 0xc
lea eax, [local_40ch]
push eax
call sym.imp.strlen;[gc]
add esp, 0x10
mov dword [local_410h], eax
; [0x7:4]=-1
; 7
cmp dword [local_410h], 7
jne 0x80485e5;[gd]
```

This is the main block. There are three named functions here:

- `printf()`
- `scanf()`
- `strlen()`

`local_40ch` and `local_410h` here were used. `local_40ch` is the second parameter for `scanf`, while the data at the `0x80486b1` address should contain the format expected. `local_40ch` contains the buffer typed in. To retrieve the data at `0x80486b1`, just enter a colon (`:`), enter `s 0x80486b1`, then return back to the visual mode. Press `q` again to view the data:

```
0x08048691 2408 /home/refun/Mastering-Reverse-Engineering-master/ch6/passcod
 offset -    0 1   2 3   4 5   6 7   8 9   A B   C D   E F   0123456789ABCDEF  commen
x08048691   0000  83c4  085b  c303  0000  0001  0002  0045   .....[.........E  ; [16]
x080486a1   6e74  6572  2070  6173  7377  6f72  643a  2000   nter password: .
x080486b1   2573  0043  6f72  7265  6374  2070  6173  7377   %s.Correct passw
x080486c1   6f72  6421  0049  6e63  6f72  7265  6374  2070   ord!.Incorrect p
x080486d1   6173  7377  6f72  6421  0000  0001  1b03  3b28   assword!.......;(  ; [17]
x080486e1   0000  0004  0000  00c4  fcff  ff44  0000  003f   ...........D...?
x080486f1   feff  ff68  0000  0044  ffff  ff94  0000  00a4   ...h...D........
x08048701   ffff  ffe0  0000  0014  0000  0000  0000  0001   ................  ; [18]
x08048711   7a52  0001  7c08  011b  0c04  0488  0100  0020   zR..|...........
x08048721   0000  001c  0000  0078  fcff  ff70  0000  0000   .......x...p....
x08048731   0e08  460e  0c4a  0f0b  7404  7800  3f1a  3b2a   ..F..J..t.x.?.;*
x08048741   3224  2228  0000  0040  0000  00cf  fdff  fff7   2$"(...@........
x08048751   0000  0000  440c  0100  4710  0502  7500  430f   ....D...G...u.C.
x08048761   0375  7c06  02e4  0c01  0041  c543  0c04  0448   .u|......A.C...H
x08048771   0000  006c  0000  00a8  feff  ff5d  0000  0000   ...l.......]....
x08048781   410e  0885  0241  0e0c  8703  410e  1086  0441   A....A....A....A
x08048791   0e14  8305  4e0e  2069  0e24  440e  2844  0e2c   ....N. i.$D.(D.,
x080487a1   410e  304d  0e20  470e  1441  c30e  1041  c60e   A.0M. G..A...A..
x080487b1   0c41  c70e  0841  c50e  0400  0010  0000  00b8   .A...A..........
x080487c1   0000  00bc  feff  ff02  0000  0000  0000  0000   ................
x080487d1   0000  0000  0000  0000  0000  0000  0000  0000   ................
x080487e1   0000  0000  0000  0000  0000  0000  0000  0000   ................
x080487f1   0000  0000  0000  0000  0000  0000  0000  0000   ................
```

The length of the data in `local_40ch` is identified and stored in `local_410h`. The value at `local_410h` is compared to 7. If equal, it follows the red line going to the `0x8048582` block, or the start of the checksum loop. If not, it follows the green line going to the `0x80485e5` block that contains code that will display **Incorrect password!**

In summary, the code would most likely look like this:

```
. . .
printf ("Enter password: ");
scanf ("%s", local_40ch);
local_410h = strlen(local_40ch);

if (local_410h != 7)
    puts ("Incorrect password!);
else
{
    int local_418h = 0;
    for (int local_414h = 0; local_414h < local_410h; local_414++)
    {
        local_418h += local_40ch[local_414h];
    }

    if (local_418h == 734)
        puts("Correct password!)
}
```

The entered password should have a **size of 7 characters** and the sum of all characters in the password should be **equal to 734**. Therefore, the password can be anything, as long as it satisfies the given conditions.

Using the ASCII table, we can determine the equivalent value of each character. If the sum is 734 from a total of 7 characters, we simply divide 734 by 7. This gives us a value of 104, or 0x68 with a remainder of 6. We can distribute the remainder, 6, to 6 of the characters, giving us this set:

Decimal	Hex	ASCII character
105	0x69	i
105	0x69	i
105	0x69	i
105	0x69	i
105	0x69	i
105	0x69	i
104	0x68	h

Let's try the password *iiiiiih* or *hiiiiii*, as follows:

```
refun@refun:~/Mastering-Reverse-Engineering-master/ch6$ ltrace ./passcode
__libc_start_main(0x804851b, 1, 0xbff4b304, 0x8048620 <unfinished ...>
printf("Enter password: ")                                                      = 16
__isoc99_scanf(0x80486b1, 0xbff4ae4c, 68, 4Enter password: iiiiiih
)                                                                               = 1
strlen("iiiiiih")                                                               = 7
puts("Correct password!"Correct password!
)                                                                               = 18
+++ exited (status 0) +++
refun@refun:~/Mastering-Reverse-Engineering-master/ch6$ ltrace ./passcode
__libc_start_main(0x804851b, 1, 0xbfeee0b4, 0x8048620 <unfinished ...>
printf("Enter password: ")                                                      = 16
__isoc99_scanf(0x80486b1, 0xbfeedbfc, 68, 4Enter password: hiiiiii
)                                                                               = 1
strlen("hiiiiii")                                                               = 7
puts("Correct password!"Correct password!
)                                                                               = 18
+++ exited (status 0) +++
refun@refun:~/Mastering-Reverse-Engineering-master/ch6$ ▮
```

Network traffic analysis

This time, we'll work on a program that receives a network connection and sends back some data. We will be using the file available at `https://github.com/PacktPublishing/Mastering-Reverse-Engineering/raw/master/ch6/server`. Once you have it downloaded, execute it from the Terminal as follows:

```
refun@refun:~/Mastering-Reverse-Engineering-master/ch6$ ./server
Genie is waiting for connections to port 9999.
```

The program is a server program that waits for connections to port 9999. To test this out, open a browser, then use the IP address of the machine where the server is running, plus the port. For example, use `127.0.0.1:9999` if you're trying this from your own machine. You might see something like the following output:

To understand network traffic, we need to capture some network packets by using tools such as `tcpdump`. `tcpdump` is usually pre-installed in Linux distributions. Open another Terminal and use the following command:

```
sudo tcpdump -i lo 'port 9999' -w captured.pcap
```

Here's a brief explanation of the parameters used:

`-i lo` uses the `loopback` network interface. We have used it here since we plan on accessing the server locally.

`'port 9999'`, with the single quotes, filters only packets that are using port 9999.

`-w captured.pcap` writes data packets to a PCAP file named `captured.pcap`.

Once `tcpdump` listens for data, try connecting to the server by visiting `127.0.0.1:9999` from the browser. If you wish to connect from outside the machine which holds the server, then re-run `tcpdump` without the `-i lo` parameter. This uses the default network interface instead. And instead of visiting using `127.0.0.1`, you'll have to use the IP address used by the default network interface.

To stop `tcpdump`, just break it using *Ctrl + C*.

To view the contents of `captured.pcap` in human readable form, use the following command:

```
sudo tcpdump -X -r captured.pcap > captured.log
```

This command should redirect the the `tcpdump` output to `captured.log`. The `-X` parameter shows the packet data in hexadecimal and ASCII. `-r captured.pcap` means read from the `PCAP` file `captured.pcap`. Opening the `captured.log` file should look something like the following:

```
 captured.log (~/) - gedit

Open ▼   ⊞                                                                                    Save

 1 15:38:11.674323 IP localhost.55704 > localhost.9999: Flags [S], seq 2962206084, win 43690,
   options [mss 65495,sackOK,TS val 3586230063 ecr 0,nop,wscale 7], length 0
 2     0x0000:  4500 003c 8334 4000 4006 b985 7f00 0001  E..<.4@.@.......
 3     0x0010:  7f00 0001 d998 270f b08f ad84 0000 0000  ......'.........
 4     0x0020:  a002 aaaa fe30 0000 0204 ffd7 0402 080a  .....0..........
 5     0x0030:  d5c1 872f 0000 0000 0103 0307            .../........
 6 15:38:11.674331 IP localhost.9999 > localhost.55704: Flags [S.], seq 616934500, ack 2962206085,
   win 43690, options [mss 65495,sackOK,TS val 3586230063 ecr 3586230063,nop,wscale 7], length 0
 7     0x0000:  4500 003c 0000 4000 4006 3cba 7f00 0001  E..<..@.@.<.....
 8     0x0010:  7f00 0001 270f d998 24c5 ac64 b08f ad85  ....'...$..d....
 9     0x0020:  a012 aaaa fe30 0000 0204 ffd7 0402 080a  .....0..........
10     0x0030:  d5c1 872f d5c1 872f 0103 0307            .../.../....
11 15:38:11.674339 IP localhost.55704 > localhost.9999: Flags [.], ack 1, win 342, options
   [nop,nop,TS val 3586230064 ecr 3586230063], length 0
12     0x0000:  4500 0034 8335 4000 4006 b98c 7f00 0001  E..4.5@.@.......
13     0x0010:  7f00 0001 d998 270f b08f ad85 24c5 ac65  ......'...$..e
14     0x0020:  8010 0156 fe28 0000 0101 080a d5c1 8730  ...V.(.........0
15     0x0030:  d5c1 872f                                .../
16 15:38:11.674366 IP localhost.9999 > localhost.55704: Flags [P.], seq 1:56, ack 1, win 342,
   options [nop,nop,TS val 3586230064 ecr 3586230064], length 55
17     0x0000:  4500 006b 82d5 4000 4006 b9b5 7f00 0001  E..k..@.@.......
18     0x0010:  7f00 0001 270f d998 24c5 ac65 b08f ad85  ....'...$..e....
19     0x0020:  8018 0156 fe5f 0000 0101 080a d5c1 8730  ...V._.........0
20     0x0030:  d5c1 8730 596f 7520 6861 7665 2063 6f6e  ...0You.have.con
21     0x0040:  6e65 6374 6564 2074 6f20 7468 6520 4765  nected.to.the.Ge
22     0x0050:  6e69 652e 204e 6f74 6869 6e67 2074 6f20  nie..Nothing.to.
23     0x0060:  7365 6520 6865 7265 2e0a 0a              see.here...
24 15:38:11.674371 IP localhost.9999 > localhost.55704: Flags [F.], seq 56, ack 1, win 342,
   options [nop,nop,TS val 3586230064 ecr 3586230064], length 0
25     0x0000:  4500 0034 82d6 4000 4006 b9eb 7f00 0001  E..4..@.@.......
26     0x0010:  7f00 0001 270f d998 24c5 ac9c b08f ad85  ....'...$.......
27     0x0020:  8011 0156 fe28 0000 0101 080a d5c1 8730  ...V.(.........0
28     0x0030:  d5c1 8730                                ...0
29 15:38:11.675539 IP localhost.55704 > localhost.9999: Flags [.], ack 56, win 342, options
   [nop,nop,TS val 3586230065 ecr 3586230064], length 0
```

Before we proceed, let's examine some basics on the two most popular network protocols, **Transmission Control Protocol (TCP)** and **User Datagram Protocol (UDP)**. TCP is a network transmission in which a communication between a sender and a receiver is established. The communication begins with a 3-way handshake, where the sender sends a SYN flag to the receiver, then the receiver sends back SYN and ACK flags to the sender, and finally, the sender sends an ACK flag to the receiver, opening the start of a communication. Further exchange of data between the sender and receiver are done in segments. Every segment has a 20-byte TCP header that contains the IP address of the sender and the receiver and any current status flags. This is followed by the size of the data being transmitted and the data itself. UDP uses a shorter header, since it only sends data and doesn't require acknowledgement from the receiver. It is not required, via UDP, to do a 3-way handshake. The primary purpose of UDP is to keep sending data to the receiver. TCP seems to be more reliable in terms of exchanging data, however. For UDP, sending data is much faster, as there are no overheads required. UDP is commonly used to transmit huge amounts of data via file transmission protocols, while TCP is used to communicate data that requires integrity.

In the preceding screenshot, lines 1 to 15 show a TCP 3-way handshake. The first connection from the localhost port at 55704 (client) to the localhost port at 9999 (server) is a SYN, denoted in the flags as S. This was responded to by an S. flag, which means SYN and ACK. The last is an ACK denoted by . in the flags. The client port at 55704 is an ephemeral port. An ephemeral port is a system generated port for client connections. The server port at 9999 is fixed in the server program.

In lines 16 to 23, we can see the actual response data from the server to the client. The server sends back a data containing a 55 character data containing the string *"You have connected to the Genie. Nothing to see here."* and 2 new line (0x0A) characters to the client. The data before the 55 character string is the packet's header containing information about the packet. The packet header, when parsed, is the information described in line 16. The TCP flags are P ., which means PUSH and ACK. The information in the packet header structure is documented in the TCP and UDP specifications. You can start to look for these specifications at RFC 675, available at https://tools.ietf.org/html/rfc675, and RFC 768, available at https://tools.ietf.org/html/rfc768. To fast-track the process, we can use Wireshark, which will be discussed later, to help us parse through the packet information.

In lines 24 to 28, FIN and ACK flags, formatted as F ., are sent from the server to the client, saying that the server is closing the connection. Lines 29 to 33 is an ACK response, ., that acknowledges the connection is being closed.

A better tool for capturing and viewing this graphically is *Wireshark*. Previously known as *Ethereal*, Wireshark has the same capabilities as `tcpdump`. Wireshark can be manually downloaded and installed from `https://www.wireshark.org/`. It can also be installed using the following `apt` command:

```
sudo apt install wireshark-qt
```

Capturing network packets requires root privileges in order to access the network interfaces. This is the reason for our use of `sudo` when running *tcpdump*. The same goes when using *Wireshark*. So, to execute *Wireshark* in Linux, we use the following command:

```
sudo wireshark
```

Besides capturing traffic and showing it in real time, you can also open and view PCAP files in *Wireshark*:

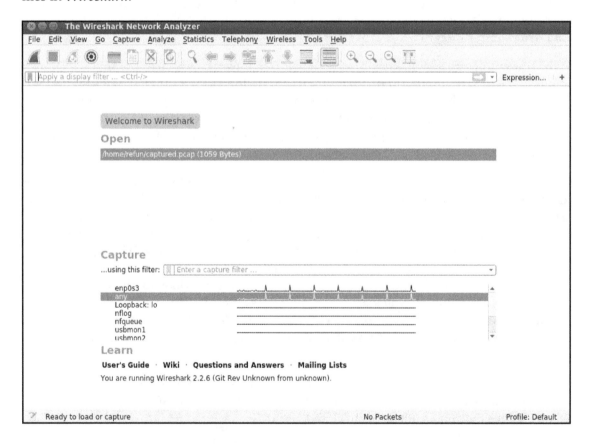

To start capturing, double-click on `any` from the list of interfaces. This essentially captures from both the default network interface and the loopback interface *lo*. What you'll see are continuous lines of network traffic packets. Wireshark has a display filter to minimize all the noise we see. For our exercise, in the filter field, enter the following display filter:

```
tcp.port == 9999
```

This should only show packets that use the TCP port at `9999`. There are more filters you can experiment on. These are documented in Wireshark's manual pages.

Clicking on a packet shows parsed information that gives you a better understanding of the packet fields, as shown in the following screenshot:

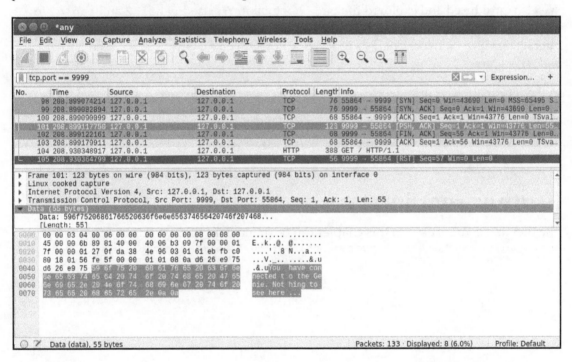

Wireshark has a wide-knowledge of standard packets. This makes Wireshark a must-have tool for every analyst.

Summary

In this chapter, our discussions revolved around reverse engineering tools that are already built into Linux systems. Debian-based operating systems, such as Ubuntu, are popular for reverse engineering purposes because of the wide community and tools available. We have focused more on how to analyze Linux' native executable, the ELF file. We started off by using GCC to compile a C program source into an ELF executable. We proceeded to analyze the executable using static info-gathering tools, including `ls`, `file`, `strings`, and `objdump`. Then we used `ltrace` and `strace` to carry out a dynamic analysis. Then we used `gdb` to debug the program, showing us Intel assembly language syntax.

We also introduced and explored the `radare2` toolkit. We used `rahash2` and `rabin2` to gather static information, and used `radare2` for disassembly and debugging in an interactive view. Network analysis tools were not left behind either, as we used `tcpdump` and `Wireshark`.

In the information security world, most files to be analyzed are executables based on Microsoft Windows, which we're going to discuss in the next chapter. We may not encounter much analysis of Linux files in the industry, but knowing how to do it will definitely come in handy when the task requires it.

Further reading

The files and sources used in this chapter can be found at `https://github.com/ PacktPublishing/Mastering-Reverse-Engineering/tree/master/ch6`.

RE for Windows Platforms

With Windows being one of the most popular operating systems in the world, most software in the cyber world has been written for it. This includes malware.

This chapter focuses on the analysis of the Windows native executable, the PE file, and evolves directly by doing file analysis, that is, gathering static information and performing dynamic analysis. We will dig deeper into understanding how the PE file behaves with the Windows operating system. The following topics will be covered in this chapter:

- Analyzing Windows PE
- Tools
- Static analysis
- Dynamic analysis

Technical requirements

This chapter requires knowledge of the Windows environment and its administration. The reader should also know how to use commands in Command Prompt. The first portion of this chapter requires the user to have basic knowledge of building and compiling C programs using Visual Studio or similar software.

Hello World

Programs in the Windows environment communicate with the system by using Windows APIs. These APIs are built around the file system, memory management (including processes, the stack, and allocations), the registry hive, network communication, and so forth. Regarding reverse engineering, a wide coverage of these APIs and their library modules is a good advantage when it comes to easily understanding how a program works when seen in its low-level language equivalent. So, the best way to begin exploring APIs and their libraries would be to develop some programs ourselves.

There are many high-level languages used by developers like C, C++, C#, and Visual Basic. C, C++, and Visual Basic (native) compile to an executable that directly executes instructions in the x86 language. C# and Visual Basic (p-code) are usually compiled to use interpreters as a layer that turns the p-code into actual x86 instructions. For this chapter, we will focus on executable binaries compiled from C/C++ and assembly language. The goal is to have a better understanding of the behavior of programs that use Windows APIs.

For this chapter, our choice for building C/C++ programs will be the Visual Studio Community edition. Visual Studio is widely used for building Microsoft Windows programs. Given that it is also a product of Microsoft, it already contains the compatible libraries required to compile programs. You can download and install Visual Studio Community edition from `https://visualstudio.microsoft.com/downloads/`.

These programs are neither harmful nor malicious. The following C programming activities can be done with Visual Studio in a bare metal machine. In case you are planning on installing Visual Studio in a Windows VM, at the time of writing this book, Visual Studio 2017 Community edition has the following recommended system requirements:

- 1.8 GHz dual core
- 4 GB of RAM
- 130 GB of disk space

These system requirements can be found at `https://docs.microsoft.com/en-us/visualstudio/productinfo/vs2017-system-requirements-vs`. You may need to perform some Windows updates and install the .NET framework. This can also be installed from the Windows 7 setup that we previously downloaded from `https://developer.microsoft.com/en-us/microsoft-edge/tools/vms/` . Please visit the Microsoft Visual Studio website for the requirements of newer versions.

There are many Visual Studio alternatives that have minimal requirements like Bloodshed Dev C++, Zeus IDE, and Eclipse. However, some of these IDE may not be up-to-date and/or may need to the compiler and its dependencies to have been properly set up.

Learning about the APIs

We'll be skipping `Hello World` here since we have already made one in the previous chapters. Instead, we'll be looking into the following example programs:

- A keylogger saved to a `filez`
- Enumerating a registry key and printing it out
- List processes and printing out

- Encrypting data and storing it in a file
- Decrypting an encrypted file
- Listening to port 9999 and sending back a message when connected

The source code for these programs can be found at https://github.com/PacktPublishing/Mastering-Reverse-Engineering/tree/master/ch7. Feel free to play with these programs, add your own code, or even create your own version. The aim here is to get you to learn how these APIs work, hand in hand.

One of the keys to determining how a program behaves is to learn how APIs are used. The use of each API is documented in the Microsoft Developer Network (MSDN) library. The programs we are about to look into are just examples of program behaviors. We use these APIs to build upon these behaviors. Our goal here is to learn how these APIs are used and interact with each other.

As a reverse engineer, it is expected and required for the reader to use the MSDN or other resources to further understand the details on how the API works. The API name can be searched in the MSDN library at https://msdn.microsoft.com.

Keylogger

A keylogger is a program that logs what keys have been pressed by a user. The log is usually stored in a file. The core API used here is GetAsyncKeyState. Every button that can be pressed from the keyboard or the mouse has an assigned ID called a virtual key code. Specifying a virtual key code, the GetAsyncKeyState gives information about whether the key has been pressed or not.

 The source code for this program can be found at https://github.com/PacktPublishing/Mastering-Reverse-Engineering/blob/master/ch7/keylogger.cpp.

For keylogging to work, we will need to check the state of each virtual key code and run them in a loop. Once a key has been identified as pressed, the virtual key code gets stored into a file. The following code does just that:

```
  while (true) {
  for (char i = 1; i <= 255; i++) {
  if (GetAsyncKeyState(i) & 1) {
  sprintf_s(lpBuffer, "\\x%02x", i);
  LogFile(lpBuffer, (char*)"log.txt");
  }
  }
```

`LogFile` here is a function that accepts two parameters: the data that it writes and the file path of the log file. `lpBuffer` contains the data and is formatted by the `sprintf_s` API as `\\x%02x`. As a result, the format converts any numbers into a two-digit hexadecimal string. The number 9 becomes `\x09`, and the number 106 becomes `\x6a`.

All we need are three Windows API functions to implement the storage of data to a log file – `CreateFile`, `WriteFile`, and `CloseHandle` – as shown in the following code:

```
void LogFile(char* lpBuffer, LPCSTR fname) {

    BOOL bErrorFlag;
    DWORD dwBytesWritten;

    HANDLE hFile = CreateFileA(fname, FILE_APPEND_DATA, 0, NULL, OPEN_ALWAYS,
FILE_ATTRIBUTE_NORMAL, NULL);
    bErrorFlag = WriteFile(hFile, lpBuffer, strlen(lpBuffer),
&dwBytesWritten, NULL);
    CloseHandle(hFile);

    return;
}
```

`CreateFileA` is used to create or open a new file given the filename and how the file will be used. Since the purpose of this exercise is to continuously log the virtual key codes of pressed keys, we need to open the file in append mode (`FILE_APPEND_DATA`). A file handle is returned to `hFile` and is used by `WriteFile`. `lpBuffer` contains the formatted virtual key code. One of the parameters `WriteFile` requires is the size of the data to be written. The `strlen` API was used here to determine the length of the data. Finally, the file handle is closed using the `CloseHandle`. It is important to close file handles to make the file available for use.

There are different keyboard variants that cater to the language of the user. Thus, different keyboards may have different virtual key codes. At the start of the program, we used `GetKeyboardLayoutNameA(lpBuffer)` to identify the type of keyboard being used. When reading the log, the type of keyboard will be used as a reference to properly identify which keys were pressed.

regenum

The regenum program, as mentioned below, aims to enumerate all values and data in a given registry key. The parameters required for the APIs depend on the result of the previous APIs. Just like how we were able to write data to a file in the keylogger program, registry enumerating APIs also require a handle. In this case, a handle to the registry key is used by the RegEnumValueA and RegQueryValueExA APIs.

 The source code for this program can be found at https://github.com/ PacktPublishing/Mastering-Reverse-Engineering/blob/master/ch7/ regenum.cpp.

```cpp
int main()
{
 LPCSTR lpSubKey = "Software\\Microsoft\\Windows\\CurrentVersion\\Run";
 HKEY hkResult;
 DWORD dwIndex;
 char ValueName[1024];
 char ValueData[1024];
 DWORD cchValueName;
 DWORD result;
 DWORD dType;
 DWORD dataSize;
 HKEY hKey = HKEY_LOCAL_MACHINE;

 if (RegOpenKeyExA(hKey, lpSubKey, 0, KEY_READ, &hkResult) ==
ERROR_SUCCESS)
 {
 printf("HKEY_LOCAL_MACHINE\\%s\n", lpSubKey);
 dwIndex = 0;
 result = ERROR_SUCCESS;
 while (result == ERROR_SUCCESS)
 {
 cchValueName = 1024;
 result = RegEnumValueA(hkResult, dwIndex, (char *)&ValueName,
&cchValueName, NULL, NULL, NULL, NULL);
 if (result == ERROR_SUCCESS)
 {
 RegQueryValueExA(hkResult, ValueName, NULL, &dType, (unsigned char
*)&ValueData, &dataSize);
 if (strlen(ValueName) == 0)
 sprintf((char*)&ValueName, "%s", "(Default)");
 printf("%s: %s\n", ValueName, ValueData);
 }
 dwIndex++;
 }
```

```
    RegCloseKey(hkResult);
    }
    return 0;
}
```

The enumeration begins by retrieving a handle for the registry key via `RegOpenKeyExA`. A successful return value should be non-zero, while its output should show a handle stored in `hkResult`. The registry key that is being targeted here is `HKEY_LOCAL_MACHINE\Software\Microsoft\Windows\CurrentVersion\Run`.

The handle in `hkResult` is used by `RegEnumValueA` to begin enumerating each registry value under the registry key. Subsequent calls to `RegEnumValueA` gives the next registry value entry. This block of code is therefore placed in a loop until it fails to return an `ERROR_SUCCESS` result. An `ERROR_SUCCESS` result means that a registry value was successfully retrieved.

For every registry value, `RegQueryValueExA` is called. Remember that we only go the registry value, but not its respective data. Using `RegQueryValueExA`, we should be able to acquire the registry data.

Finally, we have to close the handle by using `RegCloseKey`.

Other APIs that are used here are `printf`, `strlen`, and `sprintf`. `printf` was used in the program to print the target registry key, value, and data to the command-line console. `strlen` was used to get the text string length. Every registry key has a default value. Since `RegEnumValueA` will return `ERROR_SUCCEPantf`, we are able to replace the `ValueName` variable with a string called `(Default)`:

```
Windows PowerShell                                                    —  □  ×
PS C:\Users\Admin\Desktop\Mastering-Reverse-Engineering\ch7> .\regenum
HKEY_LOCAL_MACHINE\Software\Microsoft\Windows\CurrentVersion\Run
vmware-tray.exe:
SunJavaUpdateSched: "C:\Program Files (x86)\Common Files\Java\Java Update\jusched.exe"
PS C:\Users\Admin\Desktop\Mastering-Reverse-Engineering\ch7>
```

processlist

Similar to how enumerating registry values works, listing processes also works on the same concept. Since the processes in real-time change fast, a snapshot of the process list needs to be taken. The snapshot contains a list of process information at the time the snapshot was taken. The snapshot can be taken using `CreateToolhelp32Snapshot`. The result is stored in `hSnapshot`, which is the snapshot handle.

To begin enumerating the list, `Process32First` is used to acquire the first process information from the list. This information is stored in the `pe32` variable, which is a `PROCESSENTRY32` type. Subsequent process information is retrieved by calling `Process32Next`. `CloseHandle` is finally used when done with the list.

Again, `printf` is used to print out the executable file name and the process ID:

```
int main()
{
  HANDLE hSnapshot;
  PROCESSENTRY32 pe32;

  hSnapshot = CreateToolhelp32Snapshot(TH32CS_SNAPPROCESS, 0);
  pe32.dwSize = sizeof(PROCESSENTRY32);

  if (Process32First(hSnapshot, &pe32))
  {
    printf("\nexecutable [pid]\n");
    do
    {
      printf("%ls [%d]\n", pe32.szExeFile, pe32.th32ProcessID);
    } while (Process32Next(hSnapshot, &pe32));
    CloseHandle(hSnapshot);
  }
  return 0;
}
```

 The source code for this program can be found at `https://github.com/PacktPublishing/Mastering-Reverse-Engineering/blob/master/ch7/processlist.cpp`.

Encrypting and decrypting a file

Ransomware has been one of the most popular malware to spread out globally. Its core element is being able to encrypt files.

In these encrypt and decrypt programs, we are going to learn about some of the basic APIs used in encryption and decryption.

The API used to encrypt is `CryptEncrypt`, while `CryptDecrypt` is used for decryption. However, these APIs require at least a handle to the encryption key. To obtain the handle to the encryption key, a handle to the **Cryptographic Service Provider (CSP)** is required. In essence, before calling `CryptEncrypt` or `CryptDecrypt`, calling a couple of APIs is required to set up the algorithm that will be used.

In our program, `CryptAcquireContextA` is used to get a `CryptoAPI` handle of a key container from a CSP. It is in this API where the algorithm, AES, is indicated. The key that the encryption will be using will be controlled by a user-defined password which is set in the `password[]` string. To get a handle to the derived key, the APIs `CryptCreateHash`, `CryptHashData`, and `CryptDeriveKey` are used while passing the user-defined `password` to `CryptHashData`. The data to be encrypted and assigned in the `buffer` variable,is passed to `CryptEncrypt`. The resulting encrypted data is written in the same data buffer, overwriting it in the process:

```
int main()
{
  unsigned char buffer[1024] = "Hello World!";
  unsigned char password[] = "this0is0quite0a0long0cryptographic0key";
  DWORD dwDataLen;
  BOOL Final;

  HCRYPTPROV hProv;

  printf("message: %s\n", buffer);
  if (CryptAcquireContextA(&hProv, NULL, NULL, PROV_RSA_AES,
CRYPT_VERIFYCONTEXT))
  {
    HCRYPTHASH hHash;
    if (CryptCreateHash(hProv, CALG_SHA_256, NULL, NULL, &hHash))
    {
      if (CryptHashData(hHash, password, strlen((char*)password), NULL))
      {
        HCRYPTKEY hKey;
        if (CryptDeriveKey(hProv, CALG_AES_128, hHash, NULL, &hKey))_
        {
          Final = true;
```

```
            dwDataLen = strlen((char*)buffer);
            if (CryptEncrypt(hKey, NULL, Final, NULL, (unsigned
char*)&buffer, &dwDataLen, 1024))
                {
                    printf("saving encrypted buffer to message.enc");
                    LogFile(buffer, dwDataLen, (char*)"message.enc");
                }
                printf("%d\n", GetLastError());
                CryptDestroyKey(hKey);
            }
        }
        CryptDestroyHash(hHash);
    }
    CryptReleaseContext(hProv, 0);
    }
    return 0;
}
```

Using the modified version of the LogFile function, which now includes the size of the data to write, the encrypted data is stored in the message.enc file:

```
void LogFile(unsigned char* lpBuffer, DWORD buflen, LPCSTR fname) {

    BOOL bErrorFlag;
    DWORD dwBytesWritten;

    DeleteFileA(fname);

    HANDLE hFile = CreateFileA(fname, FILE_ALL_ACCESS, 0, NULL,
CREATE_ALWAYS, FILE_ATTRIBUTE_NORMAL, NULL);
    bErrorFlag = WriteFile(hFile, lpBuffer, buflen, &dwBytesWritten, NULL);
    CloseHandle(hFile);

    Sleep(10);

    return;
}
```

To gracefully close the `CryptoAPI` handles, `CryptDestroyKey`, `CryptDestroyHash`, and `CryptReleaseContext` are used.

The encrypted message `Hello World!` will now look like this:

```
Windows PowerShell                                                    —  □  ✕
PS C:\Users\Admin\Desktop\Mastering-Reverse-Engineering\ch7> .\encfile
message: Hello World!
saving encrypted buffer to message.enc0
PS C:\Users\Admin\Desktop\Mastering-Reverse-Engineering\ch7>
```

The way to decrypt the message is to use the same `CryptoAPIs`, but now use `CryptDecrypt`. This time, the contents of `message.enc` is read to the data buffer, decrypted, and then stored in `message.dec`. The CryptoAPIs are used in the same way as they were for acquiring the key handle. The buffer length stored in `dwDataLen` should initially contain the maximum length of the buffer:

```c
int main()
{
  unsigned char buffer[1024];
  unsigned char password[] = "this0is0quite0a0long0cryptographic0key";
  DWORD dwDataLen;
  BOOL Final;

  DWORD buflen;
  char fname[] = "message.enc";
  HANDLE hFile = CreateFileA(fname, GENERIC_READ, FILE_SHARE_READ, NULL,
OPEN_ALWAYS, FILE_ATTRIBUTE_NORMAL, NULL);
  ReadFile(hFile, buffer, 1024, &buflen, NULL);
  CloseHandle(hFile);

  HCRYPTPROV hProv;

  if (CryptAcquireContextA(&hProv, NULL, NULL, PROV_RSA_AES,
CRYPT_VERIFYCONTEXT))
  {
    HCRYPTHASH hHash;
    if (CryptCreateHash(hProv, CALG_SHA_256, NULL, NULL, &hHash))
    {
      if (CryptHashData(hHash, password, strlen((char*)password), NULL))
      {
        HCRYPTKEY hKey;
        if (CryptDeriveKey(hProv, CALG_AES_128, hHash, NULL, &hKey))
        {
          Final = true;
          dwDataLen = buflen;
          if ( CryptDecrypt(hKey, NULL, Final, NULL, (unsigned
```

```
char*)&buffer, &dwDataLen) )
            {
                printf("decrypted message: %s\n", buffer);
                printf("saving decrypted message to message.dec");
                LogFile(buffer, dwDataLen, (char*)"message.dec");
            }
            printf("%d\n", GetLastError());
            CryptDestroyKey(hKey);
        }
    }
    CryptDestroyHash(hHash);
    }
    CryptReleaseContext(hProv, 0);
    }
    return 0;
}
```

```
Windows PowerShell                                          —    □    ×
PS C:\Users\Admin\Desktop\Mastering-Reverse-Engineering\ch7> .\decfile
decrypted message: Hello World!%[^□
saving decrypted message to message.dec0
PS C:\Users\Admin\Desktop\Mastering-Reverse-Engineering\ch7>
```

The source code for the encryption and decryption programs can be found at the following links:

Encryption: https://github.com/PacktPublishing/Mastering-Reverse-Engineering/blob/master/ch7/encfile.cpp.

Decryption: https://github.com/PacktPublishing/Mastering-Reverse-Engineering/blob/master/ch7/decfile.cpp.

The server

In Chapter 6, *RE in Linux Platforms*, we learned about using socket APIs to control network communication between a client and a server. The same code can be implemented for the Windows operating system. For Windows, the socket library needs to be initiated by using the `WSAStartup` API before using socket APIs. In comparison to Linux functions, instead of using `write`, `send` is used to send data back to the client. Also, regarding `close`, the equivalent of this is `closesocket`, which is used to free up the socket handle.

Here's a graphical representation of how a server and a client generally communicate with the use of socket APIs. Take note that the functions shown in the following diagram are Windows API functions:

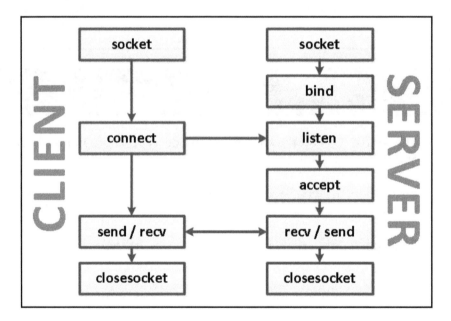

The socket function is used to initiate a socket connection. When we're done with the connection, the communication is closed via the closesocket function. The server requires that we bind the program with a network port. The listen and accept function is used to wait for client connections. The send and recv functions are used for the data transfer between the server and the client. send is used to send data while recv is used to receive data. Finally, closesocket is used to terminate the transmission. The code below shows an actual C source code of a server-side program that accepts connections and replies with You have connected to the Genie. Nothing to see here.

```c
int main()
{
 int listenfd = 0, connfd = 0;
 struct sockaddr_in serv_addr;
 struct sockaddr_in ctl_addr;
 int addrlen;
 char sendBuff[1025];


 WSADATA WSAData;

 if (WSAStartup(MAKEWORD(2, 2), &WSAData) == 0)
 {
     listenfd = socket(AF_INET, SOCK_STREAM, 0);
     if (listenfd != INVALID_SOCKET)
     {
         memset(&serv_addr, '0', sizeof(serv_addr));
         memset(sendBuff, '0', sizeof(sendBuff));
         serv_addr.sin_family = AF_INET;
         serv_addr.sin_addr.s_addr = htonl(INADDR_ANY);
         serv_addr.sin_port = htons(9999);
         if (bind(listenfd, (struct sockaddr*)&serv_addr,
sizeof(serv_addr)) == 0)
         {
             if (listen(listenfd, SOMAXCONN) == 0)
             {
                 printf("Genie is waiting for connections to port
9999.\n");
                 while (1)
                 {
                     addrlen = sizeof(ctl_addr);
                     connfd = accept(listenfd, (struct sockaddr*)&ctl_addr,
&addrlen);
                     if (connfd != INVALID_SOCKET)
                     {
                         printf("%s has connected.\n",
inet_ntoa(ctl_addr.sin_addr));
```

```
                                snprintf(sendBuff, sizeof(sendBuff), "You have
        connected to the Genie. Nothing to see here.\n\n");
                                send(connfd, sendBuff, strlen(sendBuff), 0);
                                closesocket(connfd);
                    }
                }
            }
        }
    closesocket(listenfd);
    }
  WSACleanup();
  }
  return 0;
}
```

The source code for this program can be found at `https://github.com/PacktPublishing/Mastering-Reverse-Engineering/blob/master/ch7/server.cpp`.

What is the password?

In this section, we are going to reverse the `passcode.exe` program. As a practice run, we'll gather the information we need by using static and dynamic analysis tools. We'll use some of the Windows tools that were introduced in the previous chapters. Do not be limited by the tools that we are going to use here. There are a lot of alternatives that can do the same task. The OS environment used to analyze this program is a Windows 10, 32-bit, 2 GB RAM, 2 core processor in a VirtualBox.

Static analysis

The second piece of information that you'll need to know, next to knowing the filename, is the hash of the file. Let's pick Quickhash (`https://quickhash-gui.org/`) to help us with this task. After opening the `passcode.exe` file using Quickhash, we can get the hash calculations for various algorithms. The following screenshot shows the calculated `SHA256` hash for the `passcode.exe` file:

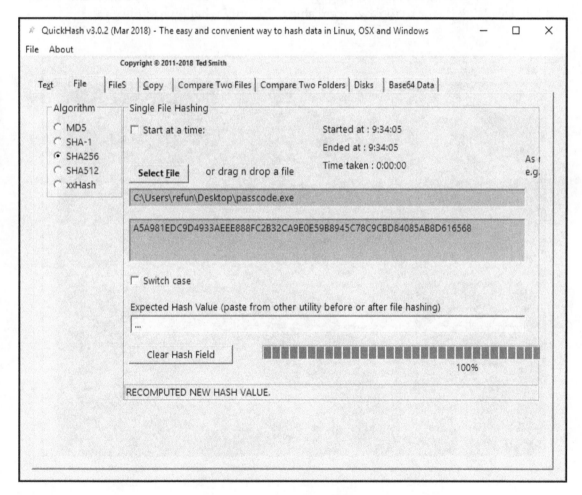

The file has a name extension of .exe. This initially sets us to use tools for analyzing Windows executable files. However, to make sure that this is indeed a Windows executable, let's use TriD to get the file type. TrID (http://mark0.net/soft-trid-e.html) is console-based and should be run on the Command Prompt. We will also need to download and extract TriD's definitions from http://mark0.net/download/triddefs.zip. In the following screenshot, we used dir and trid. By using directory listing with dir, we were able to get the file's time stamp and file size. With the trid tool, we were able to identify what type of file passcode.exe is:

```
Command Prompt                                              —  □  ✕

c:\tools\trid_w32>dir
 Volume in drive C has no label.
 Volume Serial Number is 427F-2D9B

 Directory of c:\tools\trid_w32

08/02/2018  09:41 AM    <DIR>          .
08/02/2018  09:41 AM    <DIR>          ..
04/04/2016  12:53 PM             1,182 readme.txt
04/02/2016  03:15 PM           108,544 trid.exe
08/02/2018  03:32 AM         4,437,440 triddefs.trd
08/02/2018  09:39 AM         1,283,396 triddefs.zip
               4 File(s)      5,830,562 bytes
               2 Dir(s)  25,911,054,336 bytes free

c:\tools\trid_w32>trid.exe c:\Users\refun\Desktop\passcode.exe

TrID/32 - File Identifier v2.24 - (C) 2003-16 By M.Pontello
Definitions found:  10496
Analyzing...

Collecting data from file: c:\Users\refun\Desktop\passcode.exe
 58.9% (.EXE) Win64 Executable (generic) (27625/18/4)
 14.0% (.DLL) Win32 Dynamic Link Library (generic) (6578/25/2)
  9.6% (.EXE) Win32 Executable (generic) (4508/7/1)
  4.4% (.EXE) Win16/32 Executable Delphi generic (2072/23)
  4.3% (.EXE) OS/2 Executable (generic) (2029/13)

c:\tools\trid_w32>_
```

Now that we have verified that it is a Windows executable, using CFF Explorer should give us more file structure details. Download and install CFF Explorer from `https://ntcore.com/`. Here is what you will see upon opening it:

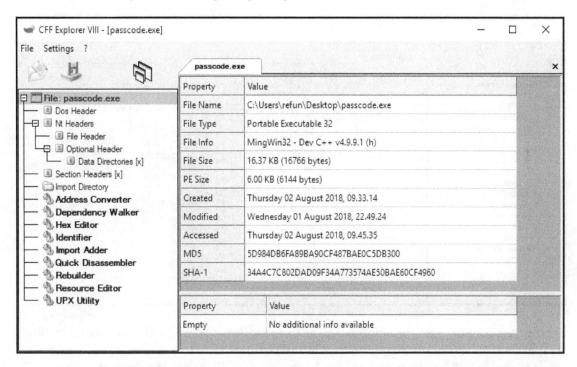

Both `TrID` and CFF Explorer identified the file as a Windows executable, but are not agreeing on their decisions. This might be confusing since TrID identified the file as a `Win64 Executable` while CFF Explorer identified it as a `Portable Executable 32`. This requires identifying the machine type from the PE header itself. The header reference for PE files can be viewed at `http://www.microsoft.com/whdc/system/platform/firmware/PECOFF.mspx`.

We can use CFF Explorer's Hex Editor to view the binary. The first column shows the file offset, the middle column shows the hexadecimal equivalent of the binary, and the right-most column shows the printable characters:

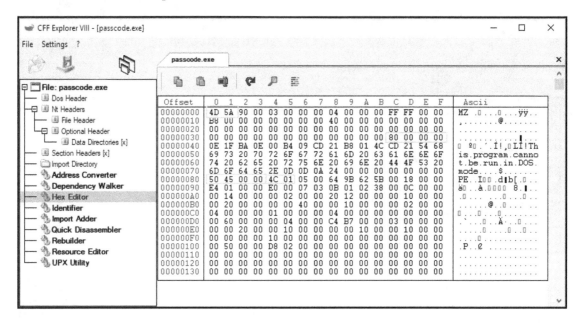

The file begins with the MZ magic header, or 0x4d5a, denoting a Microsoft executable file. At file offset 0x3c, the DWORD value, read in little endian, is 0x00000080. This is the file offset where the PE header is expected to be located. The PE header begins with a DWORD value equivalent of 0x00004550 or PE followed by two null bytes. This is followed by a WORD value that tells you on which machine type the program can run on. In this program, we get 0x014c, which is equivalent to IMAGE_FILE_MACHINE_I386 and means that it runs in Intel 386 (a 32-bit microprocessor) processors or later, but also other compatible processors.

At this point, what we already know is as follows:

```
Filename:  passcode.exe
Filesize:  16,766 bytes
MD5:    5D984DB6FA89BA90CF487BAE0C5DB300
SHA256:   A5A981EDC9D4933AEEE888FC2B32CA9E0E59B8945C78C9CBD84085AB8D616568
File Type: Windows PE 32-bit
Compiler: MingWin32 - Dev C++
```

To get to know the file better, let's run it in the sandbox.

A quick run

From the VM, open Windows sandbox, and then drop and run a copy of `passcode.exe` in it:

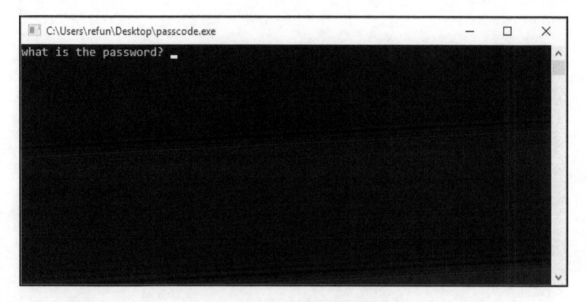

The program asks for a password. After guessing a password, the program suddenly closes. The information that we get from this event is as follows:

- The first piece of information is about the program asking for a password
- The second piece of information is that it opens Command prompt

This just means that the program should be run in the Command prompt.

Deadlisting

For the password, we may be able to find it in the text strings lying around the file itself. To get a list of strings from the file, we'll need to use SysInternal Suite's Strings (`https://docs.microsoft.com/en-us/sysinternals/downloads/strings`). Strings is a console-based tool. The list of strings at the output are printed out on the console.

> The source code for this program can be found at `https://github.com/PacktPublishing/Mastering-Reverse-Engineering/blob/master/ch7/passcode.c`.

We should redirect the output to a text file by running it as `strings.exe passcode.exe > strings.txt`:

```
strings.txt - Notepad                                    —  □  ×

File  Edit  Format  View  Help
x0@
|0@
uB1
p@@
`@@
[^_]
wrong password. try again!
correct password. bye!
what is the password?
%30[0-9a-zA-Z ]
ere
-LIBGCCW32-EH-2-SJLJ-GTHR-MINGW32
w32_sharedptr->size == sizeof(W32_EH_SHARED)
%s:%u: failed assertion `%s'
../../gcc/gcc/config/i386/w32-shared-ptr.c
GetAtomNameA (atom, s, sizeof(s)) != 0
AddAtomA
ExitProcess
FindAtomA
GetAtomNameA
SetUnhandledExceptionFilter
__getmainargs
__p__environ
```

Regardless, we still get a wrong password when we try out the strings. That being said, the strings do show us that a correct message would most likely display `correct password. bye!`. The list also shows a lot of APIs that the program uses. However, knowing that this was compiled using MingWin-Dev C++, it is possible that most of the APIs used are part of the program's initialization.

Disassembling the file using the IDA Pro 32-bit decompiler, we get to see the main function code. You can download and install IDA Pro from `https://github.com/PacktPublishing/Mastering-Reverse-Engineering/tree/master/tools/Disassembler%20Tools`. Since we are working in a Windows 32-bit environment, install the 32-bit `idafree50.exe` file. These installers were pulled from the official IDA Pro website and are hosted in our GitHub repository for the purpose of availability.

This file is a PE file, or Portable Executable. It should be opened as a Portable Executable to read the executable codes of the PE file. If opened using the MS-DOS executable, the resulting code will be the 16-bit MS-DOS stub:

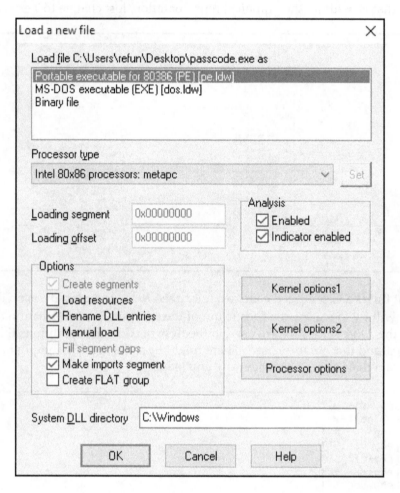

IDA Pro was able to identify the main function. It is located at the address $0x004012B8$. Scrolling down to the Graph overview shows the branching of the blocks and may give you an idea of how the program's code will flow when executed. To view the code in plain disassembly, that is, without the graphical representation, just change to **Text view** mode:

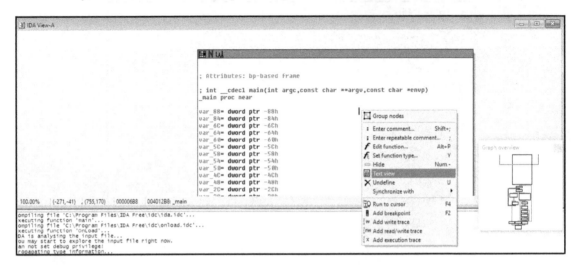

Knowing that this is a C compiled code, we only need to focus our analysis on the _main function. We will try to make pseudocode out of the analysis. The information that will be gathered are the APIs, since they are used in the flow of code, the conditions that make the jump branches, and the variables used. There might be some specific compiler code injected into the program that we may have identify and skip:

```
call     sub_401850
call     sub_4014F0
mov      [ebp+var_58], 3
mov      [ebp+var_54], 5
mov      [ebp+var_50], 7
mov      [ebp+var_4C], 0Eh
mov      [ebp+var_48], 10h
mov      [esp+88h+var_88], offset aWhatIsThePassw ; "what is the password? "
call     printf
lea      eax, [ebp+var_28]
mov      [esp+88h+var_84], eax
mov      [esp+88h+var_88], offset a3009aZaZ ; "%30[0-9a-zA-Z ]"
call     scanf
lea      eax, [ebp+var_28]
mov      [esp+88h+var_88], eax
call     strlen
cmp      eax, 11h
jnz      loc_4013F4
```

Quickly inspecting the functions sub_401850 and sub_4014F0, we can see that the _atexit API was used here. The atexit API is used to set the code that will be executed once the program terminates normally. atexit and similar APIs are commonly used by high-level compilers to run cleanup code. This cleanup code is usually designed to prevent possible memory leaks, close opened and unused handles, de-allocate allocated memory, and/or realign the heap and stack for a graceful exit:

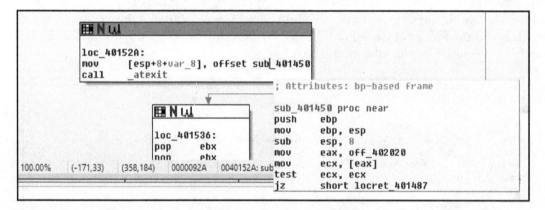

The parameter used in _atexit points to sub_401450, and contains the cleanup codes.

Continuing, we get to a call the printf function. In assembly language, calling APIs requires that its parameters are placed in sequence from the top of the stack. The push instruction is what we commonly use to store the data in the stack. This code does just the same thing. If you right-click on [esp+88h+var_88], a drop-down menu will pop out, showing a list of possible variable structures. The instruction line can be better understood as mov dword ptr [esp], offset aWhatIsThePassw:

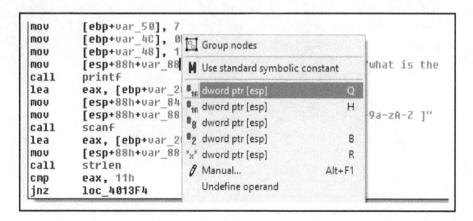

This does the same as `push offset aWhatIsThePassw`. The square brackets were used to define a data container. In this case, `esp` is the address of the container where the address of `what is the password?` gets stored. There is a difference between using `push` and `mov`. In the `push` instruction, the stack pointer, `esp`, is decremented. Overall, `printf` got the parameter it needed to display the message to the console.

The next API is `scanf`. `scanf` requires two parameters: the format of the input and the address where the input gets stored. The first parameter is located at the top of stack, and should be in the format of the input followed by the address where the input will be placed. Revising the variable structure should look like this:

```
mov      dword ptr [esp], offset aWhatIsThePassw ; "what is the password? "
call     printf
lea      eax, [ebp+var_28]
mov      [esp+4], eax
mov      dword ptr [esp], offset a3009aZaZ ; "%30[0-9a-zA-Z ]"
call     scanf
lea      eax, [ebp+var_28]
mov      [esp], eax
call     strlen
cmp      eax, 11h
jnz      loc_4013F4
```

The format given is "`%30[0-9a-zA-Z ]`", which means that `scanf` will only read 30 characters from the start of the input and that it will only accept the first set of characters that are within the square bracket. The accepted characters would only be "0" to "9", "a" to "z", "A" to "Z", and the space character. This type of input format is used to prevent exceeding a 30 character input. It is also used to prevent the rest of the code from processing non-alphanumeric characters, with the exception of the space character.

The second parameter, placed at [esp+4], should be an address to where the input will be stored. Tracing back, the value of the `eax` register is set as [ebp+var_28]. Let's just take note that the address stored at `var_28` is the inputted password.

The `strlen` API comes right after and requires only one parameter. Tracing back the value of `eax`, `var_28`, the inputted password, is the string that `strlen` will be using. The resulting length of the string is stored in the `eax` register. The string size is compared to a value of `11h` or `17`. After a `cmp`, a conditional jump is usually expected. The `jnz` instruction is used. The red line is followed if the comparison deems *false*. A green line is followed for a *true* condition. A blue line simply follows the next code block, as shown here:

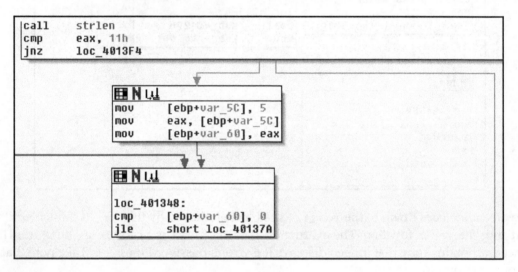

Following the red line means that the string length is equal to 17. At this point, our pseudocode is as follows:

```
main()
{
    printf("what is the password? ");
    scanf("%30[0-9a-zA-Z ]", &password);
    password_size = strlen(password);
    if (password_size == 17)
    { ... }
    else
    { ... }
}
```

It is more than likely that if the size of the password is not 17, it will say wrong password. Let's follow the green path first:

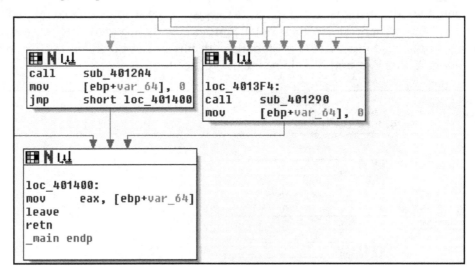

The green line goes down to the `loc_4013F4` block, followed by the `loc_401400` block that ends the _main function. The instruction at `loc_4013F4` is a call to `sub_401290`. This function contains code that indeed displays the wrong password message. Take note that a lot of lines point to `loc_4013F4`:

```
N

; Attributes: bp-based frame

sub_401290 proc near

var_8= dword ptr -8

push    ebp
mov     ebp, esp
sub     esp, 8                  ; char *
mov     [esp+8+var_8], offset aWrongPassword_  ; "\nwrong password. try again!\n"
call    printf
leave
retn
sub_401290 endp
```

Here's the continuation of building our pseudocode with this wrong password function:

```
wrong_password()
{
    printf("wrong password. try again!\n");
}

main()
{
    printf("what is the password? ");
    scanf("%30[0-9a-zA-Z ]", &password);
    password_size = strlen(password);
    if (password_size == 17)
    { ... }
    else
    {
        wrong_password();
    }
}
```

One good technique in reverse engineering is to find the shortest exit path possible. However, this takes practice and experience. This makes it easier to picture the whole structure of the code.

Now, let's analyze the rest of the code under a 17 character string size. Let's trace the branching instructions and work backwards with the conditions:

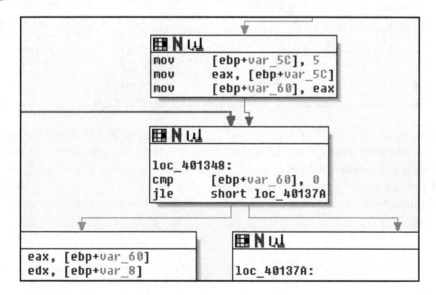

The condition for `jle` is a comparison between the values at `var_60` and 0. `var_60` is set with a value of 5, which came from `var_5c`. This prompts the code direction to follow the red line, like so:

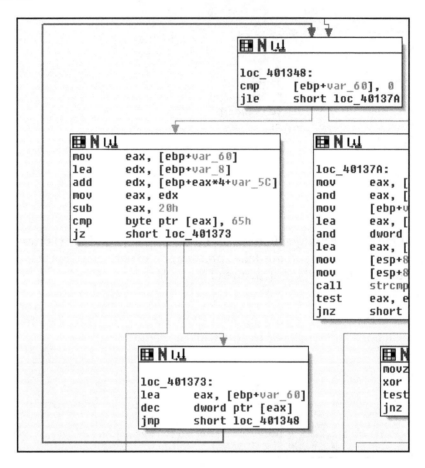

Zooming out, the code we are looking at is actually a loop that has two exit points. The first exit point is a condition that the value at `var_60` is less than or equal to 0. The second exit point is a condition where the byte pointed to by register `eax` should not be equal to 65h. If we inspect the variables in the loop further, the initial value, at `var_60`, is 5. The value at `var_60` is being decremented in the `loc_401373` block. This means that the loop will iterate 5 times.

We can also see `var_8` and `var_5c` in the loop. However, since the start of the main code, `var_8` was never set. `var_5c` was also used not as a variable, but as part of a calculated address. IDA Pro helped to identify possible variable usage as part of the `main` function's stack frame and set its base in the `ebp` register. This time, we may need to undo this variable identification by removing the variable structure only on `var_8` and `var_5c` in the loop code. This can be done by choosing the structure from the list given by right-clicking the variable names:

```
⊞ N ⊔⌋                              ⊞ N ⊔⌋
mov     eax, [ebp+var_60]           mov     eax, [ebp+var_60]
lea     edx, [ebp+var_8]            lea     edx, [ebp-8]
add     edx, [ebp+eax*4+var_5C]     add     edx, [ebp+eax*4-5Ch]
mov     eax, edx                    mov     eax, edx
sub     eax, 20h                    sub     eax, 20h
cmp     byte ptr [eax], 65h         cmp     byte ptr [eax], 65h
jz      short loc_401373            jz      short loc_401373
```

Thereby, for calculating the value in `eax`, we begin from the `lea` instruction line. The value stored to `edx` is the difference taken from `ebp` minus 8. `lea` here does not take the value stored at `ebp-8`, unlike when using the `mov` instruction. The value stored in `ebp` is the value in the `esp` register after entering the `main` function. This makes `ebp` the stack frame's base address. Referencing variables in the stack frame makes use of `ebp`. Remember that the stack is used by descending from a high memory address. This is the reason why referencing from the `ebp` register requires subtracting relatively:

```
envp= dword ptr   10h

push    ebp
mov     ebp, esp
sub     esp, 88h          ; char *
and     esp, 0FFFFFFF0h
mov     eax, 0
add     eax, 0Fh
add     eax, 0Fh
shr     eax, 4
shl     eax, 4
mov     [ebp+var_6C], eax
mov     eax, [ebp+var_6C]
call    sub_401850
call    sub_4014F0
mov     [ebp+var_58], 3
mov     [ebp+var_54], 5
mov     [ebp+var_50], 7
mov     [ebp+var_4C], 0Eh
mov     [ebp+var_48], 10h
mov     [esp+88h+var_88], offset aWhatIsThePassw ; ""
```

Now, in the add instruction line, the value to be stored in edx will be the sum of edx, and the value stored from a calculated address. This calculated address is eax*4-5Ch. eax is the value from var_60 which contains a value that decrements from 5 down to 0. But since the loop terminates when var_60 reaches 0, eax in this line will only have values from 5 down to 1. Calculating all five addresses, we should get the following output:

```
[ebp+5*4-5ch] -> [ebp-48h] = 10h
[ebp+4*4-5ch] -> [ebp-4Ch] = 0eh
[ebp+3*4-5ch] -> [ebp-50h] = 7
[ebp+2*4-5ch] -> [ebp-54h] = 5
[ebp+1*4-5ch] -> [ebp-58h] = 3
```

It also happens that the values stored at these stack frame addresses were set before calling the first printf function. At this point, given the value of eax from 5 down to 1, edx should have the resulting values:

```
eax = 5;   edx = ebp-8+10h;   edx = ebp+8
eax = 4;   edx = ebp-8+0eh;   edx = ebp+6
eax = 3;   edx = ebp-8+7;     edx = ebp-1
eax = 2;   edx = ebp-8+5;     edx = ebp-3
eax = 1;   edx = ebp-8+3;     edx = ebp-5
```

The resulting value of edx is then stored in eax by the mov instruction. However, right after this, 20h is subtracted from eax:

```
from eax = 5;   eax = ebp+8-20h;   eax = ebp-18h
from eax = 4;   eax = ebp+6-20h;   eax = ebp-1ah
from eax = 3;   eax = ebp-1-20h;   eax = ebp-21h
from eax = 5;   eax = ebp-3-20h;   eax = ebp-23h
from eax = 5;   eax = ebp-5-20h;   eax = ebp-25h
```

The next two lines of code is the second exit condition for the loop. The cmp instruction compares 65h with the value stored at the address pointed to by eax. The equivalent ASCII character of 65h is "e". If the values at the addresses pointed to by eax don't match a value of 65h, the code exits the loop. If a mismatch happens, following the red line ends up with a call to sub_401290, which happens to be the wrong password function. The addresses being compared to with the character "e" must be part of the input string.

If we made a map out of the stack frame in a table, it would look something like this:

	0	1	2	3	4	5	6	7	8	9	A	B	C	D	E	F
-60h									03	00	00	00	05	00	00	00
-50h	07	00	00	00	0e	00	00	00	10	00	00	00				
-40h																

-30h										X	X	X	e	X	e	X	e
-20h	X	X	X	X	X	X	e	X	e								
-10h																	
ebp																	

We have to consider that scanf stored the input password at ebp-var_28 or ebp-28. Knowing that there are exactly 17 characters for a correct password, we marked these input locations with X. Let's also set the addresses that should match with "e" to proceed. Remember that the string begins at offset 0, not 1.

Now that we're good with the loop, here's what our pseudocode should look like by now:

```
wrong_password()
{
    printf("wrong password. try again!\n");
}

main()
{
    e_locations[] = [3, 5, 7, 0eh, 10h];
    printf("what is the password? ");
    scanf("%30[0-9a-zA-Z ]", &password);
    password_size = strlen(password);
    if (password_size == 17)
    {

        for (i = 5; i >= 0; i--)
            if (password[e_locations[i]] != 'e')
            {
                wrong_password();
                goto goodbye;
            }
        ...
    }
    else
    {
        wrong_password();
    }
goodbye:
}
```

Moving on, after the loop, we will see another block that uses `strcmp`. This time, we corrected some of the variable structures to get a better grasp of what our stack frame would look like:

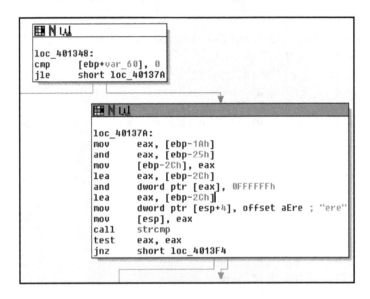

The first two instructions read DWORD values from `ebp-1Ah` and `ebp-25h`, and are used to calculate a binary, AND. Looking at our stack frame, both locations are within the inputted password string area. Eventually, a binary AND is again used on the resulting value and 0FFFFFFh. The final value is stored at `ebp-2Ch`. `strcmp` is then used to compare the value stored at `ebp-2Ch` with the string "ere". If the string comparison does not match, the green line goes to the wrong password code block.

Using the AND instruction with 0FFFFFFh means that it was only limited to 3 characters. Using AND on the two DWORDs from the password string would only mean that both should be equal, at least on the 3 characters. Thus, `ebp-1Ah` and `ebp-25h` should contain "ere":

	0	1	2	3	4	5	6	7	8	9	A	B	C	D	E	F
-60h									03	00	00	00	05	00	00	00
-50h	07	00	00	00	0e	00	00	00	10	00	00	00				
-40h																
-30h					e	r	e		X	X	X	e	r	e	X	e
-20h	X	X	X	X	X	X	e	r	e							
-10h																
ebp																

Let's mode on to the next set of code, following the red line:

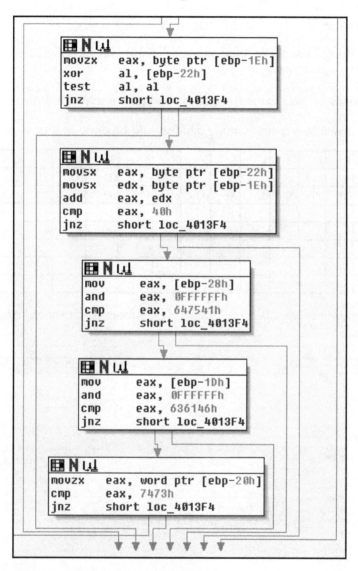

All green lines point to the wrong password code block. So, to keep moving forward, we'll have to follow the conditions that go with the red line. The first code block in the preceding screenshot uses the XOR instruction to validate that the characters at ebp-1Eh and ebp-22h are equal. The second block adds both character values from the same offsets, ebp-1Eh and ebp-22h. The sum should be 40h. In that case, the character should have an ASCII value of 20h, a space character.

The third block reads a DWORD value from ebp-28h and then uses the AND instruction to only take the first 3 characters. The result is compared with 647541h. If translated to ASCII characters, it is read as "duA".

The fourth block does the same method as the third but takes the DWORD from ebp-1Dh and compares it with 636146h, or "caF".

The last block takes a WORD value from ebp-20h and compares it with 7473h, or "ts".

Writing all these down to our stack frame table should be done in little endian:

	0	1	2	3	4	5	6	7	8	9	A	B	C	D	E	F
-60h									03	00	00	00	05	00	00	00
-50h	07	00	00	00	0e	00	00	00	10	00	00	00				
-40h																
-30h					e	r	e		A	u	d	e	r	e		e
-20h	s	t		F	a	c	e	r	e							
-10h																
ebp																

The password should be "Audere est Facere". If successful, it should run the correct password function:

```
; Attributes: bp-based frame

sub_4012A4 proc near

var_8= dword ptr -8

push    ebp
mov     ebp, esp
sub     esp, 8                ; char *
mov     [esp+8+var_8], offset aCorrectPasswor ; "\ncorrect password. bye!\n"
call    printf
leave
retn
sub_4012A4 endp
```

To complete our pseudocode, we have to compute the string's relative offsets from `ebp-28h`. `ebp-28h` is the password string's offset, 0, while the last offset, offset 16, in the string should be at `ebp-18h`:

```
wrong_password()
{
    printf("\nwrong password. try again!\n");
}


correct_password()
{
    printf("\ncorrect password. bye!\n");
}

main()
{
    e_locations[] = [3, 5, 7, 0eh, 10h];
    printf("what is the password? ");
    scanf("%30[0-9a-zA-Z ]", &password);
    password_size = strlen(password);
    if (password_size == 17)
    {
        for (i = 5; i >= 0; i--)
            if (password[e_locations[i]] != 'e')
            {
                wrong_password();
                goto goodbye;
            }
        if ( (password[6] ^ password[10]) == 0 )    // ^ means XOR
            if ( (password[6] + password[10]) == 0x40 )
                if ( ( *(password+0) & 0x0FFFFFF ) == 'duA' )
                    if ( ( *(password+11) & 0x0FFFFFF ) == 'caF' )
                        if ( ( *(password+8) & 0x0FFFF ) == 'ts' )
                        {
                            correct_password();
                            goto goodbye
                        }
    }
    wrong_password();
goodbye:
}
```

Dynamic analysis with debugging

There is nothing better than verifying what we assumed during our static analysis. Simply running the program and entering the password should finish the job:

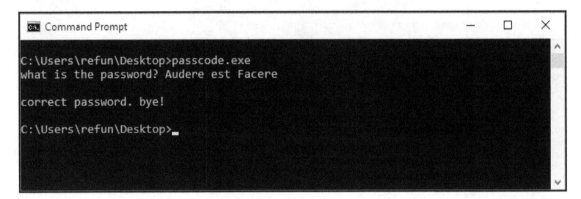

Deadlisting is as important as debugging a program. Both can be done at the same time. Debugging can help speed up the deadlisting process as it is also validated at the same time. For this exercise, we're going to redo the analysis of passcode.exe by using x32dbg from https://x64dbg.com.

After opening passcode.exe in x32dbg, registering EIP will be at a high memory region. This is definitely not in any part of the passcode.exe image:

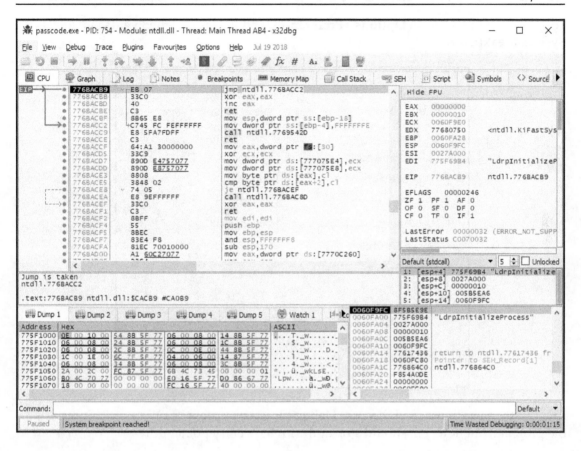

To go around this, click on **Options->Preferences,** and then under the **Events** tab, **uncheck System Breakpoint*:**

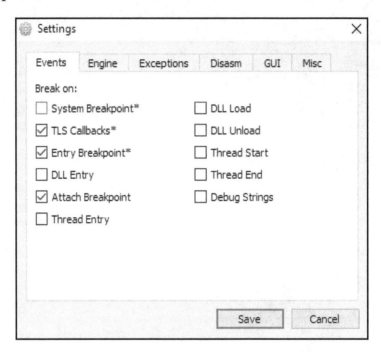

Click on the **Save** button and then use **Debug->Restart** or press Ctrl + F2. This restarts the program, but now, EIP should stop at the PE file's entry point address:

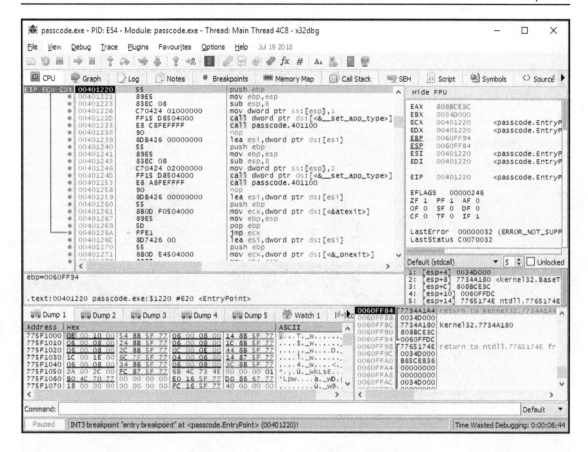

And since we also know the address of the main function, we need to set a breakpoint there and let the program run (*F9*). To do that, in the Command box, enter the following:

```
bp 004012b8
```

After running, EIP should stop at the `main` function's address. We get to see a familiar piece of code as we did during deadlisting:

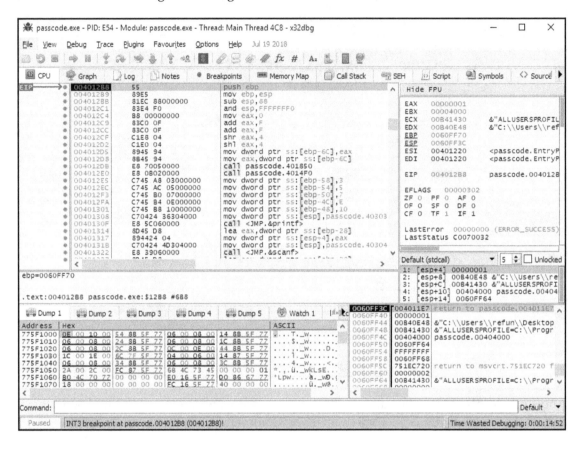

F7 and *F8* are the shortcut keys for Step in and Step over. Click on the **Debug** menu and you should see the shortcut keys assigned to the debug command. Just keep on playing with the commands; if you ever mess things up, you can always restart.

The advantage of using the Debugger is that you should easily be able to see the stack frame. There are five memory dump windows consisting of the stack frame. Let's use Dump 2 to show us the stack frame. Make two instruction steps to get `ebp` set with the stack frame's base. On the left pane, in the list of registers, right-click on **Register EBP** and then select **Follow in Dump->Dump 2**. This should bring Dump 2 forward. Since the stack moves down from a higher address, you'll have to roll the scroll bar up to show the initial data we have in the stack frame:

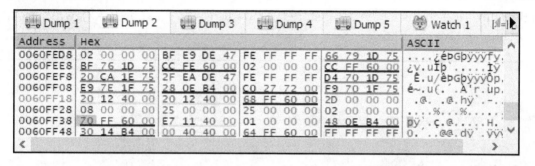

Here's the same stack frame after inputting for `scanf`. Also, during `scanf`, you'll have to switch to the command prompt window to enter the password and then switch back after. Also included in the following screenshot is the stack window, located in the right-hand pane:

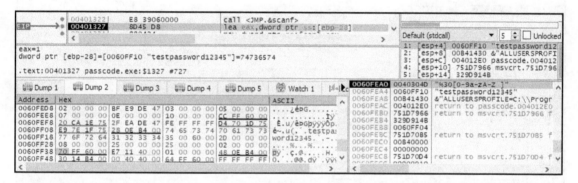

Even while in the debugger, we can change the contents of the inputted string any time, thereby forcing it to continue in the condition toward the correct password. All we need to do is right-click on the byte in the **Dump** window and select **Modify Value**. For example, in the loop that compares `65h` ("e") with the value stored in the address pointed by register `eax`, before stepping on the `cmp` instruction, we can change the value at that address.

In the following screenshot the value stored at the address `0060FF20h` (EAX), which is being modifed from 35h to 65h:

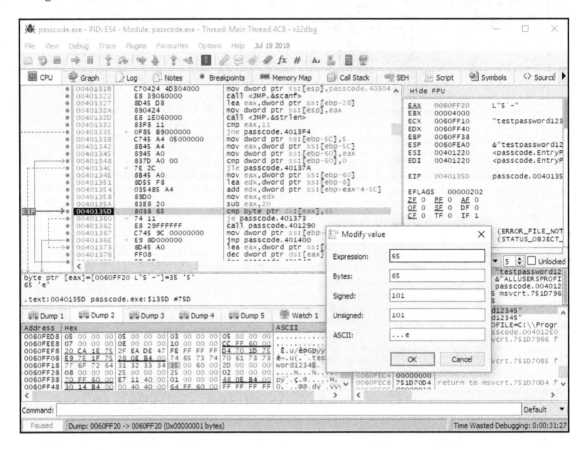

The same modification can be done by doing a binary edit through right-clicking on byte, and then selecting **Binary->Edit**.

And here's where we should end up if we have a correct password:

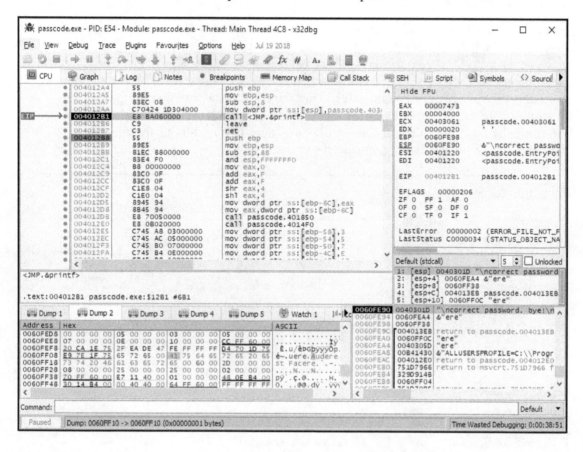

Decompilers

It may be easier if the pseudocode were automatically given to us. Certain tools exist that may be able to help us with that. Let's try and decompile `passcode.exe` (`https://github.com/PacktPublishing/Mastering-Reverse-Engineering/blob/master/ch7/passcode.exe`) using the standalone version of Snowman (`https://derevenets.com/`). Once the file has been opened, click on **View->Inspector**. This should show a box containing resolved functions from the program. Look for the function definition `_main` and select it to show the equivalent pseudocode of the assembly language. This highlights the assembly language line in the left-hand pane and the psuedocode in the middle pane:

As of the time of writing this book, the output C source may help, but not all are correctly decompiled. For instance, the loop where "e" was being compared was not decompiled correctly. The output shows a `while` loop, but we expect that the `v10` variable should have its value read from the offset calculated in the password string. However, most of the code should somehow aid us in understanding how the program should work. The decompiler engine for this is open source (`https://www.capstone-engine.org/`), so not much should be expected as support won't always be there.

The good news is that there are more powerful decompilers that exist, such as HexRays. Most institutions and some individual analysts and researchers who perform reverse engineering are willing to pay for these decompilers. HexRays is one bang for its buck for most reverse engineers.

Here's a HexRays decompiled version of `passcode.exe`:

```
    ×  | 📇    IDA View-A   📇  | 📇   Pseudocode-A   📇  | 🔘   Hex View-1   📇 | 🄰   Structures
    13   char v14; // [esp+66h] [ebp-22h]
    14   __int16 v15; // [esp+68h] [ebp-20h]
    15   char v16; // [esp+6Ah] [ebp-1Eh]
    16   char v17[7]; // [esp+6Bh] [ebp-1Dh]
    17   char v18[8]; // [esp+80h] [ebp-8h]
    18
 ● 19   _alloca((size_t)Format);
 ● 20   __main();
 ● 21   v7 = 3;
 ● 22   v8 = 5;
 ● 23   v9 = 7;
 ● 24   v10 = 14;
 ● 25   v11 = 16;
 ● 26   printf("what is the password? ");
 ● 27   scanf("%30[0-9a-zA-Z ]", Str);
 ● 28   if ( strlen(Str) != 17 )
 ● 29     goto LABEL_18;
 ● 30   v6 = 5;
 ● 31   for ( i = 5; i > 0; --i )
    32   {
 ● 33     if ( v18[*(&v6 + i) - 32] != 101 )
    34     {
 ● 35       badpass();
 ● 36       return 0;
    37     }
    38   }   |
 ● 39   *(_DWORD *)Str1 = *(_DWORD *)&Str[3] & *(_DWORD *)&v17[3] & 0xFFFFFF;
 ● 40   if ( !strcmp(Str1, "ere")
    41     && v14 == v16
    42     && v16 + v14 == 64
    43     && (*(_DWORD *)Str & 0xFFFFFF) == 'duA'
    44     && (*(_DWORD *)v17 & 0xFFFFFF) == 'caF'
    45     && v15 == 'ts' )
    46   {
 ● 47     goodpass();
    48   }
    49   else
    50   {
    51 LABEL_18:
 ● 52     badpass();
    53   }
 ● 54   return 0;
 ● 55 }
```

Decompilers are continuously developed since these tools speed up analysis. They do not decompile perfectly, but should be near the source.

Summary

In this chapter, we introduced reverse engineering, beginning with APIs, by learning how these are used in a functional program. We then used static and dynamic analysis tools to reverse a program.

Overall, there are a lot of reversing tools for Windows available for use. This also includes the vast information and research on how to use them for specific reversing situations. Reverse engineering is mostly about acquiring the resources from the World Wide Web, and from what you already know, we have already done that.

Further reading

- `https://visualstudio.microsoft.com`: this is the download site for Visual Studio
- `https://docs.microsoft.com/en-us/visualstudio/productinfo/vs2017-system-requirements-vs`: site shows recommended system requirements for installing Visual Studio
- `https://sourceforge.net/projects/orwelldevcpp/`: this site contains the binary downloads of Dev C++.
- `https://developer.microsoft.com/en-us/microsoft-edge/tools/vms/`: appliance versions of pre-installed Microsoft Windows can be downloaded here
- `http://mark0.net/soft-trid-e.html`: Download site of the TrID tool and its signature database file
- `http://www.microsoft.com/whdc/system/platform/firmware/PECOFF.mspx`: documentation of the Microsoft Portable E

8

Sandboxing - Virtualization as a Component for RE

In previous chapters, we have used virtualization software, in particular, VirtualBox or VMware, to set up our Linux and Windows environments to conduct analysis. virtualization worked fine since these virtualization software only support x86 architecture. Virtualization is a very useful component of reverse engineering. In fact, most software is built under x86 architecture. Virtualization uses the resources of the host machine's CPU via the hypervisor.

Unfortunately, there are other CPU architectures out there that doesn't support virtualization. VirtualBox nor VMware doesn't support these architectures. What if we were given a non-x86 executable to work with? And all we have is an operating system installed in an x86 machine. Well, this should not stop us from doing reverse engineering.

To work around this issue, we will be using emulators. Emulators have been around long before the hypervisor was even introduced. Emulators, basically, emulates a CPU machine. Treating this as a new machine, operating systems that run on a non-x86 architecture can be deployed. After then, we can run native executables.

In this chapter, we will learn about QEMU to deploy an non-x86 operating system. We will also learn about emulating the boot up of an x86 machine using Bochs.

Emulation

The beauty of emulation is that it can fool the operating system into thinking that it is running on a certain CPU architecture. The drawback is noticeably slow performance, since almost every instruction is interpreted. To explain CPUs briefly, there are two CPU architecture designs: **Complex Instruction Set Computing (CISC)** and **Reduced Instruction Set Computing (RISC)**. In assembly programming, CISC would only require a few instructions. For example, a single arithmetic instruction, such as MUL, executes lower-level instructions in it. In RISC, a low-level program should be carefully optimized. In effect, CISC has the advantage of requiring less memory space, but a single instruction would require more time to execute. On the other hand, RISC has better performance, since it executes instructions in a simplistic way. However, if a code is not properly optimized, programs built for RISC may not perform as fast as they should and may consume space. High-level compilers should have the ability to optimize low-level code for RISC.

Here is a short list of CPU architectures, categorized in terms of CISC and RISC:

- CISC:
  - Motorola 68000
  - x86
  - z/Architecture
- RISC:
  - ARM
  - ETRAX CRIS
  - DEC Alpha
  - LatticeMico32
  - MIPS
  - MicroBlaze
  - Nios II
  - OpenRISC
  - PowerPC
  - SPARC
  - SuperH
  - Hewlett Packard PA-RISC
  - Infineon TriCore
  - UNICORE
  - Xtensa

Popular among CISC and RISC architectures are x86 and ARM. x86 is used by Intel and AMD computers, in favor of having a minimum number of instructions used by programs. Newer devices, such as smartphones and other mobile devices, make use of ARM architecture, as it has the advantages of low power consumption with high performance.

For the purpose of discussion in this chapter, we are using ARM as the architecture that we are going to emulate on top of an x86 machine. We chose the ARM architecture since it is currently the most popular processor used in handheld devices today.

Emulation of Windows and Linux under an x86 host

We explained that installing an operating system on a VM follows the architecture of the host machine. For example, a Windows x86 build can only be installed on a VM that is itself installed on an x86 machine.

A lot of Linux operating systems, including Arch Linux, Debian, Fedora, and Ubuntu, have support for running under ARM processors. On the other hand, Windows RT and Windows Mobile were built for devices using ARM CPUs.

Since we are working on PCs using x86 processors, analyzing a non-x86-based executable still follows the same reverse engineering concepts of static and dynamic analysis. The only addition to these steps is that we would need to set up the environment for which the executable can run and learn the tools that can be used on top of this emulated environment.

Emulators

We are going to introduce two of the most popular emulators: QEMU (Quick Emulator) and Bochs.

QEMU has a reputation of being the most widely used emulator because of its support for a vast range of architectures, including x86 and ARM. It can also be installed under Windows, Linux, and macOS. QEMU is used from the command line, but there are available GUI tools, such as virt-manager, that can help set up and manage the guest operating system images. virt-manager, however, is only available for Linux hosts.

Bochs is another emulator, but is limited to only supporting x86 architecture. It is worth mentioning this emulator, as it is used to debug the **Memory Boot Record (MBR)** code.

Analysis in unfamiliar environments

Here, the reverse engineering concepts are the same. However, the availability of tools is limited. Static analysis can still be done under an x86 environment, but when we need to execute the file, it would require sandbox emulation.

It is still best to debug native executables locally in the emulated environment. But, if local debugging is slim, one alternative way is to do remote debugging. For Windows, the most popular remote debugging tools are Windbg and IDA Pro. For Linux, we usually use GDB.

Analyzing ARM-compiled executables is not far from the process that we perform with x86 executables. We follow the same steps as we did with x86:

1. Study the ARM low-level language
2. Do deadlisting using disassembly tools
3. Debug the program in the operating system environment

Studying the ARM low-level language is done in the same way that we studied x86 instructions. We just need to understand the memory address space, general purpose registers, special registers, stack, and language syntax. That would also include how API functions are called.

Tools such as IDA Pro, among other ARM disassembly tools, can be used to show the ARM disassembly code of a native ARM executable.

Linux ARM guest in QEMU

Linux ARM can be installed in an ARM CPU guest of QEMU, which runs under a Windows in an x86 CPU. Let's head straight to deploying an Arch Linux ARM, then. Running an Arch Linux instance as a QEMU guest is not that hard because of all the available resources we can download from the internet. For demo purposes, we will be using a pre-installed image of Arch Linux and running it in QEMU. Prepare to download these files:

- QEMU: `https://qemu.weilnetz.de/`
- Arch Linux image: `http://downloads.raspberrypi.org/arch/images/archlinuxarm-29-04-2012/archlinuxarm-29-04-2012.img.zip`
- System kernel: `https://github.com/okertanov/pinguin/blob/master/bin/kernel/zImage-devtmpfs`

In this book, we will install QEMU on a Windows host. While installing, **take note of where QEMU was installed**. This is particularly important, as QEMU's path will be used later.

Extract the image file from `archlinuxarm-29-04-2012.img.zip` to a new directory, and copy `zImage-devtmpfs` into the same directory.

Open a command line in the image and kernel file's directory. Then, execute the following line:

```
"c:\Program Files\qemu\qemu-system-arm.exe" -M versatilepb -cpu arm1136-r2
-hda archlinuxarm-29-04-2012.img -kernel zImage-devtmpfs -m 192 -append
"root=/dev/sda2" -vga std -net nic -net user
```

Here, change `C:\Program Files\qemu` to the path where QEMU was installed. This should fire up QEMU with Arch Linux running, as shown here:

Now, log in using these credentials:

```
alarmpi login: root
Password: root
```

You can go ahead and play with it like a regular Linux console. Arch Linux is a popular OS installed by enthusiasts of Raspberry Pi.

MBR debugging with Bochs

When we turn on a computer, the first code that runs is from the BIOS (Basic Input/Output System), a program embedded in the CPU. It performs a power-on self-test (POST) that makes sure connected hardware are working properly. The BIOS loads the master boot record (MBR) to memory and then passes code execution. The master boot record (MBR) was read from the first disk sector of the designated boot disk. The MBR contains the bootstrap loader which is responsible for loading an operating system.

If, for example, we want to debug a given MBR image, we can do that with an emulator called Bochs. Bochs can be downloaded from `http://bochs.sourceforge.net/`.

To test this out, we have provided a disk image that can be downloaded from `https://github.com/PacktPublishing/Mastering-Reverse-Engineering/blob/master/ch8/mbrdemo.zip`. This ZIP archive extracts to about 10MB. The file contains the `mre.bin` disk image and the `bochsrc` image configuration file that will be passed to Bochs.

If we open the `mre.bin` using IDA Pro, we should be able to statically analyze the MBR code. The MBR almost always starts at the `0x7c00` address. It is a 16-bit code that uses hardware interrupts to control the computer.

When loading the file in IDA Pro, make sure to change the loading offset to `0x7c00`, as shown in the following screenshot:

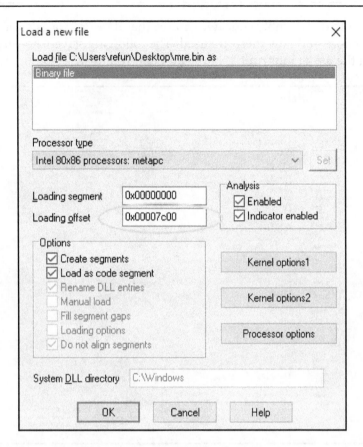

When asked about the disassembly mode, choose 16-bit mode. Since everything is still undefined, we need to turn the data into code. Select the first byte code, right-click to open the context menu, then select **Code**, as shown here:

```
seg000:7C00 seg000          segment byte public 'CODE' use16
seg000:7C00                 assume cs:seg000
seg000:7C00                 ;org 7C00h
seg000:7C00                 assume es:nothing, ss:nothing, ds:nothing, fs:nothing, gs:nothing
seg000:7C00                 db   31h
seg000:7C01                 db  0C0h    :  Enter comment...            Shift+;
seg000:7C02                 db   8Eh    ;  Enter repeatable comment...    ;
seg000:7C03                 db  0D8h  0101  Code                          C
                                      COD
seg000:7C04                 db   8Eh  0101  Byte 31h
                                      DAT
seg000:7C05                 db  0D0h  0101  Word 0C031h
                                      DAT
seg000:7C06                 db   8Eh  0101  Double word 0D88EC031h
                                      DAT
seg000:7C07                 db  0C0h
seg000:7C08                 db  0BCh  "s"  "1+Ä+Ä-Ä++"                   A
seg000:7C09                 db  0FEh
seg000:7C0A                 db   81h       Synchronize with              ▶
```

When converted into disassembly code, we can see that IDA Pro was also able to identify the interrupt functions and how these are used. The following screenshot shows 16-bit disassembly and the use of interrupt 13h to read data from disk sectors:

```
seg000:7C00                        .mmx
seg000:7C00                        .model flat
seg000:7C00
seg000:7C00 ; ====================================================================
seg000:7C00
seg000:7C00 ; Segment type: Pure code
seg000:7C00 seg000             segment byte public 'CODE' use16
seg000:7C00                        assume cs:seg000
seg000:7C00                        ;org 7C00h
seg000:7C00                        assume es:nothing, ss:nothing, ds:nothing, fs:nothing, gs:nothing
seg000:7C00                        xor    ax, ax
seg000:7C02                        mov    ds, ax
seg000:7C04                        mov    ss, ax
seg000:7C06                        mov    es, ax
seg000:7C08                        mov    sp, 81FEh
seg000:7C0B                        call   sub_7C22
seg000:7C0E                        call   sub_7C1C
seg000:7C11                        mov    si, 7C49h
seg000:7C14                        call   sub_7C39
seg000:7C17                        call   sub_7E00
seg000:7C1A
seg000:7C1A loc_7C1A:                                    ; CODE XREF: seg000:loc_7C1A↓j
seg000:7C1A                        jmp    short loc_7C1A
seg000:7C1C
seg000:7C1C ; =============== S U B R O U T I N E =======================================
seg000:7C1C
seg000:7C1C
seg000:7C1C sub_7C1C            proc near                ; CODE XREF: seg000:7C0E↑p
seg000:7C1C                        mov    ax, 3
seg000:7C1F                        int    10h            ; - VIDEO - SET VIDEO MODE
seg000:7C1F                                               ; AL = mode
seg000:7C21                        retn
seg000:7C21 sub_7C1C            endp
seg000:7C21
seg000:7C22
seg000:7C22 ; =============== S U B R O U T I N E =======================================
seg000:7C22
seg000:7C22
seg000:7C22 sub_7C22            proc near                ; CODE XREF: seg000:7C0B↑p
seg000:7C22                        mov    ah, 2
seg000:7C24                        mov    al, 1
seg000:7C26                        mov    cx, 2
seg000:7C29                        mov    dx, 80h
seg000:7C2C                        mov    bx, 7E00h
seg000:7C2F                        int    13h            ; DISK - READ SECTORS INTO MEMORY
seg000:7C2F                                               ; AL = number of sectors to read, CH = track, CL = sector
seg000:7C2F                                               ; DH = head, DL = drive, ES:BX -> buffer to fill
seg000:7C2F                                               ; Return: CF set on error, AH = status, AL = number of sectors read
seg000:7C31                        retn
seg000:7C31 sub_7C22            endp
```

To debug the MBR with Bochs, we will have to make sure that `bochsrc` contains the following line:

```
display_library: win32, options="gui_debug"
```

This line enables the use of the Bochs GUI debugger.

If we have a different disk image, we can change the file name of the disk image file in the at0-master line. In this demo, the disk image's filename is `mre.bin`:

ata0-master: type=disk, path="mre.bin", mode=flat

To emulate the disk image, execute these commands:

```
set $BXSHARE=C:\Program Files (x86)\Bochs-2.6.8
"C:\Program Files (x86)\Bochs-2.6.8\bochsdbg.exe" -q -f bochsrc
```

You might need to change `C:\Program files (x86)\Bochs-2.6.8` to the path where you have installed Bochs. Take note that, for the `$BXSHARE` environment variable, there are no quotes.

Here, Bochs was installed under a Windows environment. The paths can be changed if working in a Linux environment.

Once running, the console will be filled up with logged lines, as shown here:

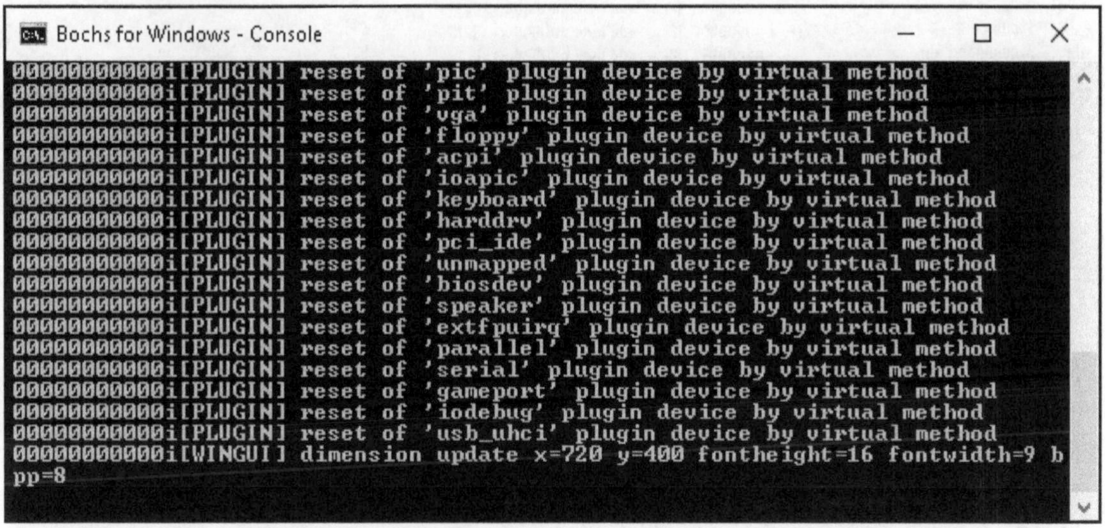

This will bring up the debugging console, which should look like the one shown in this screenshot:

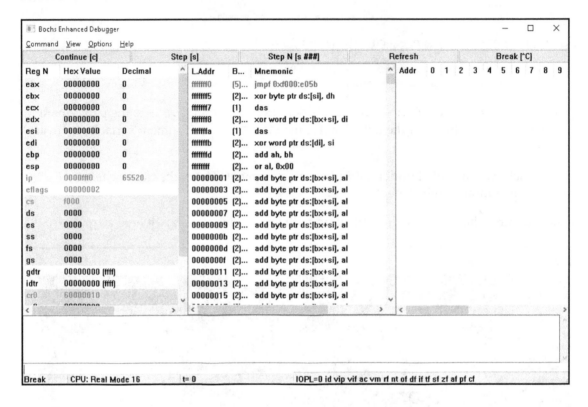

Another window that shows the output should also appear:

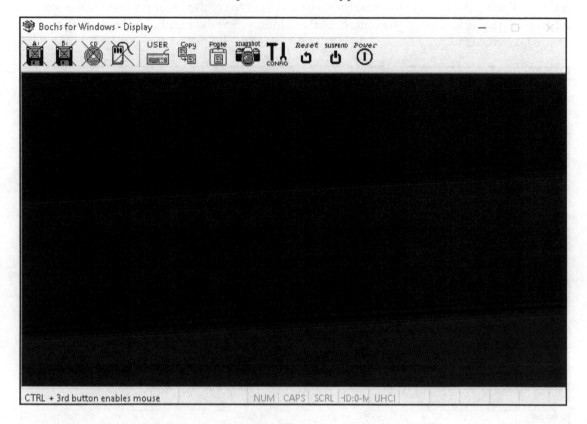

The MBR code begins at the `0x7c00` address. We will have to place a breakpoint at `0x7c00`. Bochs GUI has a command line where we get to set the breakpoints at specified addresses. This is located at the bottom of the window. See the highlighted area in the following screenshot:

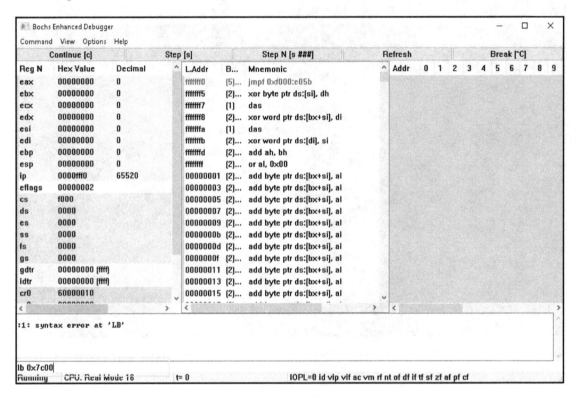

To set a breakpoint at `0x7c00`, enter `lb 0x7c00`. To see a the list of commands, enter `help`. The most common commands used are the following:

```
c              Continue/Run
Ctrl-C         Break current execution
s [count]      Step.  count is the number of instructions to step
lb address     Set breakpoint at address
bpe n          Enable breakpoint where n is the breakpoint number
bpd n          Disable breakpoint where n is the breakpoint number
del n          Delete breakpoint where n is the breakpoint number
info break     To list the breakpoints and its respective numbers
```

The GUI has also mapped keyboard keys with the commands. Select the **Command** menu to view these keys.

Press *F5* to continue the code, until it reaches the MBR code at `0x7c00`. We should now see the same disassembly code that we saw in IDA Pro. We can then start pressing *F11* to step debug on each instruction line:

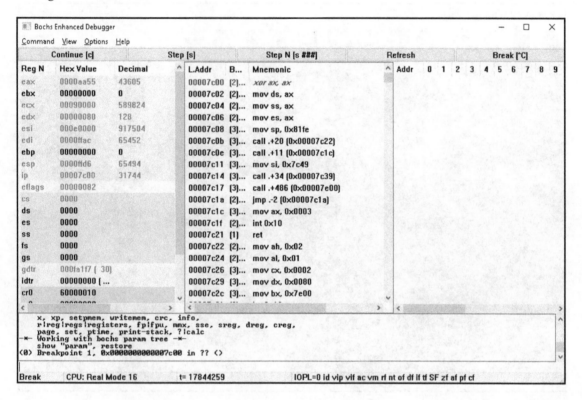

At some point, the code will enter an endless loop state. If we look at the output window, the end result should have the same message, as in the following screenshot:

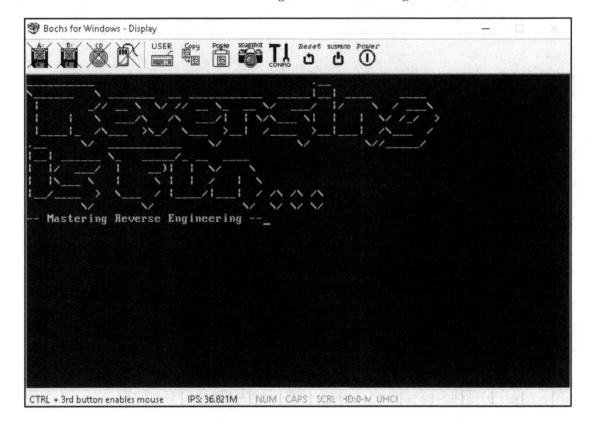

Summary

In this chapter, we have learned that, even if the file is not a Windows or a Linux x86-native executable, we can still analyze a non-x86 executable file. With static analysis alone, we can analyze a file without even doing dynamic analysis, although we still need references to understand the low-level language of non-x86 architectures, categorized as RISC or CISC. Just as we learned x86 assembly language, languages such as ARM assembly can be learned with the same concepts.

However, an analysis can still be proven with actual code execution, using dynamic analysis. To do that, we need to set up the environment where the executable will run natively. We introduced an emulation tool called QEMU that can do the job for us. It has quite a number of architectures that it can support, including ARM. Today, one of the most popular operating system using ARM architecture is Arch Linux. This operating system is commonly deployed by Raspberry Pi enthusiasts.

We also learned about debugging MBR code taken from a disk image. Using Bochs, a tool that can emulate the boot sequence of an x86 system, we were able to show how you can load and debug 16-bit code that uses hardware interrupts. In addition, some ransomware employ features that can inject or replace the MBR with malicious code. With what we learned in this chapter, nothing can stop us from reversing these pieces of code.

Further Reading

- KVM and CPU feature enablement -`https://wiki.qemu.org/images/c/c8/Cpu-models-and-libvirt-devconf-2014.pdf`
- A way for installing Windows ARM in QEMU - `https://withinrafael.com/2018/02/11/boot-arm64-builds-of-windows-10-in-qemu/`
- How to DEBUG System Code using The Bochs Emulator on a Windows PC - `https://thestarman.pcministry.com/asm/bochs/bochsdbg.html`

Binary Obfuscation Techniques

9

Binary obfuscation is a way for developers to make the code of a program difficult to understand or reverse. It is also used to hide data from being seen easily. It can be categorized as an anti-reversing technique that increases the processing time for reversing. Obfuscation can also use encryption and decryption algorithms, along with its hardcoded or code-generated cipher key.

In this chapter, we will discuss ways how data and code are obfuscated. We are going to show how obfuscation is applied in examples including simple XORs, simple arithmetic, building data in the stack, and discussions about polymorphic and metamorphic code.

In the malware world, binary obfuscation is a common technique used by viruses aiming to defeat signature-based anti-virus software. As a virus infects files, it obfuscates its code using polymorphism or metamorphism.

In this chapter, we will achieve the following learning outcomes:

- Identifying data being assembled on the stack
- Identifying data being XORed or deobfuscated prior to use
- Modifying data in text or other segments, and assembling on the heap

Data assembly on the stack

The stack is a memory space in which any data can be stored. The stack can be accessed using the stack pointer register (for 32-bit address space, the ESP register is used). Let's consider the example of the following code snippet:

```
push 0
push 21646c72h
push 6f57206fh
push 6c6c6548h
mov eax, esp
push 74h
```

```
push 6B636150h
mov edx, esp
push 0
push eax
push edx
push 0
mov eax, <user32.MessageBoxA>
call eax
```

This will eventually display the following message box:

How did that happen when no visible text strings were referenced? Before calling for the `MessageBoxA` function, the stack would look like this:

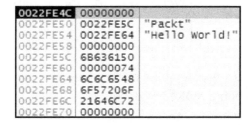

These push instructions assembled the null terminated message text at the stack.

```
push 0
push 21646c72h
push 6f57206fh
push 6c6c6548h
```

While the other string was assembled with these push instructions:

```
push 74h
push 6B636150h
```

In effect, the stack dump would look like this.

Address	Hex				ASCII
0022FE4C	00 00 00 00	5C FE 22 00	64 FE 22 00	00 00 00 00	....\b".db".....
0022FE5C	50 61 63 6B	74 00 00 00	48 65 6C 6C	6F 20 57 6F	Packt...Hello Wo
0022FE6C	72 6C 64 21	00 00 00 00	00 00 00 00	00 00 00 00	rld!............

Every after string assembly, the value of register ESP is stored in EAX and then EDX. That is, EAX points to the address of the first string. EDX points to the address of the second assembled string.

MessageBoxA accepts four parameters. The second parameter is the message text and the third is the caption text. From the stack dump shown above, the strings are located at addresses 0x22FE50 and 0x22FE54.

```
push 0
push eax
push edx
push 0
mov eax, <user32.MessageBoxA>
```

MessageBoxA has all the parameters it requires. Even though the strings were assembled at the stack, as long as data is accessible, it can be used.

Code assembly

The same concept is possible in terms of code. Here's another code snippet:

```
push c3
push 57006a52
push 50006ad4
push 8b6b6361
push 5068746a
push c48b6c6c
push 6548686f
push 57206f68
push 21646c72
push 68006a5f
mov eax, esp
call eax
mov eax, <user32.MessageBoxA>
call eax
```

This yields the same message box as before. The difference is that this code pushes `opcode` bytes into the stack, and passes code execution to it. After entering the first `call eax` instruction, the stack would look like this:

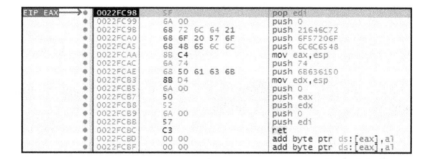

0022FC94	00401536	return to project1.00401536 from ???
0022FC98	68006A5F	
0022FC9C	21646C72	
0022FCA0	57206F68	
0022FCA4	6548686F	
0022FCA8	C48B6C6C	return to C48B6C6C from ???
0022FCAC	5068746A	
0022FCB0	8B6B6361	return to 8B6B6361 from ???
0022FCB4	50006AD4	
0022FCB8	57006A52	
0022FCBC	000000C3	

Remember that the value at the top of the stack should contain the return address set by the `call` instruction. And here's where our instruction pointer will be by now:

EIP EAX	0022FC98	5F	pop edi
	0022FC99	6A 00	push 0
	0022FC9B	68 72 6C 64 21	push 21646C72
	0022FCA0	68 6F 20 57 6F	push 6F57206F
	0022FCA5	68 48 65 6C 6C	push 6C6C6548
	0022FCAA	8B C4	mov eax,esp
	0022FCAC	6A 74	push 74
	0022FCAE	68 50 61 63 6B	push 68636150
	0022FCB3	8B D4	mov edx,esp
	0022FCB5	6A 00	push 0
	0022FCB7	50	push eax
	0022FCB8	52	push edx
	0022FCB9	6A 00	push 0
	0022FCBB	57	push edi
	0022FCBC	C3	ret
	0022FCBD	00 00	add byte ptr ds:[eax],al
	0022FCBF	00 00	add byte ptr ds:[eax],al

The `pop edi` instruction stores the return address to the `EDI` register. The same set of instructions that assemble the message text setup are used here. Finally, a `push edi`, followed by a `ret` instruction, should make it back to the return address.

The resulting stack should look like this:

0022FC70	00000000	
0022FC74	0022FC80	"Packt"
0022FC78	0022FC88	"Hello World!"
0022FC7C	00000000	
0022FC80	68636150	
0022FC84	00000074	
0022FC88	6C6C6548	
0022FC8C	6F57206F	
0022FC90	21646C72	
0022FC94	00000000	
0022FC98	68006A5F	
0022FC9C	21646C72	
0022FCA0	57206F68	
0022FCA4	6548686F	
0022FCA8	C48B6C6C	
0022FCAC	5068746A	
0022FCB0	8B6B6361	
0022FCB4	50006AD4	
0022FCB8	57006A52	
0022FCBC	000000C3	
0022FCC0	00000000	

This is then followed by a couple of instructions that invoke `MessageBoxA`.

This technique of running code in the stack is employed by numerous malware, including software vulnerability exploits. As a course of action to prevent malware code execution, some operating systems have made security updates to bar the stack from code execution.

Encrypted data identification

One of the main features of antivirus software is to detect malware using signatures. Signatures are sets of byte sequences unique to a given piece of malware. Although this detection technique is not thought of as effective for anti-virus nowadays, it may still play a vital role in detecting files, especially when an operating system is taken offline.

Simple signature detection can easily be defeated by encrypting the data and/or code of a malware. The effect would be that a new signature gets developed from a unique portion of the encrypted data. An attacker can simply re-encrypt the same malware using a different key, which would result in another signature. But still, the malware runs with the same behavior.

Of course, anti-virus software has made great improvements to defeat this technique, thereby making signature detection a technology of the past.

On the other hand, this is an obfuscation technique that eats up additional time for reversing software. Under static analysis, identifying encrypted data and decryption routines informs us what to expect in the course of our analysis, especially when debugging. To start off, we'll look into a few code snippets.

Loop codes

Decryption can easily be identified by inspecting code that runs in a loop:

```
      mov ecx, 0x10
      mov esi, 0x00402000
loc_00401000:
      mov al, [esi]
      sub al, 0x20
      mov [esi], al
      inc esi
      dec ecx
      jnz loc_00401000
```

This loop code is controlled by a conditional jump. To identify a decryption or an encryption code, it should have a source and a destination. In this code, the source starts at address 0x00402000, with the destination also at the same address. Each byte in the data is modified by an algorithm. In this case, the algorithm is a simple subtraction of 0x20 from the byte being changed. The loop ends only when 0x10 bytes of data have been modified. 0x20 is identified as the encryption/decryption key.

The algorithm can vary, using standard and binary or just standard arithmetic. As long as a source data is modified and written to a destination within a loop, we can say that we have identified a cryptographic routine.

Simple arithmetic

Besides using bitwise operations, basic mathematical operations can also be used. If addition has a subtraction counterpart, we can encrypt a file using addition and decrypt it with subtraction, and vice-versa. The following code shows decryption using addition:

```
mov ecx, 0x10
mov esi, 0x00402000
loc_00401000:
mov al, [esi]
add al, 0x10
mov [esi], al
inc esi
dec ecx
jnz loc_00401000
```

The beauty of byte values is that they can be processed as signed numbers, if, for example, given this set of encryption information:

```
data = 0x00, 0x01, 0x02, 0x0a, 0x10, 0x1A, 0xFE, 0xFF
key = 0x11
encrypt algorithm = byte subtraction
decrypt algorithm = byte addition
```

After each byte gets subtracted with 0x11, the encrypted data would be the following:

```
encrypted data = 0xEF, 0xF0, 0xF1, 0xF9, 0xFF, 0x09, 0xED, 0xEE
```

To restore it, we'll have to add the same value, 0x11, that was subtracted before:

```
decrypted data = 0x00, 0x01, 0x02, 0x0a, 0x10, 0x1A, 0xFE, 0xFF
```

If we look at the equivalent decimal values of the preceding bytes in unsigned and signed form, the data would look like the following:

```
data (unsigned) = 0, 1, 2, 10, 16, 26, 254, 255
data (signed)   = 0, 1, 2, 10, 16, 26, -2, -1
```

Here's the encrypted data shown in decimal values:

```
encrypted data (unsigned) = 239, 240, 241, 249, 255, 9, 237, 238
encrypted data (signed) = -17, -16, -15, -7, -1, 9, -19, -18
```

To sum it up, if we were to use basic arithmetical operations, we should look at it in the value's signed form.

Simple XOR decryption

XOR is the most popularly used operator when it comes to software cryptography. If we were to change the code algorithm in the previous code snippet, it would look like this:

```
mov ecx, 0x10
mov esi, 0x00402000
loc_00401000:
mov al, [esi]
xor al, 0x20
mov [esi], al
inc esi
dec ecx
jnz loc_00401000
```

What makes it popular is that the same algorithm can be used to encrypt and decrypt data. Using the same key, XOR can restore the original data back. Unlike when using SUB, the data-restoring counterpart requires an algorithm that uses ADD.

Here's a quick demonstration:

```
Encryption using the key 0x20:
   data:  0x46 = 01000110b
    key:  0x20 = 00100000b
0x46 XOR 0x20 = 01100110b = 0x66

Decryption using the same key:
   data:  0x66 = 01100110b
    key:  0x20 = 00100000b
0x66 XOR 0x20 = 01000110b = 0x46
```

Assembly of data in other memory regions

It is possible to execute data in a different memory region out of the process' image space. Similar to how code was executed at the stack space, memory spaces, such as the heap and newly allocated space, can be used to manipulate data and run the code. This is a common technique used not only by malware, but also by legitimate applications.

Accessing the heap requires calling APIs, such as `HeapAlloc` (Windows) or generally `malloc` (Windows and Linux). A default heap space is given for every process created. `Heap` is generally used when asking for a small chunk of memory space. The maximum size of a heap varies between operating systems. If the requested size of the memory space being requested for allocation doesn't fit the current heap space, `HeapAlloc` or `malloc` internally calls for `VirtualAlloc` (Windows) or `sbrk` (Linux) functions. These functions directly requests memory space from the operating system's memory manager.

Allocated memory space have defined access permissions. Just like how the segments of a program are used, these can generally have read, write, and execute permissions. If the region requires code execution, the read and execute permission should be set.

Check out the following code snippet with an implementation of decrypting data to the heap:

```
                        call GetProcessHeap
                        push 1000h                ; dwBytes
                        mov edi, eax
                        push 8 ; dwFlags
                        push edi                  ; hHeap
                        call HeapAlloc
                        push 1BEh                 ; Size
                        mov esi, eax
                        push offset unk_403018 ; Src
                        push esi                  ; Dst
                        call memcpy
                        add esp, 0Ch
                        xor ecx, ecx
                        nop
loc_401030:
                        xor byte ptr [ecx+esi], 58h
                        inc ecx
                        cmp ecx, 1BEh
                        jl short loc_401030
```

The code allocates 1000h bytes of heap space, then copies 1BEh bytes of data from the address at 0x00403018 to the allocated heap. The decryption loop can easily be identified in this code.

The algorithm uses XOR with a key value of 58h. The data size is 1BEh and the data is directly updated at the same allocated heap space. The iteration is controlled using the ECX register, while the location of the encrypted data, which is at the heap address, is stored in the ESI register.

Let's see what gets decrypted using debugging tools.

Decrypting with x86dbg

The preceding code snippet came from the HeapDemo.exe file. You can download this file from https://github.com/PacktPublishing/Mastering-Reverse-Engineering/tree/master/ch9. Go ahead and start debugging the file using x86dbg. This screenshot shows the disassembly code at the WinMain function right after loading the file in x86dbg:

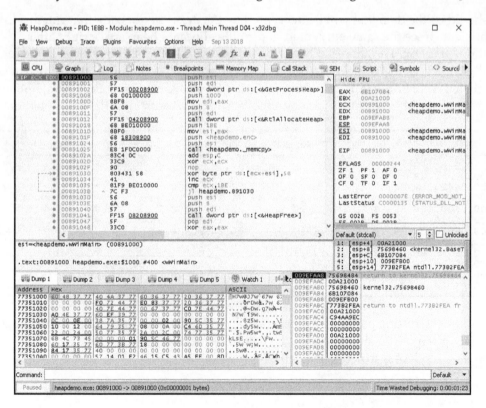

From the executable's code entry point, we encounter heap allocation with
the `GetProcessHeap` and `RtlAllocateHeap` APIs. This is followed by using a `_memcpy`
function, which copies `0x1BE` bytes of data from the address denoted by `heapdemo.enc`.
Let's take a look at the memory dump from `heapdemo.enc`. To do that, right-click on `push`
`<heapdemo.enc>`, then select **Follow in Dump**. Click on the given address, not the
Selected Address. This should change the contents in the currently focused `Dump` window:

```
Dump 1     Dump 2     Dump 3     Dump 4     Dump 5     Watch 1

Address   Hex                                                                            ASCII
00893018  14 37 2A 3D 35 78 31 28 2B 2D 35 78 3C 37 34 37  .7*=5x1(+-5x<7.
00893028  2A 78 2B 31 2C 78 39 35 3D 2C 74 78 3B 37 36 2B  *x+1,x95=,tx;7.
00893038  3D 3B 2C 3D 2C 2D 2A 78 39 3C 31 28 31 2B 3B 31  =;,=,-*x9<1(1+!
00893048  36 3F 78 3D 34 31 2C 74 78 2B 3D 3C 78 3C 37 78  6?x=41,tx+=<x<;
00893058  3D 31 2D 2B 35 37 3C 78 2C 3D 35 28 37 2A 78 31  =1-+57<x,=5(7*>
00893068  36 3B 31 3C 31 3C 2D 36 2C 78 2D 2C 78 34 39 3A  6;1<1<-6,x-,x4!
00893078  37 2A 3D 78 3D 2C 78 3C 37 34 37 2A 3D 78 35 39  7*=x=,x<747*=x!
00893088  3F 36 39 78 39 34 31 29 2D 39 76 78 0D 2C 78 3D  ?69x941)-9vx.,>
00893098  36 31 35 78 39 3C 78 35 31 36 31 35 78 2E 3D 36  615x9<x51615x.=
008930A8  31 39 35 74 78 29 2D 31 2B 78 36 37 2B 2C 2A 2D  195tx)-1+x67+,'
008930B8  3C 78 3D 20 3D 2A 3B 31 2C 39 2C 31 37 36 78 20  <x= =*:1.9.176>
```

This should be the data that will be decrypted by the next lines of code that run in a loop.
We should also see the same encrypted data at the allocated heap space right after
executing `_memcpy`. The allocated heap space's address should still be stored in the register
`ESI`. Right-click on the value of register `ESI` in the window containing a list of registers and
flags, then select **Follow in Dump**. This should show the same contents of data, but at the
heap address space. The dump shown in the following screenshot is the encrypted data:

```
Dump 1     Dump 2     Dump 3     Dump 4     Dump 5     Watch 1

Address   Hex                                                                            ASCII
00104FD0  14 37 2A 3D 35 78 31 28 2B 2D 35 78 3C 37 34 37  .7*=5x1(+-5x<7.
00104FE0  2A 78 2B 31 2C 78 39 35 3D 2C 74 78 3B 37 36 2B  *x+1,x95=,tx;7.
00104FF0  3D 3B 2C 3D 2C 2D 2A 78 39 3C 31 28 31 2B 3B 31  =;,=,-*x9<1(1+!
00105000  36 3F 78 3D 34 31 2C 74 78 2B 3D 3C 78 3C 37 78  6?x=41,tx+=<x<;
00105010  3D 31 2D 2B 35 37 3C 78 2C 3D 35 28 37 2A 78 31  =1-+57<x,=5(7*>
00105020  36 3B 31 3C 31 3C 2D 36 2C 78 2D 2C 78 34 39 3A  6;1<1<-6,x-,x4!
00105030  37 2A 3D 78 3D 2C 78  [00105017] = 353D2C78 (User Data)  *=x=,x<747*=x!
00105040  3F 36 39 78 39 34 31                                     ?69x941)-9vx.,>
00105050  36 31 35 78 39 3C 78 35 31 36 31 35 78 2E 3D 36  615x9<x51615x.=
00105060  31 39 35 74 78 29 2D 31 2B 78 36 37 2B 2C 2A 2D  195tx)-1+x67+,'
00105070  3C 78 3D 20 3D 2A 3B 31 2C 39 2C 31 37 36 78 20  <x= =*:1.9.176>
```

Now for the interesting part—decrypting. While looking at the dump of the heap, continue
doing debug steps. You should notice the values changing as the `xor byte ptr`
`ds:[ecx+esi], 58` instruction executes:

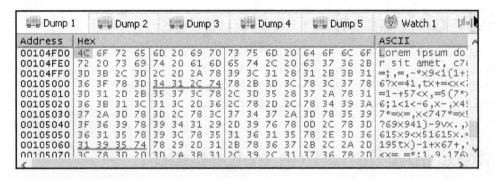

As it would be tedious to step through all these bytes for 0x1BE times, we can simply place a break point at the line after the `jl` instruction and press <u>F9</u> to continue running the instructions. This should result in this decrypted dump:

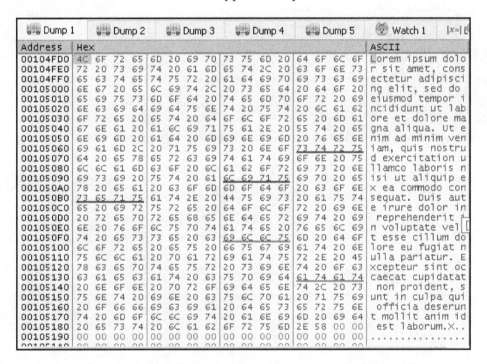

Continue debugging the code; it concludes by cleaning up the allocated heap and exiting the process. The allocated heap is freed up using the `HeapFree` API. Usually, an `ExitProcess` API is used to exit the program. This time, it uses `GetCurrentProcess` and `TerminateProcess` to do that.

Other obfuscation techniques

The obfuscation techniques we discussed are based on hiding actual strings and code using simple cryptography. Still, there are other ways to obfuscate code. As long as the concept of impeding data and code from easy extraction and analysis is present, then obfuscation still occurs. Let's discuss some more obfuscation techniques.

Control flow flattening obfuscation

The aim of control flow flattening is to make a simple code look like a complicated set of conditional jumps. Let's consider this simple code:

```
        cmp byte ptr [esi], 0x20
        jz loc_00EB100C
        mov eax, 0
        jmp loc_00EB1011
loc_00EB100C:
        mov eax, 1
loc_00EB1011:
        test eax, eax
        ret
```

When obfuscated using the control flow flattening method, it would look something like this:

```
        mov ecx, 1
        mov ebx, 0                       ; initial value of control variable
loc_00EB100A:
        test ecx, ecx
        jz loc_00EB103C                  ; jump will never happen, an endless loop
loc_00EB100E:
        cmp ebx, 0                       ; is control variable equal to 0?
        jnz loc_00EB102B
loc_00EB1013:
        cmp byte ptr [esi], 0x20
        jnz loc_00EB1024
loc_00EB1018:
        mov eax, 0
        mov ebx, 2
        jmp loc_00EB103E
loc_00EB1024:
        mov ebx, 1                       ; set control variable to 1
        jmp loc_00EB103E
loc_00EB102B:
        cmp ebx, 1                       ; is control variable equal to 1?
```

```
    jnz loc_00EB103C
loc_00EB1030:
    mov eax, 1
    mov ebx, 2                    ; set control variable to 2
    jmp loc_00EB103E
loc_00EB103C:
    jmp loc_00EB1040              ; exit loop
loc_00EB103E:
    jmp loc_00EB100A              ; loop back
loc_00EB1040:
    test eax, eax
    ret
```

The obfuscated code would ultimately have the same result as the original code. In a control flow flattening obfuscation, the flow of code is guided by a control variable. In the preceding code, the control variable is the EBX register. To graphically view the difference, here's how the original code looks:

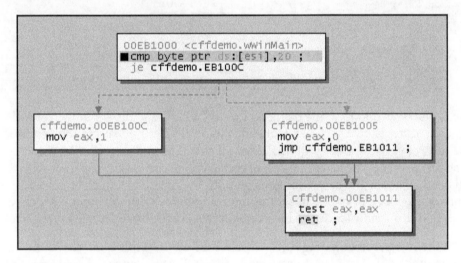

And here is how the code looks when obfuscation is applied:

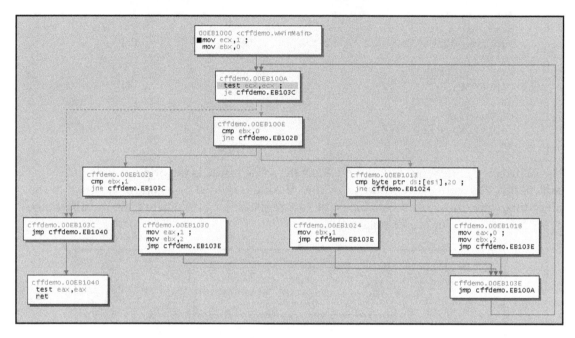

The code is placed in a loop while being controlled with the value set in the control variable, the `EBX` register. Every block of code has an ID. Before leaving the first block of code, the control variable is set with the ID of the second block of code. The flow loops around again, goes into the second block of code, and before leaving, it is set with the ID of the third block of code. The sequence goes on until the final block of code executes. Conditions in the block of code can set the control variable with the block ID it chooses to go to next. In our previous code the loop only iterates twice before it ends.

Looking at the two preceding diagrams, we can see how a simple code can look complicated when obfuscated. As a reverse engineer, the challenge is how to spot a complicated code being reduced to a more understandable code. The trick here is to identify if a control variable exists.

Garbage code insertion

Garbage code insertion is a cheap way of making code look complicated. A code is simply injected with a code or a sequence of code that actually does nothing. In the following code snippet, try to identify all of the garbage codes:

```
        mov eax, [esi]
        pushad
        popad
        xor eax, ffff0000h
        nop
        call loc_004017f
        shr eax, 4
        add ebx, 34h
        sub ebx, 34h
        push eax
        ror eax, 5
        and eax, 0ffffh
        pop eax
        jmp loc_0040180
loc_004017f:
        ret
```

Removing the garbage codes should reduce it down to this code:

```
        mov eax, [esi]
        xor eax, ffff0000h
        shr eax, 4
        jmp loc_0040180
```

A lot of malware employs this technique to quickly generate variants of its own code. It may increase the size of code, but as a result, it makes it undetectable by signature-based anti-malware software.

Code obfuscation with a metamorphic engine

A program can be coded in different ways. To "increment the value of a variable" means adding one to it. In assembly language, INC EAX would also be equivalent to ADD EAX, 1. The concept of replacing the same instruction or set of instructions with an equivalent instruction relates to metamorphism.

Here are a few examples of code that can be interchanged with each other:

`mov eax, 78h`	`push 78h` `pop eax`
`mov cl, 4` `mul cl`	`shl eax, 2`
`jmp 00401000h`	`push 00401000h` `ret`

`xchg eax, edx`	`xor eax, edx`
	`xor edx, eax`
	`xor eax, edx`

`rol eax, 7`	`push ebx`
	`mov ebx, eax`
	`shl eax, 7`
	`shr ebx, 25`
	`or eax, ebx`
	`pop ebx`

`push 1234h`	`sub esp, 4` `mov [esp], 1234h`

This concept was introduced in computer viruses that are able to infect files with a different generation of itself. The computer viruses in which this concept was introduced were Zmist, Ghost, Zperm, and Regswap. The challenge that the metamorphic engines in these viruses face is to make the infected files still work like the original and prevent them from being corrupted.

So, how does metamorphic code differ from a polymorphic code? First off, both techniques were brought up to thwart anti-virus software from detecting several generations of malware. Anti-virus software usually detects malware using signatures. These signatures are unique sequences of bytes found in the malware file. To prevent the anti-virus from further detection, encryption is used to hide the whole virus code, or portions of it. A stub code responsible for decrypting the self-encrypted code of the virus. The following diagram shows a representation of the file generations of a polymorphic virus:

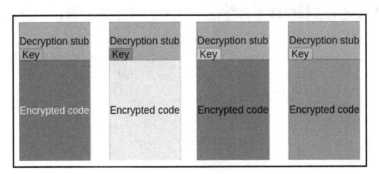

As we can see, the stub usually comes with the same code, but the key changes. This leaves the encrypted code different from the previous generation. In the preceding diagram, we depicted the difference by changing the encrypted code's color. If a code involves decryption and encryption, it can be called a polymorphic code. Some anti-virus software employs the use of code emulation or adds specific decryption algorithms to decrypt the virus code, enabling the signatures to be matched for detection.

For metamorphic code, no encryption is involved. The concept is about substituting a code with a different code that results with the same behavior. For each generation of the virus code, the code changes. A polymorphic code can easily be identified because of the stub code. But easy identification of metamorphic code is impossible, since it would just look like a regular set of code. Here's a representation of, file generations of a metamorphic code:

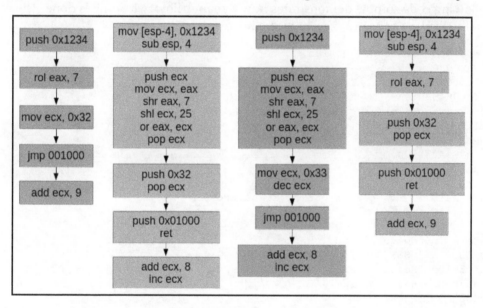

All these metamorphic generation will yield the same result retaining its code sequence. It is hard for anti-virus signatures to detect metamorphic viruses, since the code itself changes. Metamorphic code can only be identified by comparing two variations. In metamorphic viruses, the generation of new code involves a metamorphic engine, which comes along with the code itself. Even the engine's lines of code themselves can be modified.

Dynamic library loading

During static analysis, we can immediately see imported functions that are available for the program's use. It is possible to only see two API functions in the import table, but have the program use dozens of APIs. In Windows, these two API functions are LoadLibrary and GetProcAddress, while in Linux, these are dlopen and dlsym.

LoadLibrary only requires the name of the library where the desired API function name is located. GetProcAddress is then responsible for retrieving the address of the API function from the library with that API name. With the library loaded, a program can call the API function using the API's address.

The following code snippet demonstrates how dynamic library loading is done. The code eventually displays a "hello world message box:

```
; code in the .text section
push 00403000h
call LoadLibrary
push 00403010h
push eax
call GetProcAddress
push 0
push 00403030h
push 00403020h
push 0
call eax                   ; USER32!MessageBoxA


; data in the .data section
00403000h "USER32.DLL", 0
00403010h "MessageBoxA", 0
00403020h "Hello World!", 0
00403030h "Packt Demo", 0
```

Some programs have the text strings encrypted, including the name of the API functions, and get decrypted at runtime before doing dynamic import. This prevents tools such as Strings or BinText from listing down the APIs that the program might use. An analyst would be able to see these loaded functions while doing debug sessions.

Use of PEB information

The **Process Environment Block** (**PEB**) contains useful information about the running process. This includes the list of modules loaded for the process, the chain of **Structured Error Handlers** (**SEH**), and even the program's command line parameters. Instead of using API functions, such as `GetCommandLine` and `IsDebuggerPresent`, here, the obfuscation technique directly reads this information from PEB.

For instance, the `IsDebuggerPresent` API contains the following code:

```
; Exported entry 910.  IsDebuggerPresent



; BOOL __stdcall IsDebuggerPresent()
public _IsDebuggerPresent@0
_IsDebuggerPresent@0 proc near
mov      eax, large fs:30h
movzx    eax, byte ptr [eax+2]
retn
_IsDebuggerPresent@0 endp
```

Using the following code alone will return a value of 1 or 0 in the EAX register. It is in the FS segment where the PEB and **Thread Information Block** (**TIB**) are found. This code shows that the debug flag can be found at offset 2 of the PEB.

```
mov eax, large fs:30h
movzx eax, byte ptr [eax+2]
```

There are different ways for an obfuscation to be implemented. It can be implemented based on the creativity of the developer. As long as the goal of concealing the obvious is present, it will make it hard for reverse engineers to analyze the binary. A better understanding of various obfuscation techniques will definitely helps us overcome the analysis of complicated code during reversing.

Summary

In this chapter, we have understood what obfuscation is all about. As a means of hiding data, simple cryptography is one of the most commonly used techniques. Identifying simple decryption algorithms requires looking for the cipher key, the data to decrypt, and the size of the data. After identifying these decryption parameters, all we need to do is place a breakpoint at the exit point of the decryption code. We can also monitor the decrypted code using the memory dump of the debugging tool.

We cited a few methods used in obfuscation, such as control flow flattening, garbage code insertion, metamorphic code, dynamically importing API functions, and directly accessing the process information block. Identifying obfuscated codes and data helps us overcome the analysis of complicated code. Obfuscation was introduced as a way to conceal information.

In the next chapter, we'll continue introducing the same concept, but in particular, we'll look how they are implemented in an executable file using Packer tools and encryption.

10
Packing and Encryption

As a continuation of what we have learned about obfuscation, we will now introduce a set of tools which are categorized to defend software from reverse engineering. The result of using these tools, such as packers and crypters, is a transformed version of the original executable file which still behaves exactly as the original flow of code behavior did. Based on the tool used, we will discuss what a transformed executable would look like and how execution of the transformed file takes place.

We have picked the UPX tool to demonstrate how packers work at low-level and to show techniques that can be used to reverse it.

 There are many free packers available in the internet that are commonly used by malicious author to pack their software (fsg, yoda, aspack), but for the sake of simplicity we will focus on the simplest of them all UPX.

This chapter will use Windows as our environment and will be debugging with x86Dbg or OllyDbg. We will also show how the Volatility tool may come in handy. We will touch on obfuscation in the scripting language, and then use a bit of Cyber Chef to decipher data.

We will cover the following topics in this chapter:

- Unpacking with the UPX tool
- Identifying unpacking stubs, and setting breakpoints for memory extraction using debuggers
- Dumping memory, and extracting programs executing in memory
- Identifying and decrypting segments using keys within executables

A quick review on how native executables are loaded by the OS

For better understanding on how packers modify files, let us have a quick review of how executable files are loaded by the operating system. Native executables are better known as PE files for Windows and ELF files for Linux. These files are compiled down to their low-level format; that is, using assembly language like x86 instructions. Every executable is structured with a header, code section, data section, and other pertinent sections. The code section contains the actual low-level instruction codes, while the data section contains actual data used by the code. The header contains information about the file, the sections, and how the file should be mapped as a process in the memory. This is shown in the following diagram:

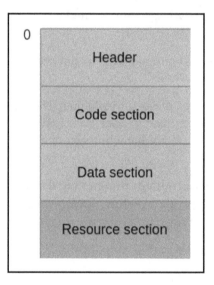

The **header** information can be classified as raw and virtual. Raw information consists of appropriate information about the physical file, such as file offsets and size. The offsets are relative to file offset 0. While virtual information consists of appropriate information regarding memory offsets in a process, virtual offsets are usually relative to the image base, which is the start of the process image in memory. The image base is an address in the process space allocated by the operating system. Basically, the header tells us how the operating system should map the file (raw) and its sections to the memory (virtual). In addition, every section has an attribute which tells us whether the section can be used for reading, writing, or executing. *In* chapter 4, *Static and Dynamic Reversing*, under Memory Regions and Mapping of a Process, we showed how a raw file gets mapped in virtual memory space. The following figure shows how the file on a disk (left) would look when mapped in virtual memory space (right):

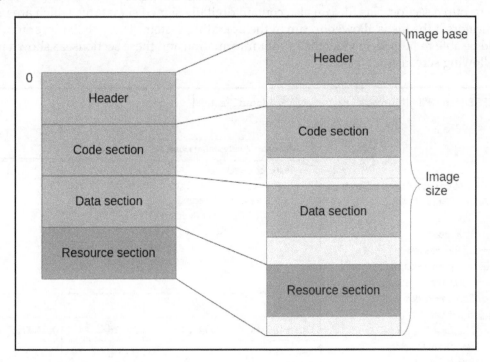

The libraries or modules containing functions required by the code are also listed in a portion of the file that can be seen in sections other than the code and data sections. This is called the import table. It is a list of API functions and the libraries it is from. After the file is mapped, the operating system loads all the libraries in the same process space. The libraries are loaded in the same manner as the executable file but in a higher memory region of the same process space. More about where the libraries are loaded can be found in `Chapter 4`, *Static and Dynamic Reversing,* under Memory Regions and Mapping of a Process.

When everything is mapped and loaded properly, the OS reads the entry point address from the header then passes the code execution to that address.

There are other sections of the file that make the operating system behave in a special manner. An example of this is the icons displayed by the file explorer, which can be found in the resource section. The file can also contain digitally signed signatures which are used as indicators if the file is allowed to run in the operating system. The CFF Explorer tool should be able to help us to view the header information and these sections, as shown in the following screenshot:

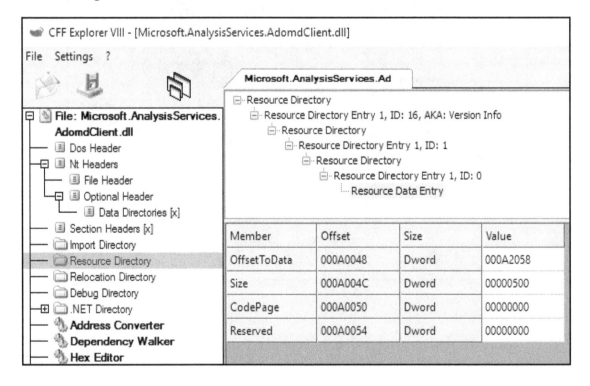

We have covered the basics so far but all these structures are well documented by Microsoft and the Linux community. The structure of the Windows PE file can be found in the following link: `https://docs.microsoft.com/en-us/windows/desktop/debug/pe-format`. While the structure for a Linux ELF file can be found in the following link: `http://refspecs.linuxbase.org/elf/elf.pdf`.

Packers, crypters, obfuscators, protectors and SFX

Executable files can have the code packed, encrypted and obfuscated but remain executable with all of the program intact. These techniques are primarily aimed at protecting the program from being reversed. The rule is that if the original program works properly, it can be reversed. For the rest of the chapter, we will define the term host or original program as the executable file, data, or code before it gets packed, encrypted, obfuscated or protected.

Packers or compressors

Packers, also known as compressors, are tools used to compress the host down to a smaller size. The concept of compressing data helps us to reduce the time taken to transfer any data. At the obfuscation side, compressed data will most likely not show complete readable text.

In the following figure, the left pane shows the code's binary and data before getting compressed, while the one on the right shows its compressed form. Notice that the text strings are not completely found in the compressed form:

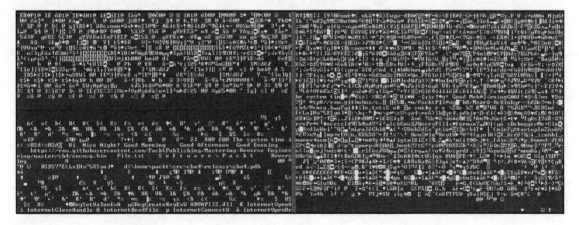

Given that the code and data are now compressed, executing the file would require a code that decompresses it. This code is called the decompression code stub.

In the following figure, the original structure of the file is shown at the left with the program entry point in the code section. A probable packed version would have a new structure (right) with the entry point starting in the decompression stub:

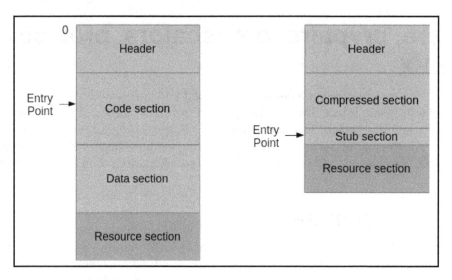

When the packed executable is executed, the stub runs first and, afterwards, passes the code execution to the decompressed code. The entry point in the header should point to the address of the stub.

Packers reduce the size of some of the sections and thus must change values in the file header. The raw location and size of the sections are modified. As a matter of fact, some packers would treat the file as one big section containing both the code and data within it. The trick is to set this one big section with readable, writable, and executable attributes. However, this may run the risk of having improper error handling, especially when code accidentally writes to a supposedly read-only area, or executes code to a supposedly non-executable area.

The end result of a packed file is to get the host behavior intact with a packed file having a smaller file size.

Crypters

Obfuscation by encryption is done by crypters. Packers compress the sections while crypters encrypt the sections. Similar to packers, crypters have a stub used to decrypt encrypted code and data. As a result, crypters may instead increase the file size of the host.

The following image shows a file `crypted` by `Yoda Crypter`:

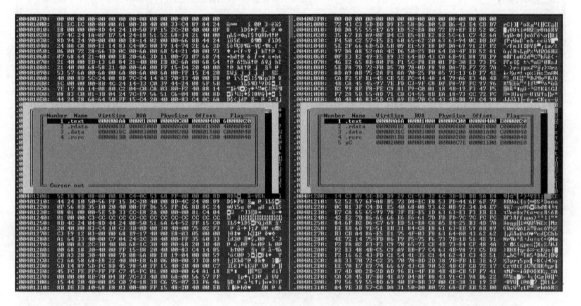

The section offsets and sizes have been retained but encrypted. The stub was placed in a newly added section named *yC*. If we compare how the original opcode bytes look with the encrypted bytes, we'll notice that opcode bytes have zero bytes spread out. This is a trait that can be used to identify encrypted bytes.

Another trait for packers and crypters is about how they import API functions. Using CFF Explorer to check out the Import Directory, we only see two imported APIs: LoadLibrary and GetProcAddress. Both functions are from Kernel32.DLL, and notice that it has its name in mixed character casing: KeRnE132.Dll, as shown in the following example:

yodacrypted.exe						
Module Name	Imports	OFTs	TimeDateStamp	ForwarderChain	Name RVA	FTs (IAT)
00001E28	N/A	00001E00	00001E04	00001E08	00001E0C	00001E10
szAnsi	(nFunctions)	Dword	Dword	Dword	Dword	Dword
KeRnEl32.dLl	2	00000000	00000000	00000000	00005028	00005035

OFTs	FTs (IAT)	Hint	Name			
Dword	Dword	Word	szAnsi			
N/A	0000503F	0000	LoadLibraryA			
N/A	0000504D	0000	GetProcAddress			

With only these two API functions, every function it requires can be dynamically loaded.

The following image shows the GetProcAddress API:

```
004052A3  .  50              PUSH EAX
004052A4  .  C3              RETN
004052A5  $  50              PUSH EAX               ASCII "GetModuleHandleA"
004052A6  .  56              PUSH ESI
004052A7  .  8BD5            MOV EDX,EBP
004052A9  .  81C2 9B334000   ADD EDX,0040339B
004052AF  .  FF12            CALL DWORD PTR DS:[EDX]  kernel32.GetProcAddress
004052B1  .  C3              RETN
004052B2  .  8BD5            MOV EDX,EBP
```

While the following image shows the LoadLibrary API:

```
00405197  .  8BD5            MOV EDX,EBP
00405199  .  81C2 9F334000   ADD EDX,0040339F
0040519F  .  8D02            LEA EAX,[EDX]
004051A1  .  50              PUSH EAX               ASCII "Kernel32.dll"
004051A2  .  8BD5            MOV EDX,EBP
004051A4  .  81C2 97334000   ADD EDX,00403397
004051AA  .  FF12            CALL DWORD PTR DS:[EDX]  kernel32.LoadLibraryA
004051AC  .  8BD5            MOV EDX,EBP
004051AE  .  81C2 AC334000   ADD EDX,004033AC
004051B4  .  8BF0            MOV ESI,EAX
```

Looking at the stub, we expected it to have a loop code that contains the decryption algorithm. The following image shows the decryption algorithm used by Yoda Crypter:

```
00405456  >AC            LODS BYTE PTR DS:[ESI]
00405457   90            NOP
00405458   34 6E         XOR AL,6E
0040545A   34 E9         XOR AL,E9
0040545C   C0C8 3E       ROR AL,3E
0040545F   34 2B         XOR AL,2B
00405461   04 97         ADD AL,97
00405463   2C 9E         SUB AL,9E
00405465   02C1          ADD AL,CL
00405467   FEC8          DEC AL
00405469   EB 01         JMP SHORT 0040546C
0040546B   E9            DB E9
0040546C  >EB 01         JMP SHORT 0040546F
0040546E   C2            DB C2
0040546F  >C0C0 E1       ROL AL,0E1
00405472   02C1          ADD AL,CL
00405474   04 A0         ADD AL,0A0
00405476   04 19         ADD AL,19
00405478   34 CF         XOR AL,CF
0040547A   34 C1         XOR AL,C1
0040547C   EB 01         JMP SHORT 0040547F
0040547E   C2            DB C2
0040547F  >02C1          ADD AL,CL
00405481   04 D5         ADD AL,0D5
00405483   F8            CLC
00405484   EB 01         JMP SHORT 00405487
00405486   E8            DB E8
00405487  >AA            STOS BYTE PTR ES:[EDI]
00405488  ^E2 CC         LOOP SHORT 00405456
0040548A   C3            RETN
```

Obfuscators

Obfuscators are also classified as code modifiers which change the structure of the code while retaining the flow of the program. In the previous chapter, we introduced the control flow flattening (CFF) technique. The CFF technique converts a small code to run in a loop which gets controlled by a control flag. However, obfuscation is not limited to the CFF technique. The compiled file structure can also be modified, especially for a psuedocode based execution, like Visual Basic and .NET compiled programs.

One of the main techniques to obfuscate is to garble, or encrypt, the name of functions so that decompilers wouldn't be able to recognize the function correctly. Examples of these high-level obfuscating tools are Obfuscar, CryptoObfuscator and Dotfuscator.

The renaming of variable names with random generated text strings, converting the code text to hexadecimal text, and splitting text for the code to concatenate the text are some obfuscation techniques used for scripts such as JavaScript and visual basic scripts.

The following screenshot gives an example of an obfuscated JavaScript code using an online obfuscation tool:

The original code is at the left while its obfuscated version is at the right.

Protectors

The protectors employ the combination of packers and crypters, and other anti-reversing features. Protected software usually has multiple layers of decompression and decryption that may use cipher algorithms like `blowfish`, `sha512`, or `bcrypt`. Some sophisticated protectors even use their own code virtualization which is similar to the pseudocode concept. Protectors are usually sold commercially and used for anti-piracy.

Examples of Windows executable protectors are `Themida`, `VMProtect`, `Enigma`, and `Asprotect`.

SFX Self-extracting archives

We usually archive our files using ZIP and RAR. But, did you know that these archived files can be turned into a self-extracting executable (SFX)? The intention for these tools is to easily produce installers for any software requiring multiple files, such as the main program and its dependent library modules. Embedded in the SFX archive is an SFX script. This script is responsible for instructing which directories the files are destined to be extracted to. This can be seen in the following diagram:

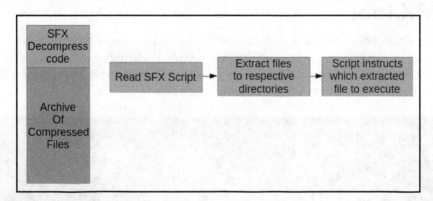

Usually, SFX have scripting features that can:

- Extract archived files
- Run a file from the extracted files
- Run any file from the system
- Delete files
- Make registry entries
- Visit sites from the internet
- Create files

Basically, it can pretty much do what a regular program can do to the system. Examples of SFX tools are Winzip SFX, RARSFX and NSIS.

Unpacking

At this stage, using x86dbg, we are going to unpack a packed executable. In this debugging session, we will be unpacking a UPX packed file. Our target will be to reach the original host's entry point. Besides this UPX packed file, we have provided packed samples in our GitHub page that can be used for practice.

The UPX tool

The Ultimate Packer for eXecutables, also known as UPX, can be downloaded from https://upx.github.io/. The tool itself can pack Windows executables. It is also able to restore or unpack UPX packed files. To see it in action, we used the tool on the file original.exe. This is shown in the following example:

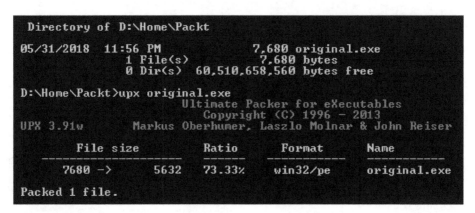

Notice that the original file size reduced after being packed.

Debugging though the packer

Major modifications in the file, especially in the PE file header, have been made by the packer. To better understand how packers work, let us compare the host and the packed version of the executable file. Using the CFF tool, let us inspect the header differences.

The figure above shows the NT header difference between the original and the UPX packed version:

Member	Offset	Size	Value	Meaning	Member	Offset	Size	Value	Meaning
original.exe				×	**upxed.exe**				
Machine	000000F4	Word	014C	Intel 386	Machine	000000F4	Word	014C	Intel 386
NumberOfSections	000000F6	Word	0004		NumberOfSections	000000F6	Word	0003	
TimeDateStamp	000000F8	Dword	5B101B3F		TimeDateStamp	000000F8	Dword	5B101B3F	
PointerToSymbolTa	000000FC	Dword	00000000		PointerToSymbolTa	000000FC	Dword	00000000	
NumberOfSymbols	00000100	Dword	00000000		NumberOfSymbols	00000100	Dword	00000000	
SizeOfOptionalHea	00000104	Word	00E0		SizeOfOptionalHea	00000104	Word	00E0	
Characteristics	00000106	Word	0103	Click here	Characteristics	00000106	Word	0103	Click here

The only difference here is the number of sections, which was reduced from four down to three, as demonstrated by the following example:

Member	Offset	Size	Value	Meaning	Member	Offset	Size	Value	Meaning
original.exe					**upxed.exe**				
Magic	00000108	Word	010B	PE32	Magic	00000108	Word	010B	PE32
MajorLinkerVersion	0000010A	Byte	08		MajorLinkerVersion	0000010A	Byte	08	
MinorLinkerVersion	0000010B	Byte	00		MinorLinkerVersion	0000010B	Byte	00	
SizeOfCode	0000010C	Dword	00000C00		SizeOfCode	0000010C	Dword	00001000	
SizeOfInitializedData	00000110	Dword	00000E00		SizeOfInitializedData	00000110	Dword	00001000	
SizeOfUninitializedData	00000114	Dword	00000000		SizeOfUninitializedData	00000114	Dword	00005000	
AddressOfEntryPoint	00000118	Dword	0000157E	.text	AddressOfEntryPoint	00000118	Dword	00006B90	UPX0
BaseOfCode	0000011C	Dword	00001000		BaseOfCode	0000011C	Dword	00006000	
BaseOfData	00000120	Dword	00002000		BaseOfData	00000120	Dword	00007000	
ImageBase	00000124	Dword	00400000		ImageBase	00000124	Dword	00400000	
SectionAlignment	00000128	Dword	00001000		SectionAlignment	00000128	Dword	00001000	
FileAlignment	0000012C	Dword	00000200		FileAlignment	0000012C	Dword	00000200	
MajorOperatingSystemVers	00000130	Word	0004		MajorOperatingSystemVers	00000130	Word	0004	
MinorOperatingSystemVers	00000132	Word	0000		MinorOperatingSystemVers	00000132	Word	0000	
MajorImageVersion	00000134	Word	0000		MajorImageVersion	00000134	Word	0000	
MinorImageVersion	00000136	Word	0000		MinorImageVersion	00000136	Word	0000	
MajorSubsystemVersion	00000138	Word	0004		MajorSubsystemVersion	00000138	Word	0004	
MinorSubsystemVersion	0000013A	Word	0000		MinorSubsystemVersion	0000013A	Word	0000	
Win32VersionValue	0000013C	Dword	00000000		Win32VersionValue	0000013C	Dword	00000000	
SizeOfImage	00000140	Dword	00005000		SizeOfImage	00000140	Dword	00008000	
SizeOfHeaders	00000144	Dword	00000400		SizeOfHeaders	00000144	Dword	00001000	
CheckSum	00000148	Dword	00004A92		CheckSum	00000148	Dword	00000000	
Subsystem	0000014C	Word	0002	Windows GUI	Subsystem	0000014C	Word	0002	Windows GUI
DllCharacteristics	0000014E	Word	0000	Click here	DllCharacteristics	0000014E	Word	0000	Click here
SizeOfStackReserve	00000150	Dword	00100000		SizeOfStackReserve	00000150	Dword	00100000	
SizeOfStackCommit	00000154	Dword	00001000		SizeOfStackCommit	00000154	Dword	00001000	
SizeOfHeapReserve	00000158	Dword	00100000		SizeOfHeapReserve	00000158	Dword	00100000	
SizeOfHeapCommit	0000015C	Dword	00001000		SizeOfHeapCommit	0000015C	Dword	00001000	
LoaderFlags	00000160	Dword	00000000		LoaderFlags	00000160	Dword	00000000	
NumberOfRvaAndSizes	00000164	Dword	00000010		NumberOfRvaAndSizes	00000164	Dword	00000010	

In the optional header comparison in the preceding example, the changes are:

- SizeOfCode: `0x0C00 to 0x1000`
- SizeOfInitializedData: `0x0e00 to 0x5000`
- AddressOfEntryPoint: `0x157e to 0x6b90`
- BaseOfCode: `0x1000 to 0x6000`
- BaseOfData: `0x2000 to 0x7000`
- SizeOfImage: `0x5000 to 0x8000`
- SizeOfHeaders: `0x0400 to 0x1000`
- CheckSum: `0x4a92` to `0`

The image below shows a comparison between the data directory table of the original and UPXed version of the program.

original.exe					upxed.exe				
Member	Offset	Size	Value	Section	Member	Offset	Size	Value	Section
Export Directory RVA	00000168	Dword	00000000		Export Directory RVA	00000168	Dword	00000000	
Export Directory Size	0000016C	Dword	00000000		Export Directory Size	0000016C	Dword	00000000	
Import Directory RVA	00000170	Dword	0000234C	.rdata	Import Directory RVA	00000170	Dword	000071B4	UPX0
Import Directory Size	00000174	Dword	00000078		Import Directory Size	00000174	Dword	0000017C	
Resource Directory RVA	00000178	Dword	00004000	.rsrc	Resource Directory RVA	00000178	Dword	00007000	UPX0
Resource Directory Size	0000017C	Dword	000001B0		Resource Directory Size	0000017C	Dword	000001B4	
Exception Directory RVA	00000180	Dword	00000000		Exception Directory RVA	00000180	Dword	00000000	
Exception Directory Size	00000184	Dword	00000000		Exception Directory Size	00000184	Dword	00000000	
Security Directory RVA	00000188	Dword	00000000		Security Directory RVA	00000188	Dword	00000000	
Security Directory Size	0000018C	Dword	00000000		Security Directory Size	0000018C	Dword	00000000	
Relocation Directory RVA	00000190	Dword	00000000		Relocation Directory RVA	00000190	Dword	00000000	
Relocation Directory Size	00000194	Dword	00000000		Relocation Directory Size	00000194	Dword	00000000	
Debug Directory RVA	00000198	Dword	00002110	.rdata	Debug Directory RVA	00000198	Dword	00000000	
Debug Directory Size	0000019C	Dword	0000001C		Debug Directory Size	0000019C	Dword	00000000	
Architecture Directory RVA	000001A0	Dword	00000000		Architecture Directory RVA	000001A0	Dword	00000000	
Architecture Directory Size	000001A4	Dword	00000000		Architecture Directory Size	000001A4	Dword	00000000	
Reserved	000001A8	Dword	00000000		Reserved	000001A8	Dword	00000000	
Reserved	000001AC	Dword	00000000		Reserved	000001AC	Dword	00000000	
TLS Directory RVA	000001B0	Dword	00000000		TLS Directory RVA	000001B0	Dword	00000000	
TLS Directory Size	000001B4	Dword	00000000		TLS Directory Size	000001B4	Dword	00000000	
Configuration Directory RVA	000001B8	Dword	00002240	.rdata	Configuration Directory RVA	000001B8	Dword	00006D20	UPX0
Configuration Directory Size	000001BC	Dword	00000040		Configuration Directory Size	000001BC	Dword	00000048	
Bound Import Directory RVA	000001C0	Dword	00000000		Bound Import Directory RVA	000001C0	Dword	00000000	
Bound Import Directory Size	000001C4	Dword	00000000		Bound Import Directory Size	000001C4	Dword	00000000	
Import Address Table Directory	000001C8	Dword	00002000	.rdata	Import Address Table Directory	000001C8	Dword	00000000	
Import Address Table Directory ...	000001CC	Dword	000000F4		Import Address Table Directory ...	000001CC	Dword	00000000	
Delay Import Directory RVA	000001D0	Dword	00000000		Delay Import Directory RVA	000001D0	Dword	00000000	
Delay Import Directory Size	000001D4	Dword	00000000		Delay Import Directory Size	000001D4	Dword	00000000	
.NET MetaData Directory RVA	000001D8	Dword	00000000		.NET MetaData Directory RVA	000001D8	Dword	00000000	
.NET MetaData Directory Size	000001DC	Dword	00000000		.NET MetaData Directory Size	000001DC	Dword	00000000	

The previous example shows that the changes in the data directory are:

- Import Directory RVA: 0x234c to 0x71b4
- Import Directory Size: 0x0078 to 0x017c
- Resource Directory RVA: 0x4000 to 0x7000
- Resource Directory Size: 0x01b0 to 0x01b4
- Debug Directory RVA: 0x2110 to 0
- Debug Directory Size: 0x001c to 0
- Configuration Directory RVA: 0x2240 to 0x6d20
- Configuration Directory Size: 0x40 t0 0x48
- Import Address Directory RVA: 0x2000 to 0
- Import Address Directory Size: 0xf4 t0 0

The image below shows a comparison between the header sections between the original and the UPXed version of the program.

original.exe

Name	Virtual Size	Virtual Address	Raw Size	Raw Address	Reloc Address	Linenumbers	Relocations N...	Linenumbers ...	Characteristics
Byte[8]	Dword	Dword	Dword	Dword	Dword	Dword	Word	Word	Dword
.text	0000AAAA	00001000	0000C00	00000400	00000000	00000000	0000	0000	60000020
.rdata	000008B2	00002000	0000A00	00001000	00000000	00000000	0000	0000	40000040
.data	0000038C	00003000	00000200	00001A00	00000000	00000000	0000	0000	C0000040
.rsrc	000001B0	00004000	00000200	00001C00	00000000	00000000	0000	0000	40000040

upxed.exe

Name	Virtual Size	Virtual Address	Raw Size	Raw Address	Reloc Address	Linenumbers	Relocations N...	Linenumbers ...	Characteristics
Byte[8]	Dword	Dword	Dword	Dword	Dword	Dword	Word	Word	Dword
UPX0	00005000	00001000	00000000	00000400	00000000	00000000	0000	0000	E0000080
UPX1	00001000	00006000	0000E00	00000400	00000000	00000000	0000	0000	E0000040
.rsrc	00001000	00007000	00000400	00001200	00000000	00000000	0000	0000	C0000040

The previous example shows that almost all of the information in the original section header has changed in the UPXed version. The raw and virtual offsets, sizes, and characteristics have changed.

For the UPX0 section, the meaning of the bit flags in the **Characteristics** field are listed in the following example:

The following example shows that the number of imported API functions has been reduced, but the original static import library files are still the same:

original.exe						
Module Name	Imports	OFTs	TimeDateStamp	ForwarderChain	Name RVA	FTs (IAT)
szAnsi	(nFunctions)	Dword	Dword	Dword	Dword	Dword
ADVAPI32.dll	2	000023C4	00000000	00000000	000024DC	00002000
WININET.dll	5	000024A0	00000000	00000000	0000254C	000020DC
KERNEL32.dll	18	000023D0	00000000	00000000	00002590	0000200C
USER32.dll	1	00002498	00000000	00000000	000025AC	000020D4
MSVCR80.dll	30	0000241C	00000000	00000000	000025D2	00002058

upнed.exe						
Module Name	Imports	OFTs	TimeDateStamp	ForwarderChain	Name RVA	FTs (IAT)
szAnsi	(nFunctions)	Dword	Dword	Dword	Dword	Dword
KERNEL32.DLL	6	00000000	00000000	00000000	00007268	0000722C
ADVAPI32.dll	1	00000000	00000000	00000000	00007275	00007248
MSVCR80.dll	1	00000000	00000000	00000000	00007282	00007250
USER32.dll	1	00000000	00000000	00000000	0000728E	00007258
WININET.dll	1	00000000	00000000	00000000	00007299	00007260

The following figure shows the API functions that will be imported for KERNEL32.dll. They have totally different API functions:

original.exe					upxed.exe			
Module Name	Imports	OFTs	TimeDateStamp	Forwarde	Module Name	Imports	OFTs	TimeDateStamp
00001590	N/A	00001374	00001378	0000137C	00001468	N/A	000013B4	000013B8
szAnsi	(nFunctions)	Dword	Dword	Dword	szAnsi	(nFunctions)	Dword	Dword
ADVAPI32.dll	2	000023C4	00000000	00000000	KERNEL32.DLL	6	00000000	00000000
WININET.dll	5	000024A0	00000000	00000000	ADVAPI32.dll	1	00000000	00000000
KERNEL32.dll	18	000023D0	00000000	00000000	MSVCR80.dll	1	00000000	00000000

OFTs	FTs (IAT)	Hint	Name		OFTs	FTs (IAT)	Hint	Name
Dword	Dword	Word	szAnsi		Dword	Dword	Word	szAnsi
0000288E	0000288E	01CA	GetSystemTimeAsFileTime		N/A	000072A4	0000	LoadLibraryA
00002878	00002878	0143	GetCurrentProcessId		N/A	000072B2	0000	GetProcAddress
00002862	00002862	0146	GetCurrentThreadId		N/A	000072C2	0000	VirtualProtect
00002852	00002852	01DF	GetTickCount		N/A	000072D2	0000	VirtualAlloc
00002838	00002838	02A3	QueryPerformanceCounter		N/A	000072E0	0000	VirtualFree
00002824	00002824	0239	IsDebuggerPresent		N/A	000072EE	0000	ExitProcess
00002558	00002558	0034	CloseHandle					
00002566	00002566	03A4	WriteFile					
00002572	00002572	0173	GetLocalTime					
00002582	00002582	0053	CreateFileA					
00002806	00002806	034A	SetUnhandledExceptionFilter					
000027EA	000027EA	036E	UnhandledExceptionFilter					
000027C2	000027C2	035E	TerminateProcess					
000027B0	000027B0	01B7	GetStartupInfoA					
00002792	00002792	0226	InterlockedCompareExchange					
0000278A	0000278A	0356	Sleep					
00002774	00002774	0229	InterlockedExchange					
000027D6	000027D6	0142	GetCurrentProcess					

As for the resource directory contents, it looks like the size did not change except for the offset, as can be seen in the following example:

original.exe				upxed.exe			

Resource Directory				Resource Directory			
Resource Directory Entry 1, ID: 24, AKA: Configuration Files				Resource Directory Entry 1, ID: 24, AKA: Configuration Files			
Resource Directory				Resource Directory			
Resource Directory Entry 1, ID: 1				Resource Directory Entry 1, ID: 1			
Resource Directory				Resource Directory			
Resource Directory Entry 1, ID: 1033				Resource Directory Entry 1, ID: 1033			
Resource Data Entry				Resource Data Entry			

Member	Offset	Size	Value	Member	Offset	Size	Value
OffsetToData	00001C48	Dword	00004058	OffsetToData	00001248	Dword	0000705C
Size	00001C4C	Dword	00000155	Size	0000124C	Dword	00000155
CodePage	00001C50	Dword	000004E4	CodePage	00001250	Dword	000004E4
Reserved	00001C54	Dword	00000000	Reserved	00001254	Dword	00000000

The following list shows the changes on which the traits are based in the packed file:

- There are three sections, namely UPX0, UPx1 and .rsrc:
    - UPX0 has virtual section properties but has no raw section properties. This only means that the section will be allocated by the operating system but no data will be mapped to it from the file. This section is set with read, write, and execute flags.
    - The entry point address is within the UPX1 section. The stub should be located in this section, along with the compressed code and data.
    - The .rsrc section seems to retain its contents. Retaining the resource section should still give out the proper icons and program details read by the operating system's file explorer.
- With the packer having its own structure causing major changes in the sections, some header fields, like the BaseOfCode and BaseOfData, were totally modified.
- Virtual sizes were aligned based on the SectionAlignment. For example, the .rsrc's virtual size was originally 0x1b0, aligning it with the SectionAlignment, which should make it 0x1000.
- The ImageSize has increased since a stub was inserted by the packer.

The entry point is the sum of the `ImageBase` and `AddressOfEntryPoint`. The original entry point is located at `0x0040157e`. This address is located within the range of `UPX0`, which begins at `0x00401000` with a size of `0x5000`. The stub is located at the packed file's entry point in the `UPX1` section. The outcome we are expecting is that the packer decompresses the code, dynamically imports the API functions, and finally passes the code execution to the original entry point. To hasten our debugging, what we should be looking for is an instruction, or a set of instructions, that will pass execution to `0x0040157e`, which is the original entry point.

Let us see this in action by opening `upxed.exe` in `x86dbg`. We start off at the entry point at `0x00406b90`, as shown in the following screenshot:

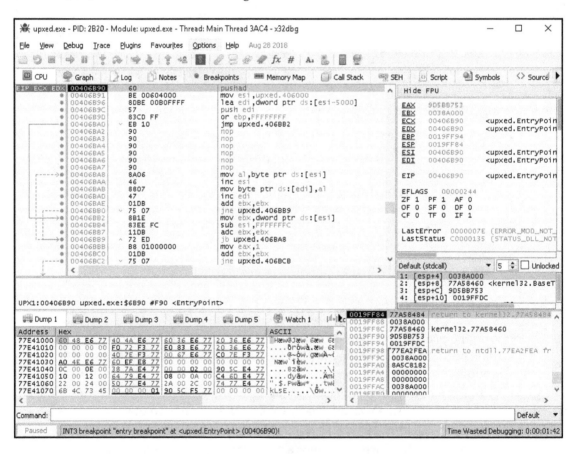

The operating system maps the file to the memory, and we have all the virtual sections allocated as well. The first instruction uses `pushad` to save all the initial flag states. If it saves all the flags, it should restore these flags before it jumps towards the original entry point. The next instruction stores the address `0x00406000` to register `esi`. This address is the start of the `UPX1` section. This is where the compressed data is. The next line stores `0x00401000` to register edi. It is easy to tell that the compressed data will be decompressed from `esi` to `edi`. With debugging on, the decompression codes are from `0x00406b91` to `0x00406c5d`.

Before placing a breakpoint at `0x00406c62`, set a dump window with the address `0x00401000`. This should help us view a decompressed portion of the host. Running through the code until `0x00406c62` should complete the decompression. This is shown in the following screenshot:

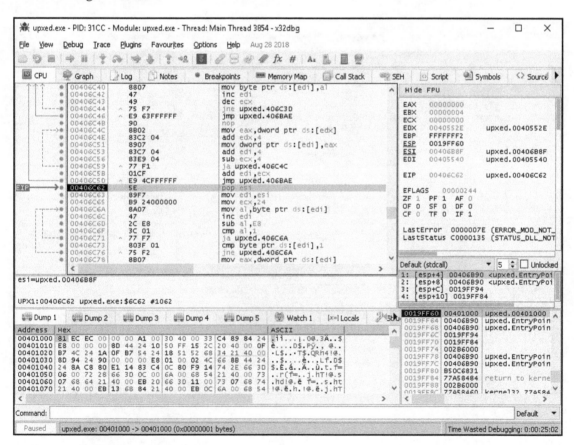

The next set of instructions fixes call instructions using relative jump addresses. This code runs from 0x00406c65 to 0x00406c94. Just place another breakpoint, or instead use a Run until selection at the 0x00406c96 line, to run through the loop of this call fixing code.

The next lines are the portion of the packer that dynamically load the API functions used by the host. The code stores 0x00405000 to register edi. This address contains data where it can locate the list of names of the original modules and API function names associated with each module.

For every module name, it uses LoadLibraryA to load the libraries that the host will use later. This is shown in the following screenshot:

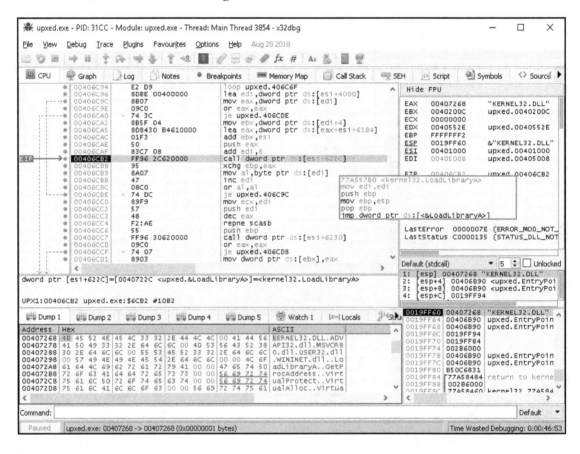

Right after loading a module, it uses `GetProcAddress` to retrieve the addresses of the APIs the host will use, as shown in the following screenshot:

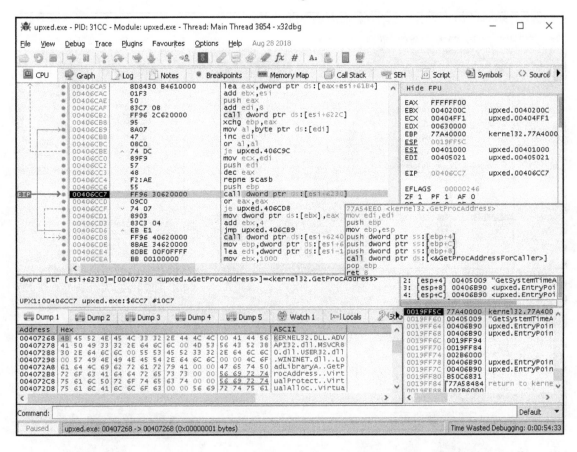

Every retrieved API address is stored at the host import table which is located at `0x00402000`. Restoring the function addresses to the same import table address should make the host call the APIs without any issues. Placing a breakpoint at `0x00406cde` should execute the dynamic import routine.

The next routine is about to set the mapped header's access permission to read-only, preventing it from being written to or code executed, as shown in the following screenshot:

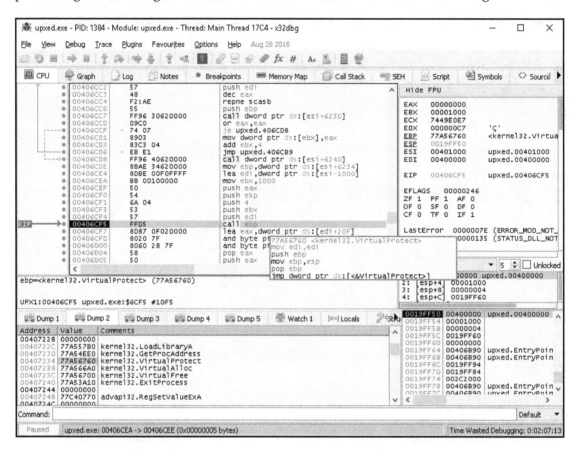

VirtualProtect is used to set memory access flags and also takes four parameters. The following code shows the parameters according to MSDN:

```
BOOL WINAPI VirtualProtect(
  _In_   LPVOID lpAddress,
  _In_   SIZE_T dwSize,
  _In_   DWORD  flNewProtect,
  _Out_  PDWORD lpflOldProtect
);
```

The first call to VirtualProtect is set with an `lpAddress` equal to `0x00400000`, dwSize with `0x1000` bytes, and the protect flags with a value of 4. The value 4 denotes the constant for PAGE_READWRITE. The succeeding calls to VirtualProtect are set with a protect flag PAGE_READONLY. This is shown in the following screenshot:

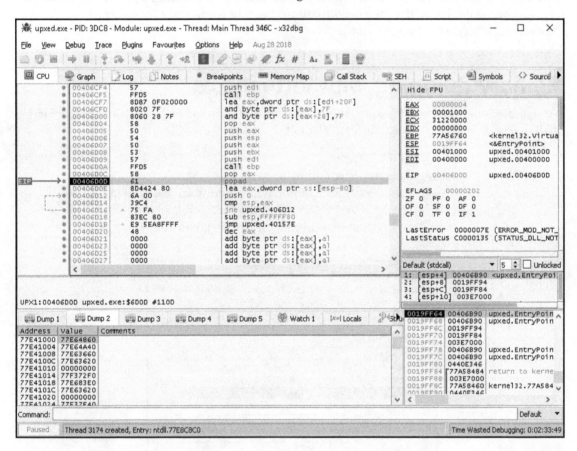

Remember that, at the start of the code, we encountered a `pushad` instruction. At this point, we are on its counterpart instruction, `popad`. This is most likely the part where execution will be passed to the original entry point. Looking at the `jmp` instruction at `0x00406D1B`, the address jumps to an address in the UPX0 section. Looking at our host-packed comparison, the original entry point is indeed located at `0x0040157e`.

Reaching the original entry point should conclude debugging the packer code.

Dumping processes from memory

A packed file's data cannot be seen in plain sight, but if we let it run, everything is expected to be unpacked in its process space. What we aim to do is to produce a version of the file in its unpacked state. To do that, we need to dump the whole memory then extract the executable's process image to a file.

Memory dumping with VirtualBox

We will be using Volatility to dump the process from a suspended VirtualBox image. First of all, we need to learn how to dump a VirtualBox image:

1. Enable the VirtualBox's debug menu:
   - For Windows VirtualBox hosts:
     - Enter a new environment variable named VBOX_GUI_DBG_ENABLED and set it to true. This is shown in the following screenshot:

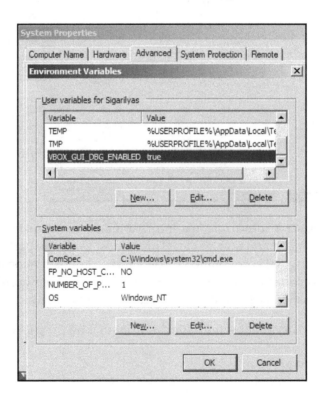

- For Linux hosts:
    - Edit/etc/environment as a root user
    - Add a new entry `VBOX_GUI_DBG_ENABLED=true`
    - Execute the command: `source /etc/environment`
    - Restart VirtualBox if already opened

2. Run the packed executable in the Windows guest. We are going to run `upxed.exe` from our GitHub page.

3. From the VBoxDbg console, execute these lines to save the whole memory dump to a file. Note that there should be a dot before the `pgmphystofile` command, as shown in the following example:

    1. `.pgmphystofile memory.dmp`

    2. memory.dmp is the filename and is stored at the logged-in user's home directory. That is the `%userprofile%` folder in Windows and the `~/` folder in Linux.

Next, we will be using Volatility to parse the memory dump and extract the data we need.

Extracting the process to a file using Volatility

Volatility can be downloaded from `https://www.volatilityfoundation.org/releases`. For this section, our VirtualBox host is in a Linux Ubuntu machine. The Volatility command parameters shown here should also be the same when used in Windows.

First, we need to identify the exact operating system version using Volatility using the `imageinfo` parameter, as shown in the following examples:

```
vol -f ~/memory.dmp imageinfo
```

```
> ./volatility_2.6_lin64_standalone -f ~/memory.dmp imageinfo
Volatility Foundation Volatility Framework 2.6
INFO    : volatility.debug    : Determining profile based on KDBG search...
          Suggested Profile(s) : Win7SP1x86_23418, Win7SP0x86, Win7SP1x86
                    AS Layer1 : IA32PagedMemory (Kernel AS)
                    AS Layer2 : FileAddressSpace (/home/niangao/memory.dmp)
                     PAE type : No PAE
                          DTB : 0x185000L
                         KDBG : 0x82d29c28L
          Number of Processors : 1
    Image Type (Service Pack) : 1
              KPCR for CPU 0 : 0x82d2ac00L
          KUSER_SHARED_DATA : 0xffdf0000L
          Image date and time : 2018-10-10 09:25:12 UTC+0000
     Image local date and time : 2018-10-10 02:25:12 -0700
```

Again, `~/memory.dmp` is the file path of the memory we just dumped. The result should show a list of the identified OS profile. For Windows 7 SP1 32-bit, we would be using `Win7SP1x86` as our profile for succeeding `Volatility` commands.

Next, we will have to list down the running processes and identify which is our packed executable. To list down running processes, we will be using the `pslist` parameter, as shown in the following examples:

```
volatility --profile=Win7SP1x86 -f ~/memory.dmp pslist
```

```
> ./volatility_2.6_lin64_standalone --profile Win7SP1x86 -f ~/memory.dmp pslist
Volatility Foundation Volatility Framework 2.6
Offset(V)    Name                  PID    PPID    Thds    Hnds    Sess    Wow64   Start                       Exit
----------   ----                  ---    ----    ----    ----    ----    -----   -----                       ----
0x8469c020   System                  4       0     109     550    ------      0   2018-10-10 12:22:41 UTC+0000
0x86ba5d40   smss.exe              392       4       2      29    ------      0   2018-10-10 12:22:41 UTC+0000
0x8f0db4c8   csrss.exe             468     460       9     456       0       0   2018-10-10 12:22:47 UTC+0000
0x8f12d530   csrss.exe             520     508       9     195       1       0   2018-10-10 12:22:49 UTC+0000
0x8f112530   wininit.exe           528     460       3      76       0       0   2018-10-10 12:22:49 UTC+0000
0x8f0e6530   winlogon.exe          556     508       4     109       1       0   2018-10-10 12:22:49 UTC+0000
0x8f1b6d40   services.exe          616     528       8     196       0       0   2018-10-10 12:22:50 UTC+0000
0x8f1959d8   lsass.exe             624     528       9     698       0       0   2018-10-10 12:22:51 UTC+0000
0x86ba3b18   lsm.exe               632     528      11     202       0       0   2018-10-10 12:22:51 UTC+0000
0x8f150d40   svchost.exe           720     616      10     345       0       0   2018-10-10 12:22:56 UTC+0000
0x8f2098c0   DFServ.exe            776     616      12     145       0       0   2018-10-10 12:22:57 UTC+0000
0x8f210478   VBoxService.ex        816     616      13     117       0       0   2018-10-10 12:22:59 UTC+0000
0x8f219d40   svchost.exe           888     616       6     263       0       0   2018-10-10 09:23:01 UTC+0000
0x8f247400   svchost.exe           980     616      24     514       0       0   2018-10-10 09:23:02 UTC+0000
0x8f251860   svchost.exe          1028     616      27     486       0       0   2018-10-10 09:23:02 UTC+0000
0x8f251cb0   svchost.exe          1052     616      31     488       0       0   2018-10-10 09:23:02 UTC+0000
0x8f2567a8   svchost.exe          1076     616      41    1005       0       0   2018-10-10 09:23:02 UTC+0000
0x8f272718   audiodg.exe          1156     980       5     117       0       0   2018-10-10 09:23:03 UTC+0000
0x8f3a4030   svchost.exe          1316     616      24     524       0       0   2018-10-10 09:23:05 UTC+0000
0x8f138030   spoolsv.exe          1428     616      13     264       0       0   2018-10-10 09:23:09 UTC+0000
0x8f0a4a58   svchost.exe          1488     616      21     310       0       0   2018-10-10 09:23:10 UTC+0000
0x8f0efa08   armsvc.exe           1592     616       5      61       0       0   2018-10-10 09:23:12 UTC+0000
0x8f13aad0   svchost.exe          1636     616      31     298       0       0   2018-10-10 09:23:13 UTC+0000
0x98468350   svchost.exe          2040     616       5      97       0       0   2018-10-10 09:23:19 UTC+0000
0x846cfd40   taskhost.exe          432     616      10     178       1       0   2018-10-10 09:23:20 UTC+0000
0x8f115d40   taskeng.exe          1696    1076       6      81       0       0   2018-10-10 09:23:21 UTC+0000
0x9849c5f8   dwm.exe              2088    1028       5      69       1       0   2018-10-10 09:23:22 UTC+0000
0x984b5460   explorer.exe         2112     680      38     784       1       0   2018-10-10 09:23:22 UTC+0000
0x98554c20   DFLocker.exe         2340     776       2      54       0       0   2018-10-10 09:23:31 UTC+0000
0x987c1610   FrzState2k.exe       2448     776       6      93       1       0   2018-10-10 09:23:36 UTC+0000
0x987c3d40   VBoxTray.exe         2468    2112      14     166       1       0   2018-10-10 09:23:37 UTC+0000
0x985bd7e8   SearchIndexer.       2688     616      13     529       0       0   2018-10-10 09:23:42 UTC+0000
0x9863b380   svchost.exe          3016     616      11     350       0       0   2018-10-10 09:23:49 UTC+0000
0x98669ad0   wmpnetwk.exe         3256     616      18     447       0       0   2018-10-10 09:23:53 UTC+0000
0x986d0d40   WmiPrvSE.exe         4084     720       8     116       0       0   2018-10-10 09:24:09 UTC+0000
0x8f17ebd8   upxed.exee           2656    2112       1      46       1       0   2018-10-10 09:24:53 UTC+0000
```

Looking at the second column's last line in the previous screenshot, we find `upxed.exe`. We need to note down the **process ID (PID)** which has a value of `2656`. Now that we have retrieved the PID of our packed executable, we can dump the process to file using the `procdump` parameter, as shown in the following code:

```
volatility --profile=Win7SP1x86 -f ~/memory.dmp procdump -D dump/ -p 2656
```

`procdump` will save the process executable in the `dump/` folder set by the `-D` parameter, as shown in the following screenshot:

```
> mkdir dump
> ./volatility_2.6_lin64_standalone --profile=Win7SP1x86 -f ~/memory.dmp procdump -D dump/ -p 2656
Volatility Foundation Volatility Framework 2.6
Process(V) ImageBase   Name                  Result
---------- ---------   ------------------    ------
0x8f17ebd8 0x00400000  upxed.exee            OK: executable.2656.exe
> ls dump/
total 16K
drwxrwxr-x 2 niangao niangao 4.0K Oct 10 05:47 .
drwx------ 3 niangao niangao 4.0K Oct 10 05:47 ..
-rw-rw-r-- 1 niangao niangao 5.5K Oct 10 05:47 executable.2656.exe
```

Volatility has a wide range of features to choose from. Feel free to explore these arguments as these may help in fitting analysis situations.

How about an executable in its unpacked state?

Now that we have an executable file from Volatility, running this back in our Windows guest sandbox gives us the following message:

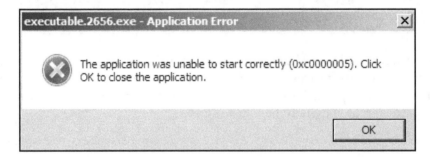

Remember that the packed executable has its own PE header and stub and not that of the original host's. The header, stub and compressed data were directly mapped to the process space. Every API function was dynamically imported. Even with the code and data decompressed, the entry point set in the header is still of the packed executables and not of the original hosts.

Fortunately, x86dbg has a plugin known as Scylla. After reaching the original entry point, which means we are in the unpacked state, we can rebuild the process being debugged into a brand new executable file. The new executable file is already unpacked and can be executed alone.

This still requires us to debug the packed executable until we reach the original entry point (OEP). Once at the OEP, open up Scylla from the plugins' drop-down menu. This should open up the Scylla window, as shown in the following example:

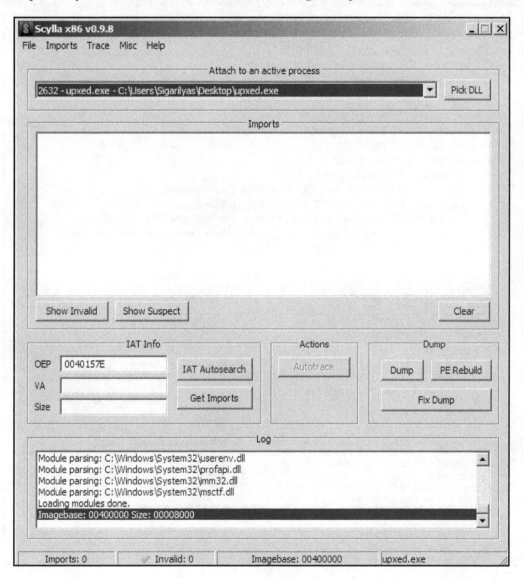

The active process is already set to the `upxed.exe` process. The OEP is also set to where the instruction pointer is. The next thing to do is click on **IAT Autosearch** to make Scylla parse the process space and locate the most probable import table. This fills up the **VA** and `Size` fields in the **IAT info** frame with the probable import table location and size. Click on `Get Imports` to make Scylla scan for the imported library and API functions. This is shown in the following screenshot:

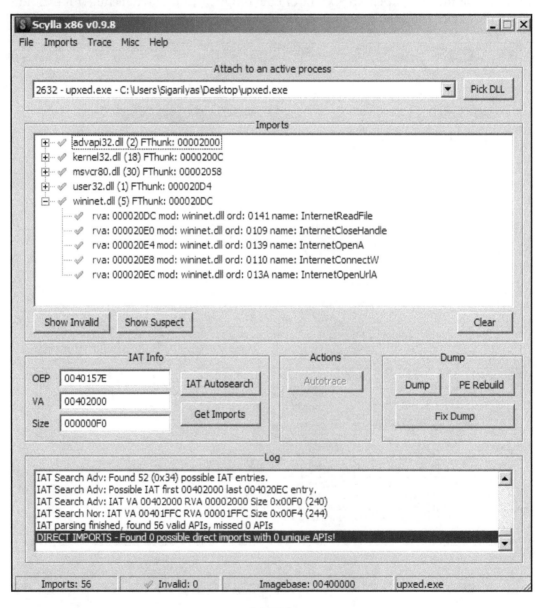

Expand one of the libraries and it will show the API functions it found. Now, under the **Dump frame**, click on the **Dump** button. This brings up a dialog that asks where to save the executable file. This simply dumps the executable file's process. We still need to apply the IAT info and imports. Click on **Fix Dump** and open the dumped executable file. This produces a new file with the _SCY appended to the file name, as shown in the following screenshot:

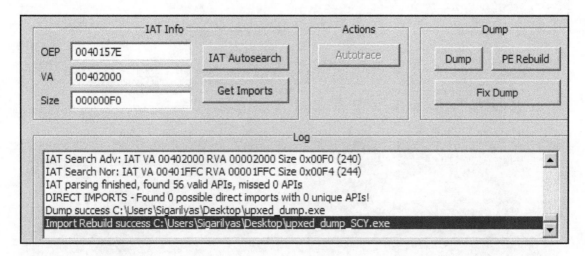

Running this new executable file should give us the same result as the original host's behavior.

In Volatility, we did not have enough information to reconstruct the executable file. Using x86dbg and Scylla, though requiring us to get past debugging the packer stub, we were able to have a reconstructed executable file.

Other file-types

Nowadays, websites usually convert binary data to printable ASCII text in order for the site developers to easily embed this data along with the HTML scripts. Others simply convert data to something that is not easy for humans to read. In this section, we will aim to decode data that has been hidden from plain understandable form. In Chapter 13 *Reversing various File-types*, we will deal more with how to reverse other File-Types besides Windows and Linux executables. In the meantime, we will just decode obvious data.

Let us head to our browsers and visit `www.google.com`, at the time of writing (we stored a copy of the source at `https://github.com/PacktPublishing/Mastering-Reverse-Engineering/blob/master/ch10/google_page_source.txt`), viewing the source would show us a portion that has a `b64` encoded text, as in the following screenshot:

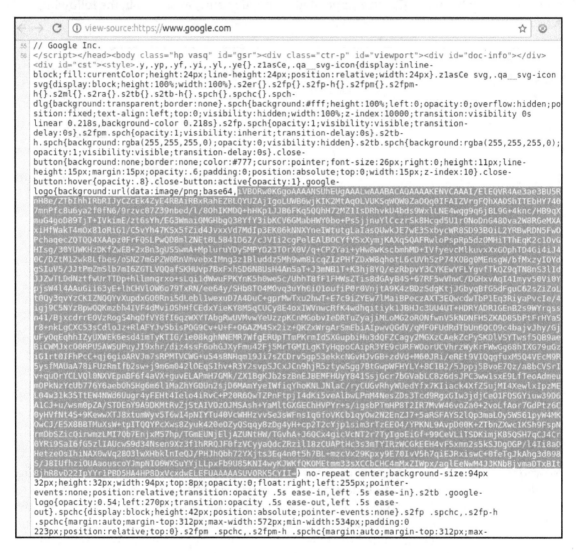

Using Cyberchef, a tool which can help decode various types of encoded data including base 64, we can deduce this data to something we understand. Just copy and paste the base-64 data into the input box then double-click *From Base64*. This should display the decoded binary content in the output box, as shown in the following screenshot:

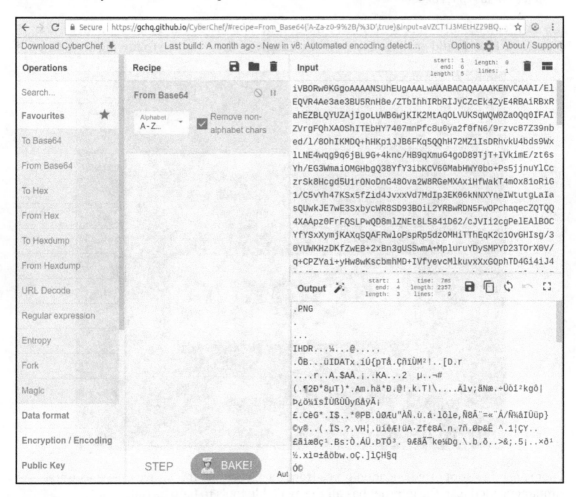

Notice that the output has a PNG written at the beginning. This is most likely a PNG image file. In addition, if we carefully look at the source code, we can see that the type of data was also indicated before the base-64 encoded data, as shown in the following example:

```
data:image/png;base64
```

If we click on the disk icon, we can save the output data to a file and name it with a `.png` extension. That should enable us to view the image, as shown in the following screenshot:

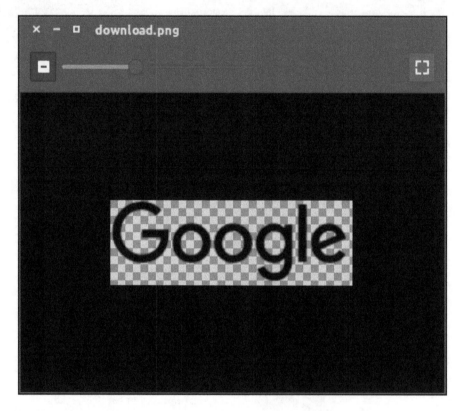

There are other supported encoded types from the Cyberchef tool. If we ever encounter similar encoded text, the internet has all the available tools to help us out.

Summary

Reverse engineering is about how we work with the tools in their proper situations. Even with packed, encrypted, and obfuscated executables, hidden information can still be extracted.

In this chapter, we introduced various concepts of how data can be hidden using packers, crypters, obfuscators, protectors, and even SFX tools. We encountered a packed file produced by the UPX tool which we were still able to reverse using a debugger. Being aware of where the instruction pointer is, we can determine if we are already at the original entry point. As a general rule, if the instruction pointer has jumped from a different section, we can say that we are already at the original entry point.

Using another solution to viewing the unpacked state of a program, we used Volatility with a memory dump from a VirtualBox guest and extracted the process of the executable that we just ran. Using the Scylla tool, we were also able to rebuild an unpacked state of the packed executable.

We ended this chapter by introducing the CyberChef tool, which is able to decode popular encoded data like base-64. This tool might come in useful when we encounter encoded data not only in scripts found in websites but in every executable we encounter.

In the next chapter, we will proceed further in our journey by identifying malicious behaviors executed by malware.

11
Anti-analysis Tricks

Anti-debugging, anti-virtual-machine (VM), anti-emulation, and anti-dumping are all tricks that attempt to analysis put a halt to an analysis. In this chapter, we will try to show the concepts of these anti-analysis methods. To help us identify these codes, we will explain the concept and show the actual disassembly codes that makes it work. Being able to identify these tricks will help us to avoid them. With initial static analysis, we would be able to skip these codes.

In this chapter, we will achieve the following learning outcomes:

- Identifying anti-analysis tricks
- Learning how to overcome anti-analysis tricks

Anti-debugging tricks

Anti-debugging tricks are meant to ensure that the codes are not working under the influence of a debugger. Say we have a program with an anti-debugging code in it. The behavior of the program is just as if it were running without an anti-debugging code. The story becomes different, however, when the program is being debugged. While debugging, we encounter code that goes straight to exiting the program or jumps into code that doesn't make sense. This process is illustrated in the following diagram:

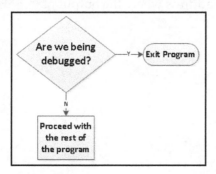

Developing anti-debugging code requires understanding the traits of the program and the system, both when normally running and when being debugged. For example, the **Process Environment Block** (**PEB**) contains a flag that is set when a program is being run under a debugger. Another popular trick is to use a **Structured Exception Handler** (**SEH**) to continue code that forces an error exception while debugging. To better understand how these work, let's discuss these tricks in a little more detail.

IsDebuggerPresent

IsDebuggerPresent is a Kernel32 API function that simply tells us whether the program is under a debugger. The result is placed in the eax register with a value of either true (1) or false (0). When used, the code looks something like this:

```
call IsDebuggerPresent
test eax, eax
jz notdebugged
```

The same concept applies with the CheckRemoteDebuggerPresent API. The difference is that it checks whether either another process or its *own* process is being debugged. CheckRemoteDebuggerPresent requires two arguments: a handle to a process and an output variable that tells us whether the process is being debugged or not. The following code checks whether its own process is being debugged:

```
call GetCurrentProcess
push edi
push eax
call CheckRemoteDebuggerPresent
cmp dword ptr [edi], 1
jz beingdebugged
```

The GetCurrentProcess API is used to retrieve the handle to the running process. This usually returns a -1 (0xFFFFFFFF) value, which is the handle to its own process. The edi register should be a variable address where the output of CheckRemoteDebuggerPresent will be stored.

Debug flags in the PEB

A thread is the basic unit of execution. The process itself is run as a thread entity that is capable of triggering multiple threads in the same process space. The information about the currently running thread is stored in the the Thread Environment Block (TEB). The TEB is also called the Thread Information Block (TIB) and contains information such as the thread ID, structured error handling frame, stack base address and limit, and the address pointing to information about the process the thread is running under. Information about the process is stored in the Process Environment Block (PEB).

The PEB contains information like pointer to tables that lists the loaded modules, command line parameters used to run the process, information taken from the PE header, and if it is being debugged. The TIB and PEB structures are documented by Microsoft at https://docs.microsoft.com/en-us/windows/desktop/api/winternl/.

PEB has fields that can be used to identify whether a process is being debugged: the BeingDebugged and NtGlobalFlag flags. In PEB, these are located at the following locations:

Offset	Information
0x02	BeingDebugged (1 for True) - BYTE
0x68	GlobalNTFlag (usually 0x70 when debugged) - DWORD

Internally, IsDebuggerPresent works with this code:

```
mov eax,dword ptr fs:[18]
mov eax,dword ptr ds:[eax+30]
movzx eax,byte ptr ds:[eax+2]
ret
```

Let's check what is happening with the IsDebuggerPresent code:

```
mov eax, dword ptr fs:[18]
```

The preceding line retrieves the address of the **Thread Environment Block** (**TEB**) from the **Thread Information Block** (**TIB**). The FS segment contains TIB. TEB address is stored at offset 0x18 of TIB. TIB is stored in the eax register.

The following line retrieves PEB address and stores it in the eax register. The PEB address is located at offset 0x30 of TEB:

```
mov eax, dword ptr ds:[eax+30]
```

The byte at offset 2 of PEB contains a Boolean value of 1 or 0, indicating whether the process is being debugged or not:

```
movzx eax, byte ptr ds:[eax+2]
```

If we wanted to create our own function, but applied this with GlobalNTFlag, we can make the code look like this:

```
mov eax, dword ptr fs:[18]
mov eax, dword ptr ds:[eax+0x30]
mov eax, dword ptr ds:[eax+0x68]
cmp eax, 0x70
setz al
and eax, 1
```

The first three lines of the preceding block basically retrieve GlobalNTFlag at offset 0x68 of PEB.

The following cmp instruction will set the zero flag to 1 if the value of eax is equal to 0x70:

```
cmp eax, 0x70
```

The setz instruction will set the al register with what ZF is, which should either be 0 or 1:

```
setz al
```

Finally, the and instruction will only retain the first bit for the eax register, which, as a result, clears the register, but retains a value of either 1 or 0, for true or false:

```
and eax, 1
```

Debugger information from NtQueryInformationProcess

Querying process information using the `NtQueryInformationProcess` function gives us another way to identify if the process is under a debugger. As sourced from MSDN, the `NtQueryInformationProcess` syntax declaration is the following:

```
NTSTATUS WINAPI NtQueryInformationProcess(
  _In_       HANDLE ProcessHandle,
  _In_       PROCESSINFOCLASS ProcessInformationClass,
  _Out_      PVOID ProcessInformation,
  _In_       ULONG ProcessInformationLength,
  _Out_opt_  PULONG ReturnLength
);
```

More information about this function can be found at https://docs.microsoft.com/en-us/windows/desktop/api/winternl/nf-winternl-ntqueryinformationprocess.

Specific information is returned based on what ID is supplied in the second argument, `PROCESSINFOCLASS`. `PROCESSINFOCLASS` is an enumerated list of IDs that we want to query. The IDs we need in order to determine whether the process is being debugged are the following:

- `ProcessDebugPort` (7)
- `ProcessDebugObjectHandle` (30)
- `ProcessDebugFlags` (31)

In essence, if the output result, filled in the `ProcessInformation` from the third argument, gives us a non-zero result, then it means that the process is being debugged.

Timing tricks

Normally, the time it takes for a program to execute lines of instructions from address A to address B would only take less than a second. But if these instructions were being debugged, a human would probably take about a second per line. Debugging from address A to address B would at least take a couple of seconds.

Essentially, the concept works just like a stopwatch. If the time it takes for a few lines of code is too long, the trick assumes that the program is being debugged.

Timing tricks can be applied as an anti-debugging method in any programming language. Setting a stopwatch would only require a function that can read time. Here are some examples of how timing tricks can be implemented in x86 assembly:

```
rdtsc
mov ebx, eax
nop
nop
nop
nop
nop
nop
nop
nop
rdtsc
sub eax, ebx
cmp eax, 0x100000
jg exit
```

In x86 processors means **Read Time-Stamp Counter (RDTSC)**. Every time the processor is reset (either by a hard reset or power-on), the timestamp counter is set to 0. The timestamp counter increments for every processor clock cycle. In the preceding chunk of RDTSC code, the result of the first RDTSC instruction is stored in the ebx register. After a set of nop instructions, the value stored in ebx is subtracted from the result of the second RDTSC instruction. This takes the difference between the first and second TSC. If the difference is greater than 0x100000, the code jumps to exit. If the program were not being step debugged, the difference should be about less than 0x500.

On the other hand, GetSystemTime and GetLocalTime, which are API functions that can retrieve time, can also be used to implement timing tricks. To identify these tricks, the code has to contain two time-retrieving functions.

Passing code execution via SEH

One of the most popular anti-debugging tricks is to use SEH to pass code execution. It is popular trick used in Windows computer viruses. But before we discuss how this trick is used for anti-debugging, let us discuss how SEH works a little.

Exceptions are usually triggered from errors, such as reading bytes from inaccessible memory regions, or by something as simple as division by zero. They can also be triggered by debugger interrupts, INT 3 and INT 1. When an exception occurs, the system jumps right to the exception handler. Normally, the exception handler's job is to do something about the error.

Usually, this job gives an error message notification, leading to a graceful termination of the program. In programming terms, this is try-except or `try-catch` handling. The following is an example of exception handling in Python programming:

```
try:
    print("Hello World!")
except:
    print("Hello Error!")
```

An SEH record contains two elements: the address of the exception handler and the address of the next SEH record. The next SEH record contains the address of the SEH record next to it. Overall, the SEH records are chained to each other. This is called the SEH chain. If the current handler was not able to handle the exception, then the next handler takes over. A program crash can happen if ever the SEH records were exhausted. This process is shown here:

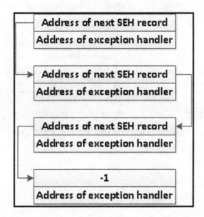

As we can see, the last SEH record contains a −1 (0xFFFFFFFF for 32-bit address space) value at the SEH record pointer field.

Now that we know how SEH works, how can this be abused for anti-debugging? Using our try-except Python code, abusing it would look something like this:

```
x = 1
try:
    x = x / 0
    print("This message will not show up!")
except:
    print("Hello World!")
```

What we did was force an error (a division-by-zero error, to be precise) to cause an exception. The exception handler displays the Hello World! message. But how does it work in x86 assembly language?

To set up our new SEH, we need to first identify where the current SEH is. For every process, there is an SEH chain set up by the Windows OS. The current SEH record can be retrieved from offset 0 of TIB, as denoted by the FS segment register.

The following assembly code retrieves the address of the current SEH record to the eax register:

```
mov eax, dword ptr FS:[0]
```

To change the handler, we can simply change the address of the current SEH record at FS:[0] with our SEH record. Let's assume that the handling code's address will be at 0x00401000, and that the current SEH record, is located at 0x00200000 has these values in it:

Next SEH record	0xFFFFFFFF
Current handler address	0x78000000

The next thing to do is build our SEH record, which we can store in the stack. With FS:[0] returning the 0x00200000 value, and our handler located at 0x00401000, here's a way to build the SEH record from the stack:

```
push 0x00401000
push dword ptr FS:[0]
```

The stack should look like something like this:

ESP	0x00200000
ESP+4	0x00401000

All we need to do is update the value of FS:[0] to the address of this SEH record, which is the register ESP register (that is, top of the stack):

```
mov dword ptr FS:[0], esp
```

The preceding code should add our SEH to the SEH chain.

Causing exceptions

The next thing to do is develop a code that forcefully causes an exception. We have a few known ways to do that:

- Use debug breakpoints (INT 3 / INT 1)

- Access inaccessible memory spaces

- Divide by zero

The aim of an SEH anti-debugging trick is to direct the debug analysis to an error. This makes an analyst try to trace back to what might have caused the error, eventually wasting time. And, if the analyst is familiar with SEH, it would be easy to pinpoint where the handler is and set a breakpoint there.

Step debugging works because of Interrupt 1, while breakpoints are set using Interrupt 3. When the execution of code encounters an INT 3 instruction, a debug exception occurs. To invoke an Interrupt 1 exception, the trap flag has to be set first.

When reading data from inaccessible memory, a read error occurs. There are already known memory regions, such as the kernel space, that are not allowed to be directly accessed from the user-mode process. Most of these regions are protected with a PAGE_GUARD flag. The PAGE_GUARD flag can be set with a VirtualAlloc or VirtualProtect function. That means we can produce our own inaccessible memory region. Typically, the region from offset 0 of the process space is not accessible. The following line of code will cause an access violation exception:

```
mov al, [0]
```

In mathematics, doing actual division by zero is an infinite task. The system explicitly identifies this kind of error and causes an exception. An example line for this is the following:

```
mov eax, 1
xor cl, cl
div cl
```

What the preceding code does is set the eax register to 1, set the cl register to 0, and then divides eax with cl, causing a divide-by-zero exception.

A typical SEH setup

Based on what we've learned, let's make use of a regular flow of code, then use SEH as an anti-debugging trick. The following code will be our original code:

```
push eax
mov eax, 0x12345678
mov ebx, 0x87654321
and eax, ebx
pop eax
```

After placing the SEH anti-debugging trick, the code would look something like this:

```
    mov eax, dword ptr FS:[0]
    push 0x00401000
    push eax
    mov dword ptr FS:[0], esp
    mov al, [0]

RDTSC (with CPUID to force a VM Exit)

VMM instructions i.e. VMCALL

VMEXIT
0x00401000:
    push eax
    mov eax, 0x12345678
    mov ebx, 0x87654321
    and eax, ebx
    pop eax
```

What we did here was to manually set up the SEH. Fortunately, Windows has a feature that can also set up exception handlers called Vectored Exception Handler. The API that registers a new handle is AddVectoredExceptionHandler. A C source code that implements this can be found at https://docs.microsoft.com/en-us/windows/desktop/debug/using-a-vectored-exception-handler.

Anti-VM tricks

This trick's aim is to exit the program when it identifies that it is running in a virtualized environment. The most typical way to identify being in a VM is to check for specific virtualization software artifacts installed in the machine. These artifacts may be located in the registry or a running service. We have listed a few specific artifacts that can be used to identify being run inside a VM.

VM running process names

The easiest way for a program to determine whether it is in a VM is by identifying known file names of running processes. Here's a list for each of the most popular pieces of VM software:

Virtualbox	VMWare	QEMU	Parallels	VirtualPC
vboxtray.exe vboxservice.exe vboxcontrol.exe	vmtoolsd.exe vmwaretray.exe vmwareuser VGAuthService.exe vmacthlp.exe	qemu-ga.exe	prl_cc.exe prl_tools.exe	vmsrvc.exe vmusrvc.exe

Existence of VM files and directories

Identifying the existence of at least one of the VM software's files can tell if the program is running in a virtual machine. The following table contains a list of files that can be used to identify if the program is running in a VirtualBox or VMware guest:

Virtualbox	VMWare
%programfiles%\oracle\virtualbox guest additions system32\drivers\VBoxGuest.sys system32\drivers\VBoxMouse.sys system32\drivers\VBoxSF.sys system32\drivers\VBoxVideo.sys system32\vboxdisp.dll system32\vboxhook.dll system32\vboxmrxnp.dll system32\vboxogl.dll system32\vboxoglarrayspu.dll system32\vboxoglcrutil.dll system32\vboxoglerrorspu.dll system32\vboxoglfeedbackspu.dll system32\vboxoglpackspu.dll system32\vboxoglpassthroughspu.dll	%programfiles%\VMWare system32\drivers\vm3dmp.sys system32\drivers\vmci.sys system32\drivers\vmhgfs.sys system32\drivers\vmmemctl.sys system32\drivers\vmmouse.sys system32\drivers\vmrawdsk.sys system32\drivers\vmusbmouse.sys

Default MAC address

The first three hexadecimal numbers of the VM's default MAC address can also be used. But, of course, if the MAC address were changed, these won't work:

VirtualBox	VMWare	Parallels
08:00:27	00:05:69 00:0C:29 00:1C:14 00:50:56	00:1C:42

Registry entries made by VMs

Information and configuration of software are usually done in the registry. This also counts for the VM guest software, which makes registry entries. Here's a short list of registry entries by VirtualBox:

```
HARDWARE\ACPI\DSDT\VBOX__
HARDWARE\ACPI\FADT\VBOX__
HARDWARE\ACPI\RSDT\VBOX__
SOFTWARE\Oracle\VirtualBox Guest Additions
SYSTEM\ControlSet001\Services\VBoxGuest
SYSTEM\ControlSet001\Services\VBoxMouse
SYSTEM\ControlSet001\Services\VBoxService
SYSTEM\ControlSet001\Services\VBoxSF
SYSTEM\ControlSet001\Services\VBoxVideo
```

Here are registry entries known to be from VMWare:

```
SOFTWARE\VMware, Inc.\VMware Tools
```

A Linux emulation with Wine has the following registry entry:

```
SOFTWARE\Wine
```

The existence of Microsoft's Hyper-V' can also be identified from the registry:

```
SOFTWARE\Microsoft\Virtual Machine\Guest
```

VM devices

These are virtual devices created by the VM. Here are the accessible devices created by VirtualBox and VMWare:

VirtualBox	VMWare
\\.\VBoxGuest \\.\VBoxTrayIPC \\.\VBoxMiniRdrDN	\\.\HGFS \\.\vmci

CPUID results

CPUID is an x86 instruction that returns information about the processor it is running under. Before running the instruction, the type of information, called a leaf, is required and stored in register EAX. Depending on the leaf, it returns values in registers EAX, EBX, ECX, and EDX. Every bit stored in the registers may tells if a certain CPU feature is available or not. Details about the returned CPU information can be found at https://en.wikipedia.org/wiki/CPUID.

One of then pieces of CPUID returned information is a flag that tells whether the system is running on a hypervisor. Hypervisor is a CPU feature that supports running VM guests. For anti-VM, if this flag were enabled, it would mean that the process is in a VM guest.

The following x86 code checks whether the hypervisor flag is enabled:

```
mov eax, 1
cpuid
bt ecx, 31
jc inhypervisor
```

The preceding code retrieves information from CPUID leaf 1. The 31st bit result in the ecx register is placed in the carry flag. If the bit is set to 1, the system is running on a hypervisor.

Besides the hypervisor information, some specific VM software can be identified from the guest OS. The CPUID instruction can return a unique string ID to identify the VM software the guest is under. The following code checks whether it is running in a VMWare guest:

```
mov eax, 0x40000000
cpuid
cmp ebx, 'awMV'
jne exit
cmp ecx, 'MVer'
```

```
jne exit
cmp edx, 'eraw'
jne exit
```

When values of the `ebx`, `ecx`, and `edx` registers are concatenated, it would read as `VMwareVMware`. Here is a list of known string IDs used by other VM software:

VirtualBox 4.x	VMware	Hyper-V	KVM	Xen
VBoxVBoxVBox	VMwareVMware	Microsoft Hv	KVMKVMKVM	XenVMMXenVMM

Anti-emulation tricks

Anti-emulation or anti-automated analysis are methods employed by a program to prevent moving further in its code if it identifies that it is being analyzed. The behavior of a program can be logged and analyzed using automated analysis tools such as Cuckoo Sandbox, Hybrid Analysis, and ThreatAnalyzer. The concept of these tricks is in being able to determine that the system in which a program is running is controlled and was set up by a user.

Here are some things that distinguish a user-controlled environment and an automated analysis controlled system from each other:

- A user-controlled system has mouse movement.
- User controlled systems can include a dialog box that waits for a user to scroll down and then click on a button.
- The setup of an automated analysis system has the following attributes:
  - A low amount of physical memory
  - A low disk size
  - The free space on the disk may be nearly depleted
  - The number of CPUs is only one
  - The screen size is too small

Simply setting up a task that requires a user's manual input would determine that the program is running in a user-controlled environment. Similar to anti-VM, the VM guest setup would make use of the lowest possible requirements, such that it doesn't eat up the VM host's computer resources.

Another anti-analysis trick checks for running analysis tools. These tools include the following:

- OllyDBG (`ollydbg.exe`)
- WinDbg (`windbg.exe`)
- IDA Pro (`ida.exe`, `idag.exe`, `ida64.exe`, `idag64.exe`)
- SysInternals Suite Tools, which includes the following:
    - Process Explorer (`procexp.exe`)
    - Process Monitor (`procmon.exe`)
    - Regmon (`regmon.exe`)
    - Filemon (`filemon.exe`)
    - TCPView (`tcpview.exe`)
    - Autoruns (`autoruns.exe`, `autorunsc.exe`)
- Wireshark (`wireshark.exe`)

A way around these tricks is for automated analysis to trick them back. For example, there are ways to mimic mouse movement and even read dialog window properties, scroll, and click buttons. A simple work-around for anti-analysis trick is to rename the tool we're using to monitor behaviors.

Anti-dumping tricks

This method does not stop dumping memory to a file. This trick instead prevents the reverser from easily understanding the dumped data. Here are some examples of how this could be applied:

- Portions of the PE header have been modified, so that the process dump gives the wrong properties.

- Portions of PEB, such as SizeOfImage, have been modified, so that the process dumping tool dumps wrong.

- Dumping is very useful for seeing decrypted data. Anti-dumping tricks would re-encrypt the decrypted code or data after use.

To overcome this trick, we can either identify or skip the code that modifies data. For re-encryption, we can also skip the code that re-encrypts, to leave it in a decrypted state.

Summary

Malware have been evolving by adding new techniques to evade anti-virus and reverse engineering. These techniques include process hollowing, process injection, process doppelganging, code anti-debugging, and anti-analysis. Process hollowing and process doppelganging techniques basically overwrites the image of a legit process with a malicious image. This masks the malicious program with a legit process. Process injection, on the other hand, inserts and runs code in a remote process space.

Anti-debugging, anti-analysis, and the other tricks discussed in this chapter are obstacles for reverse engineering. But knowing the concept for these tricks enables us to overcome them. Doing static analysis with deadlisting, we can identify and then skip the tricky code, or in the case of SEH, place a breakpoint at the handler.

We discussed anti-debugging tricks and their technique of using errors to cause exceptions and hold the rest of its code at the handler. We also discussed other tricks, including anti-VM and anti-emulation tricks, which are able to identify being in an analysis environment.

In the next chapter, we will be using what we have learned here with an actual reverse engineering analysis of an executable file.

12
Practical Reverse Engineering of a Windows Executable

Reverse engineering is very common when dealing with malware analysis. In this chapter, we will look at an executable program and determine its actual behavioral flow using the tools we have learned so far. We will head straight from static analysis to dynamic analysis. This will require that we have our lab set up ready so that it will be easier to follow through.

The target file that will be analyzed in this chapter has behaviors that were seen in actual malware. Regardless of a file being malware or not, we have to handle every file we analyze carefully in an enclosed environment. Let's get started on performing some reversing.

We will cover the following topics in this chapter:

- Practical static analysis
- Practical dynamic analysis

Things to prepare

The file we are about to analyze can be downloaded from `https://github.com/PacktPublishing/Mastering-Reverse-Engineering/blob/master/ch12/whatami.zip`. It is a password-protected zip file and the password is "`infected`", without the quotes.

We need to prepare our Windows lab setup. The analysis discussed in this chapter runs the program in a VirtualBox guest running a Windows 10 32-bit operating system . The following tools additionally need to be prepared:

- IDA Pro 32-bit: A copy of the free version can be downloaded from `https://github.com/PacktPublishing/Mastering-Reverse-Engineering/blob/master/tools/Disassembler%20Tools/32-bit%20idafree50.exe`.

- x86dbg: The latest version can be downloaded from `https://x64dbg.com`. A copy of of an older version is available at `https://github.com/PacktPublishing/Mastering-Reverse-Engineering/blob/master/tools/Debuggers/x64dbg%20-%20snapshot_2018-04-05_00-33.zip`.

- Fakenet: The official version can be downloaded at `https://github.com/fireeye/flare-fakenet-ng`. A copy can also be downloaded from `https://github.com/PacktPublishing/Mastering-Reverse-Engineering/tree/master/tools/FakeNet`

- SysInternals Suite: `https://docs.microsoft.com/en-us/sysinternals/downloads/`

- Snowman: `https://derevenets.com/`

- HxD: `https://mh-nexus.de/en/hxd/`

- CFF Explorer: `https://ntcore.com/`

We may need other tools as we proceed with our analysis. If you find tools that are more comfortable to use, feel free to use them.

Initial static analysis

To help us out in terms of our static info gathering, here is a list of the information that we need to obtain:

- File properties (name, size, other info)
- Hash (MD5, SHA1)
- File type (including header information)
- Strings
- Deadlisting (highlight where we need information)

At the end of the initial analysis, we will have to summarize all the information we retrieved.

Initial file information

To get the filename, file size, hash calculations, file type, and other information regarding the file, we will be using CFF Explorer. When opening the file, we might encounter an error message when using the latter, as can be seen in the following screenshot:

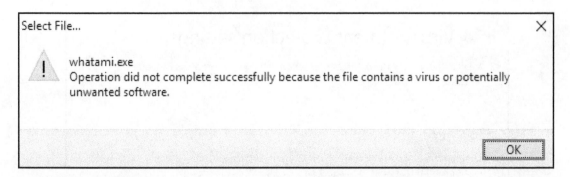

This error is caused by MS Windows' virus protection feature. Since we are in a sandboxed environment (under a virtualized guest environment), it should be okay to disable this. Disabling this feature in a production environment can expose risks for the computer getting compromised by malware.

To disable this feature in Windows, select **Start->Settings->Windows Security->Virus & threat protection->Virus & threat protection** settings. Then turn off **Real-time protection**. You might as well turn off both **Cloud-delivered protection** and **Automatic sample submission** to **prevent any security settings** from blocking activities that the program that is being analyzed might perform.

The following screenshot shows **Real-time protection** disabled:

Chapter 12

Opening the file with CFF Explorer reveals a lot of information, including packer identification of the file being UPX packed:

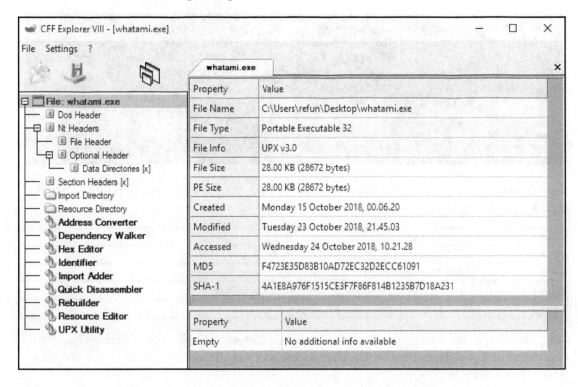

From the preceding result, we can tabulate the following file information:

Filename	whatami.exe
File size	28,672 bytes
MD5	F4723E35D83B10AD72EC32D2ECC61091
SHA-1	4A1E8A976F1515CE3F7F86F814B1235B7D18A231
File type	Win32 PE file – packed with UPX v3.0

We will have to download the UPX tool and try to decompress the file. The UPX tool can be downloaded from `https://upx.github.io/`. Using UPX, extract the file using the "-d" option, as follows:

```
upx -d whatami.exe
```

The result after decompressing the file, demonstrated as follows, tells us that the file originally had a size of 73,728 bytes:

```
C:\Users\refun\Desktop>upx-3.95-win32\upx.exe -d whatami.exe
                    Ultimate Packer for eXecutables
                      Copyright (C) 1996 - 2018
UPX 3.95w      Markus Oberhumer, Laszlo Molnar & John Reiser   Aug 26th 2018

        File size       Ratio      Format       Name
    --------------------  ------   -----------   -----------
       73728 <-     28672   38.89%    win32/pe      whatami.exe

Unpacked 1 file.
```

So, if we re-open the file in CFF Explorer, our file information table would now include the following:

Filename	whatami.exe
File size	73,728 bytes
MD5	18F86337C492E834B1771CC57FB2175D
SHA-1	C8601593E7DC27D97EFC29CBFF90612A265A248E
File type	Win32 PE file – compiled by Microsoft Visual C++ 8

Let's see what notable strings we can find using SysInternals' strings tool. Strings is a command-line tool. Just pass the filename as the tool's argument and redirect the output to a file. Here is how we use it:

```
strings.exe whatami.exe > filestrings.txt
```

By removing noisy strings or text that are not relevant, we obtained the following:

```
!This program cannot be run in DOS mode.
Rich
.text
`.rdata
@.data
.rsrc
hey
how did you get here?
calc
ntdll.dll
NtUnmapViewOfSection
KERNEL32.DLL
MSVCR80.dll
USER32.dll
```

```
Sleep
FindResourceW
LoadResource
LockResource
SizeofResource
VirtualAlloc
FreeResource
IsDebuggerPresent
ExitProcess
CreateProcessA
GetThreadContext
ReadProcessMemory
GetModuleHandleA
GetProcAddress
VirtualAllocEx
WriteProcessMemory
SetThreadContext
ResumeThread
GetCurrentProcess
GetSystemTimeAsFileTime
GetCurrentProcessId
GetCurrentThreadId
GetTickCount
QueryPerformanceCounter
SetUnhandledExceptionFilter
TerminateProcess
GetStartupInfoW
UnhandledExceptionFilter
InterlockedCompareExchange
InterlockedExchange
_XcptFilter
exit
_wcmdln
_initterm
_initterm_e
_configthreadlocale
__setusermatherr
_adjust_fdiv
__p__commode
__p__fmode
_encode_pointer
__set_app_type
_crt_debugger_hook
?terminate@@YAXXZ
_unlock
__dllonexit
_lock
_onexit
```

```
_decode_pointer
_except_handler4_common
_invoke_watson
_controlfp_s
_exit
_cexit
_amsg_exit
??2@YAPAXI@Z
memset
__wgetmainargs
memcpy
UpdateWindow
ShowWindow
CreateWindowExW
RegisterClassExW
LoadStringW
MessageBoxA
WHATAMI
t<assembly xmlns="urn:schemas-microsoft-com:asm.v1" manifestVersion="1.0">
  <dependency>
    <dependentAssembly>
      <assemblyIdentity type="win32" name="Microsoft.VC80.CRT"
version="8.0.50727.6195" processorArchitecture="x86"
publicKeyToken="1fc8b3b9a1e18e3b"></assemblyIdentity>
    </dependentAssembly>
  </dependency>
</assembly>PAD
```

We highlighted a number of text strings. As a result, we may be expecting a number of messages to pop up by using the MessageBoxA function. With APIs such as LoadResource and LockResource, we may also encounter code that will process some data from the resource section. A suspended process may also be invoked after seeing APIs such as CreateProcess and ResumeThread. Anti-debugging may also be expected using the IsDebuggerPresent API. The program may have been compiled to use GUI-based code using CreateWindowExW and RegisterClassExW, but we do not see the window messaging loop functions: GetMessage, TranslateMessage, and DispatchMessage.

All these are just assumptions that we can better understand following further analysis. Now, let's try to do deadlisting on the file using IDA Pro.

Deadlisting

After opening up `whatami.exe` in IDA Pro, auto-analysis recognizes the `WinMain` function. In the following screenshot, we can see that the first three APIs that will be executed are `LoadStringW`, `RegisterClassExW`, and `CreateWindowEx`:

```
; int __stdcall wWinMain(HINSTANCE hInstance, HINSTANCE hPrevInstance, LPWSTR lpCmdLine, int nShowCmd)
_wWinMain@16 proc near

var_30= WNDCLASSEXW ptr -30h
hInstance= dword ptr  4
hPrevInstance= dword ptr  8
lpCmdLine= dword ptr  0Ch
nShowCmd= dword ptr  10h

sub     esp, 30h
push    esi
mov     esi, [esp+34h+hInstance]
push    edi
push    64h             ; cchBufferMax
push    offset ClassName ; lpBuffer
push    6Dh             ; uID
push    esi             ; hInstance
call    ds:LoadStringW
xor     edi, edi
lea     eax, [esp+38h+var_30]
push    eax             ; WNDCLASSEXW *
mov     [esp+3Ch+var_30.cbSize], 30h
mov     [esp+3Ch+var_30.style], 3
mov     [esp+3Ch+var_30.lpfnWndProc], offset sub_4010C0
mov     [esp+3Ch+var_30.cbClsExtra], edi
mov     [esp+3Ch+var_30.cbWndExtra], edi
mov     [esp+3Ch+var_30.hInstance], esi
mov     [esp+3Ch+var_30.hIcon], edi
mov     [esp+3Ch+var_30.hCursor], edi
mov     [esp+3Ch+var_30.hbrBackground], 6
mov     [esp+3Ch+var_30.lpszMenuName], 6Dh
mov     [esp+3Ch+var_30.lpszClassName], offset ClassName
mov     [esp+3Ch+var_30.hIconSm], edi
call    ds:RegisterClassExW
push    edi             ; lpParam
push    esi             ; hInstance
push    edi             ; hMenu
push    edi             ; hWndParent
push    edi             ; nHeight
push    80000000h       ; nWidth
push    edi             ; Y
push    80000000h       ; X
push    0CF0000h        ; dwStyle
push    offset WindowName ; lpWindowName
push    offset ClassName ; lpClassName
push    edi             ; dwExStyle
mov     dword_403374, esi
call    ds:CreateWindowExW
```

When `CreateWindowExW` is executed, the window properties are taken from the configuration set by `RegisterClassExW`. The `ClassName`, which is used as the name of the window, is taken from the file's text string resource using `LoadStringW`. However, our concern here would only be the code pointed to by `lpfnWindProc` takes us. When `CreateWindowExW` is executed, the code pointed to by the `lpfnWndProc` parameter is executed.

Before we proceed, take a look at sub_4010C0. Let's see the code that comes after CreateWindowExW:

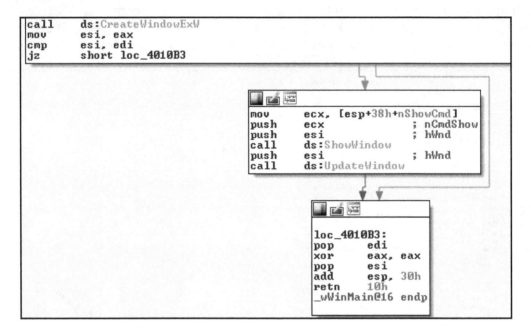

The preceding screenshot shows that after CreateWindowExW, ShowWindow and UpdateWindow are the only APIs that may be executed. However, there are indeed no window messaging APIs that were expected to process window activities. This would entail us assuming that the intention of the program was only to run code at the address pointed to by the lpfnWndProc parameter.

Double clicking on dword_4010C0, which is the address of lpfnWndProc, will show a set of bytes that have not been properly analyzed by IDA Pro. Since we are sure that this area should be a code, we will have to tell IDA Pro that it is a code. By pressing 'c' at address 0x004010C0, IDA Pro will start converting the bytes to readable assembly language code. Select Yes when IDA Pro asks us to convert to code:

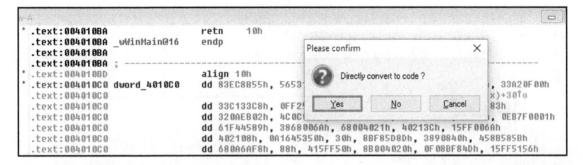

Scrolling down, we will encounter another unrecognized code at 0x004011a0. Just perform the same procedure:

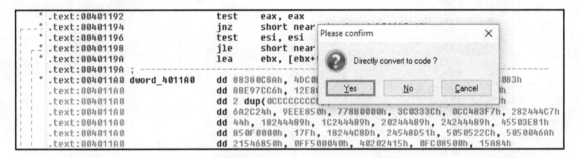

Scrolling down again will bring us to data that can no longer be converted. This should be the last part of the code. Let's tell IDA Pro that this code should be a treated as a function. To do that, highlight lines from 0x004010C0 to 0x004011C0, right-click on the highlighted lines, and then select "Create function..." to turn the set of code into a function.

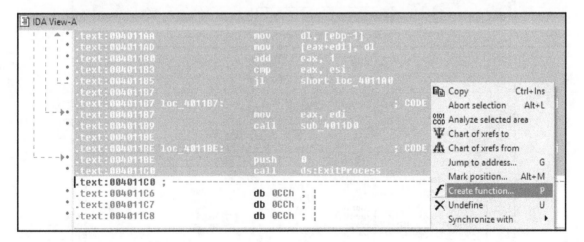

Turning the code into a function will help our deadlisting see a graphical view of the code. To do that, right-click and select Graph view. The following screenshot shows the first set of code of the function. What interests us here is how the `rdtsc` and `cpuid` instructions were used:

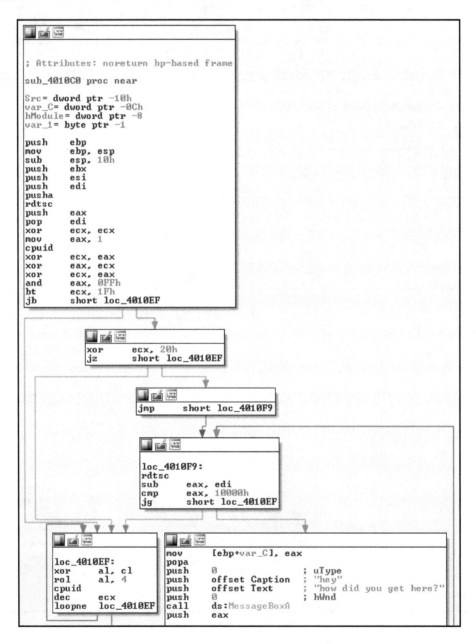

In Chapter 11, *Identification with POC Malware*, under anti-debugging tricks, we discussed rdtsc being used as a timing trick. The difference is calculated right after the second rdtsc. In the following code, the expected duration should only be less than or equal to 0x10000, or 65,536 cycles. If we get to pass that timing trick, a message box will appear.

Leaf 1 (set in the register eax) is passed to the first execution of a cpuid instruction. Again, in Chapter 11, cpuid can be used for anti-VM tricks. The result is placed in register eax. This is followed by three xor instructions that eventually exchange the values of the eax and ecx registers.

```
xor ecx, eax
xor eax, ecx
xor ecx, eax
```

The bt instruction moves the 31st (0x1F) bit to the carry flag. If the 31st bit is set, it means that we are running in a hypervisor environment. We will need to take note of this line during our debugging session later. We want to make the result with the 31st bit set to 0.

This may be followed by another check on the 5th bit using xor ecx, 20h. With the 5th bit set, it would mean that VMX (Virtual Machine eXtensions) instructions are available. If the VMX instructions are available, it would also mean that the system is capable of running virtualization. Usually, VMX is only available at the host VM, and the program can assume that it is running on the physical machine. For bitwise logic, if the 5th bit of ecx is set, an xor 20h should make it a zero. But if the other bits of register ecx were set, register ecx would not have a zero value. We should also take note on this for our debug session.

Two main tricks were shown here – a timing-trick and an anti-VM trick. Overall, if we deduce what we analyzed, the program can either go in two directions: the loop at loc_4010EF, which makes no sense, and the MessageBoxA code.

If we take a closer look, the whole anti-debug and anti-VM tricks are enclosed by `pusha` and `popa` instructions. Essentially, we can skip the whole trick codes and jump right to the `MessageBoxA` code, as can be seen in the following screenshot:

```
push    0                       ; uType
push    offset Caption          ; "hey"
push    offset Text             ; "how did you get here?"
push    0                       ; hWnd
call    ds:MessageBoxA
push    eax
push    ebx
mov     eax, large fs:30h
lea     ebx, [ebp+hModule]
mov     eax, [eax+8]
mov     [ebx], eax
pop     ebx
pop     eax
mov     eax, [ebp+hModule]
push    0Ah                     ; lpType
push    88h                     ; lpName
push    eax                     ; hModule
call    ds:FindResourceW
mov     ecx, [ebp+hModule]
mov     esi, eax
push    esi                     ; hResInfo
push    ecx                     ; hModule
call    ds:LoadResource
mov     ebx, eax
push    ebx                     ; hResData
call    ds:LockResource
mov     edx, [ebp+hModule]
push    esi                     ; hResInfo
push    edx                     ; hModule
mov     [ebp+Src], eax
call    ds:SizeofResource
push    4                       ; flProtect
push    3000h                   ; flAllocationType
mov     esi, eax
push    esi                     ; dwSize
push    0                       ; lpAddress
call    ds:VirtualAlloc
mov     edi, eax
mov     eax, [ebp+Src]
push    esi                     ; Size
push    eax                     ; Src
push    edi                     ; Dst
call    memcpy
add     esp, 0Ch
push    ebx                     ; hResData
call    ds:FreeResource
call    ds:IsDebuggerPresent
test    eax, eax
jnz     short loc_4011BE
```

The `MessageBoxA` code is followed by functions that read an `RCDATA` (`0x0A`) resource type with an ordinal name of `0x88` (`136`). Using CFF Explorer, click on **Resource Editor** and expand `RCData`. We should be able to see the data being read here, as shown in the following screenshot:

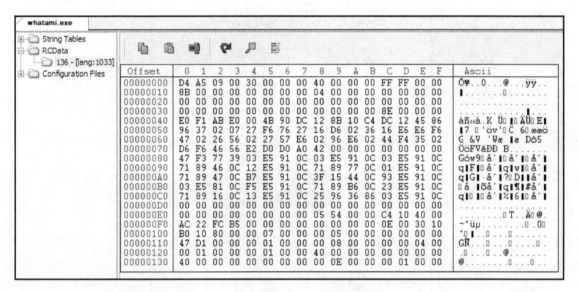

The data is copied, using `memcpy`, to a memory space allocated using `VirtualAlloc`. The allocated size is the size indicated in the RCData's properties. The size can be seen by expanding `RCData` in the Resource Directory in `CFF` Explorer. The address of the copied data is left to the `edi register`.

We also see `IsDebuggerPresent` being used here, another anti-debugging trick. Following the green line ends up to an `ExitProcess`.

The following screenshot is where the red line goes to:

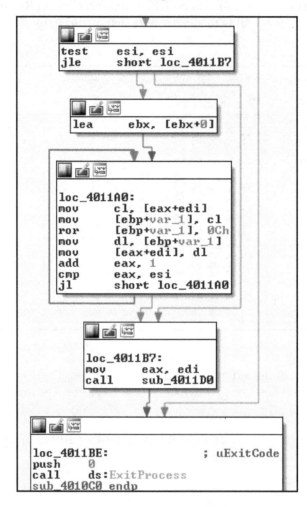

```
test       esi, esi
jle        short loc_4011B7


lea        ebx, [ebx+0]


loc_4011A0:
mov        cl, [eax+edi]
mov        [ebp+var_1], cl
ror        [ebp+var_1], 0Ch
mov        dl, [ebp+var_1]
mov        [eax+edi], dl
add        eax, 1
cmp        eax, esi
jl         short loc_4011A0


loc_4011B7:
mov        eax, edi
call       sub_4011D0


loc_4011BE:                    ; uExitCode
push       0
call       ds:ExitProcess
sub_4010C0 endp
```

The loop at `loc_4011A0` seems to be decrypting the data. Remember that the address of the data is in register edi. The decryption algorithm uses a `ror 0x0c` (rotate 12 bits to the right). After decryption, it stores the data address to register `eax` and then calls the `sub_4011D0` function.

Knowing the location and size of the decrypted data, we should be able to create a memory dump during our debug session.

Inside `sub_4011DO`, the address stored in eax is transferred to the esi register, and subsequently to register edi. We then encounter a call to `CreateProcessA` that runs "calc":

```
sub_4011D0 proc near

var_60= dword ptr -60h
lpContext= dword ptr -5Ch
Buffer= byte ptr -58h
ProcessInformation= _PROCESS_INFORMATION ptr -54h
Dst= dword ptr -44h

sub      esp, 60h
push     ebx
push     esi
push     edi
push     44h              ; Size
mov      edi, eax
lea      eax, [esp+70h+Dst]
push     0                ; Val
push     eax              ; Dst
call     memset
mov      esi, [edi+3Ch]
xor      eax, eax
add      esi, edi
add      esp, 0Ch
mov      [esp+6Ch+Dst], 44h
mov      [esp+6Ch+ProcessInformation.hProcess], eax
mov      [esp+6Ch+ProcessInformation.hThread], eax
mov      [esp+6Ch+ProcessInformation.dwProcessId], eax
mov      [esp+6Ch+ProcessInformation.dwThreadId], eax
cmp      dword ptr [esi], 4550h
jnz      loc_401393
```

```
lea      ecx, [esp+6Ch+ProcessInformation]
push     ecx              ; lpProcessInformation
lea      edx, [esp+70h+Dst]
push     edx              ; lpStartupInfo
push     eax              ; lpCurrentDirectory
push     eax              ; lpEnvironment
push     4                ; dwCreationFlags
push     eax              ; bInheritHandles
push     eax              ; lpThreadAttributes
push     eax              ; lpProcessAttributes
push     offset CommandLine ; "calc"
push     eax              ; lpApplicationName
call     ds:CreateProcessA
test     eax, eax
jz       loc_401393
```

The process named "`calc`" is actually the Windows default calculator application. The sixth parameter of `CreateProcessA`, `dwCreationFlags`, is what interests us here. The value of 4 denotes CREATE_SUSPENDED. The calculator was run as a process in suspended mode. This means that it is not running and was only loaded in the calculator's own process space.

If we were to make a block diagram of `sub_4011D0` with the sequence of API functions, we would have something like this.

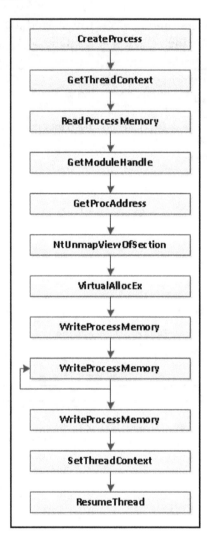

The sequence of APIs demonstrates a behavior called process hollowing. Process hollowing is a technique, commonly used by malware, to mask its code under a legitimate process. This technique creates a process in a suspended state, and then its memory is unmapped and replaced with a different process image. In this case, the legitimate process is Calculator.

The NtUnmapViewOfSection API is a function that unmaps or removes the PE image layout from a given process space. This API comes from the NTDLL.DLL library file. Instead of using LoadLibrary, the GetModuleHandle was used. LoadLibrary is used to load a library that has not yet been loaded, while GetModuleHandle is used to retrieve the handle of an already loaded library. In this case, the program assumed that NTDLL.DLL was already loaded.

The following screenshot shows the disassembly code that retrieves the function address of NtUnmapViewOfSection:

```
push    offset ModuleName ; "ntdll.dll"
call    ds:GetModuleHandleA
push    offset ProcName   ; "NtUnmapViewOfSection"
push    eax               ; hModule
call    ds:GetProcAddress
mov     ecx, [esi+34h]
mov     edx, [esp+1Ch]
push    ecx
push    edx
call    eax
```

The decrypted data from the resource section's RCData is passed to sub_4011D0. Every call to WriteProcessMemory reads chunks of data from the decrypted data. Given this, we are expecting the decrypted data to be that of a Win32 PE file.

To summarize, the code initially creates a window. However, the registered window properties are almost empty, except for the callback, Wndproc. The Wndproc callback is the code that initially executes when the window is created. As a result, the creation of a window using RegisterClassEx and CreateWindow APIs were just used to pass code execution. In other words, the whole window creation was the simple equivalent of a jmp instruction.

Here's another diagram outlining the flow of code at the Wndproc callback:

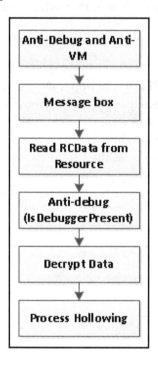

In the first section of the Wndproc code, we encountered anti-debug (timing tricks with rdtsc) and anti-vm (cpuid bit 31 and 5) tricks. Once we get passed that, a message box appears. The data from the resource's RCData is copied to an allocated memory. We encounter another anti-debugging trick using the IsDebuggerPresent API. The data is decrypted and passed to a process-hollowing code using Calculator.

Our next target for analysis would be the decrypted image executed using process hollowing. We will start directly with debugging.

Debugging

We will be using x86dbg for our debug session. Remember that we decompressed the file using UPX. It would be wise to open the decompressed version instead of the original whatami.exe file. Opening the compressed will be fine but we will have to go through debugging the UPX packed code.

Unlike IDA Pro, x86dbg is not able to recognize the WinMain function where the real code starts. In addition, after opening the file, the instruction pointer may still be somewhere in the NTDLL memory space. And to avoid being in an NTDLL region during startup, we may need to make a short configuration change in x86dbg.

Select Options->Preference. Under the Events tab, uncheck System Breakpoint and TLS Callbacks. Click on the Save button and then select Debug->Restart. This should now bring us to the entry point of whatami.exe at the following address: 0x004016B8.

Since we already know the WinMain address from IDA Pro, we can just place a breakpoint at that address. The WinMain address is at 0x00401000. Press CTRL+G, then type 0x00401000, then press F2 to place a breakpoint, and finally press F9 to run the program.

Here is a screenshot of where we should be at this point:

We have observed in our static analysis that `RegisterClassExW` and `CreateWindowExW` were used to set the WndProc as a window handler where more interesting codes are placed. Make a breakpoint at the WndProc address, `0x004010c0`, and then press F9. This should bring us to the following screenshot, where the anti-debug and anti-VM codes are located:

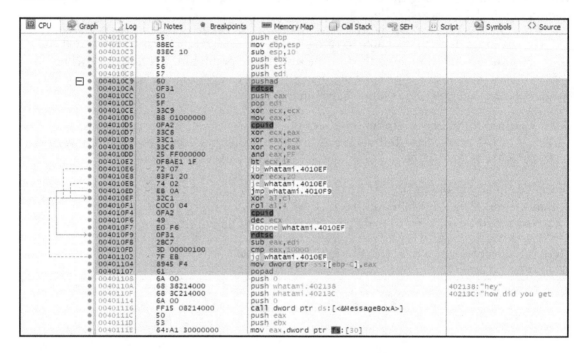

We highlighted the anti-debug and anti-VM codes here. These codes run begins from the pushad instruction up to the popad instruction. What we can do here is skip the anti-debug and anti-VM codes. Press F7 or F8 until we are at address `0x004010C9`. Select line `0x00401108`, the line right after `popad`, and then right-click on it to bring up the context menu. Select Set New Origin Here. This brings the instruction pointer, register EIP, to this address.

We should now be at the code that displays the following message using the `MessageBoxA` function. Just keep on pressing F8 until the following message appears:

You will have to click on the OK button for debugging to proceed. The next portion of the code will retrieve the RCData from the resource section. Keep on pressing F8 until we reach line 0x0040117D, a call to memcpy. If we look carefully at the three parameters to be passed for memcpy, register edi should contain the source address of the data to be copied, register eax should contain the destination address, and register esi should contain the size of data to be copied. To get a memory view of what the destination will contain, select the value of EDI in the right-hand pane, and then right-click on it to show the context menu. Select Follow in Dump. We should now be able to view Dump 1's memory space, as demonstrated in the following screenshot:

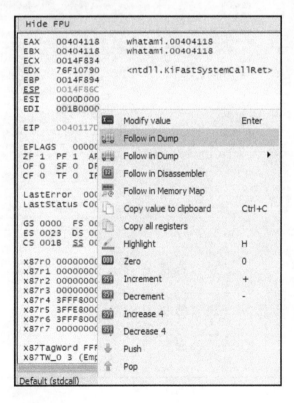

Press F8 to proceed with the memcpy. The following screenshot shows the current location:

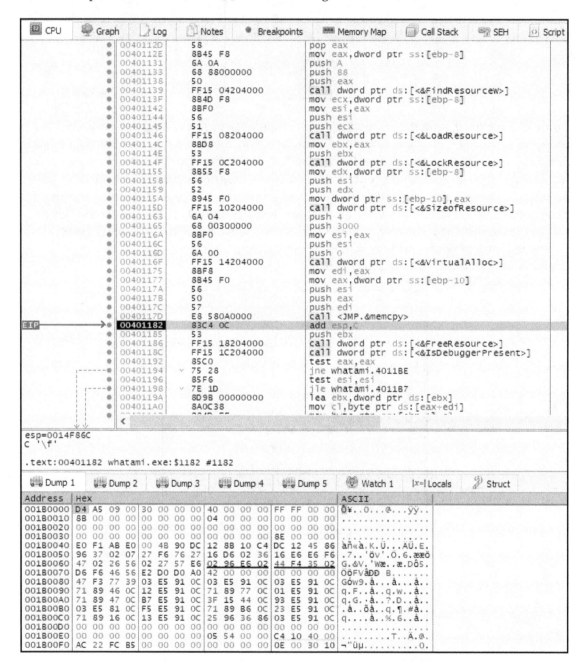

Keep on pressing F8 until we are at the line (0x00401192) after the call to
IsDebuggerPresent. Register EAX is expected to be set to 1, which indicates a "True"
value. We will need to change that to "False", with a zero value. To do that, double-click
on the value of register EAX, and then change 1 to 0. In effect, this should not let the code
jump straight to the ExitProcess call.

The next code would be the decryption routine. The arrows in the far left-hand pane show a
loopback code. The algorithm uses a ror instruction. Keep on pressing F8 while observing
Dump 1. We can slowly see the data being decrypted, starting with an MZ header. You
can place a breakpoint at address 0x004011B7, where the decryption code ends and
reveals entirely decrypted data, shown as follows:

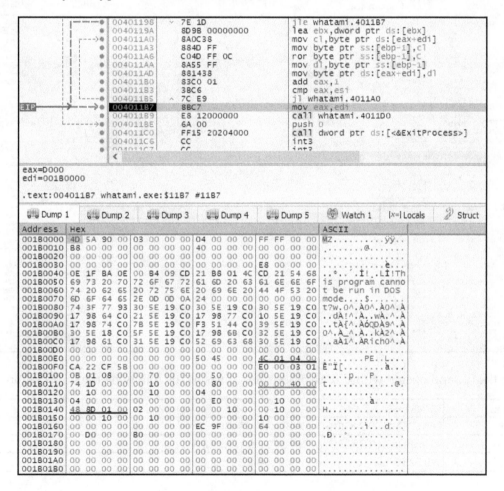

The decrypted data is a `Win32` PE file with a size of `0x0D000` (53,248 bytes). What we can do here is dump this decrypted memory to a file. To do that, click on the Memory Map tab or select View->Memory Map. This shows us the process memory space with the addresses of memory sections and its respective size. The memory address where the decrypted data is, in our case, `0x001B000`. This address may be different to other analyzes. Select the decrypted data's memory address with a size of `0x00D000`, right-click to bring up the context menu, and then select Dump Memory to File. Refer to the following example:

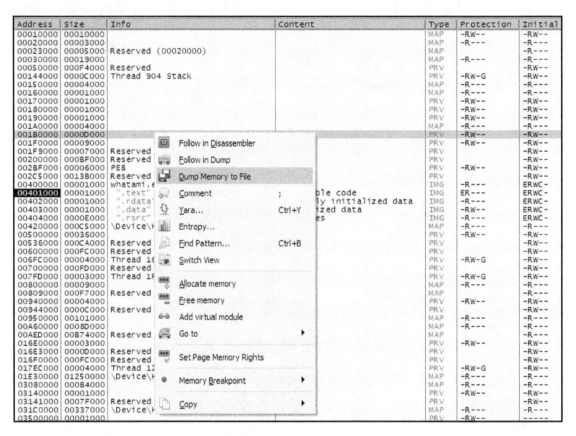

Save the file and open it with CFF Explorer. This gives us the following file information:

File size	53,248 bytes
MD5	DD073CBC4BE74CF1BD0379BA468AE950
SHA-1	90068FF0C1C1D0A5D0AF2B3CC2430A77EF1B7FC4
File type	Win32 PE file – compiled by Microsoft Visual C++ 8

In addition, viewing the import directory shows us four library modules: KERNEL32, ADVAPI32, WS2_32, and URLMON. The following CFF Explorer screenshot shows that registry and cryptography APIs are being imported from ADVAPI32:

whatami_001B0000.bin						
Module Name	Imports	OFTs	TimeDateStamp	ForwarderChain	Name RVA	FTs (IAT)
0000A384	N/A	0000A000	0000A004	0000A008	0000A00C	0000A010
szAnsi	(nFunctions)	Dword	Dword	Dword	Dword	Dword
KERNEL32.dll	71	0000A084	00000000	00000000	0000A29E	00008034
ADVAPI32.dll	12	0000A050	00000000	00000000	0000A384	00008000
WS2_32.dll	12	0000A1A4	00000000	00000000	0000A392	00008154
urlmon.dll	1	0000A1D8	00000000	00000000	0000A3B4	00008188

OFTs	FTs (IAT)	Hint	Name
Dword	Dword	Word	szAnsi
0000A360	0000A360	008A	CryptDeriveKey
0000A350	0000A350	009D	CryptHashData
0000A342	0000A342	01CB	RegCloseKey
0000A32C	0000A32C	00A0	CryptReleaseContext
0000A318	0000A318	008B	CryptDestroyHash
0000A304	0000A304	01F7	RegQueryValueExA
0000A2F4	0000A2F4	0089	CryptDecrypt
0000A2E6	0000A2E6	01EB	RegOpenKeyA

The presence of WS2_32 means that the program might use network socket functions. URLDownloadToFile is the single API imported from URLMON. We are expecting a file to be downloaded.

Going back to our debug session, there are two call instructions left. The one option is a call to ExitProcess, which will terminate the currently running process. The other is a call to address 0x004011D0. Use F7 to do a debug step causing the debugger to enter the call instruction. This is the function that does the process-hollowing routine. The following screenshot is where we should be at after entering 0x004011D0:

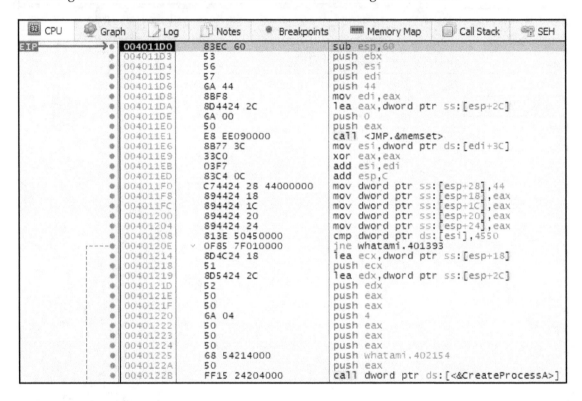

Continue pressing F8 until after the call to CreateProcessA. Open Windows Task Manger, and take a look at the list of processes. You should see calc.exe in suspended status, shown as follows:

Name	PID	Status	User name	CPU	Memory (p...	Description
ApplicationFrameHo...	6028	Running	refun	00	4,016 K	Application Frame Host
browser_broker.exe	2968	Running	refun	00	420 K	Browser_Broker
calc.exe	5572	Suspended	refun	00	24 K	Windows Calculator
CFF Explorer.exe	4408	Running	refun	00	2,120 K	Common File Format Ex...
csrss.exe	400	Running	SYSTEM	00	428 K	Client Server Runtime Pr...
csrss.exe	488	Running	SYSTEM	01	432 K	Client Server Runtime Pr...
ctfmon.exe	3984	Running	refun	00	2,312 K	CTF Loader
dasHost.exe	2292	Running	LOCAL SE...	00	556 K	Device Association Fra...
dllhost.exe	5116	Running	refun	00	1,288 K	COM Surrogate
dwm.exe	916	Running	DWM-1	00	27,940 K	Desktop Window Mana...
explorer.exe	3404	Running	refun	00	22,324 K	Windows Explorer
fontdrvhost.exe	696	Running	UMFD-0	00	80 K	Usermode Font Driver H
fontdrvhost.exe	704	Running	UMFD-1	00	1,036 K	Usermode Font Driver H
idag.exe	1284	Running	refun	00	6,236 K	The Interactive Disasse...
lsass.exe	616	Running	SYSTEM	00	2,336 K	Local Security Authority...

Continue pressing F8 until we reach the line that calls ResumeThread (0x0040138C). What happened is that the unknown PE file has just replaced the image of the Calculator process. If we take a look back at the block diagram of sub_4011D0, we are currently in the process hollowing behavior of this program. While Calculator is in suspended mode, no code is being executed yet. So before hitting F8 on the ResumeThread line, we will have to attach the suspended Calculator and place breakpoints at the entry point or at its WinMain address. To do that, we will have to open up another x86dbg debugger, then select **File->Attach**, and look for calc. If you cannot see that, you will need to run as an administrator by selecting File->Restart.

Let's use IDA Pro to help us identify the `WinMain` address. Open the dumped memory in IDA Pro and, following the automated analysis, we'll be at the `WinMain` function. Change the view to Text view and then take note of the `WinMain` address, as in the following screenshot:

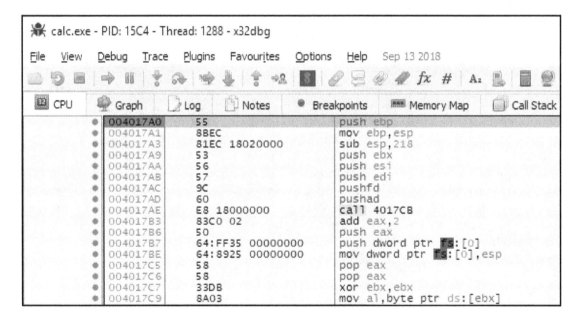

```
IDA View-A
  .text:004017A0 ;   __stdcall wWinMain(x, x, x, x)
  .text:004017A0 _wWinMain@16    proc near                 ; CODE XREF: ___tmainCRTStartup+171↓p
  .text:004017A0                 push    ebp
  .text:004017A1                 mov     ebp, esp
  .text:004017A3                 sub     esp, 218h
  .text:004017A9                 push    ebx
  .text:004017AA                 push    esi
  .text:004017AB                 push    edi
  .text:004017AC                 pushf
  .text:004017AD                 pusha
```

In `x86dbg`, place a breakpoint at `0x004017A0`, as shown in the following screenshot:

```
calc.exe - PID: 15C4 - Thread: 1288 - x32dbg

File   View   Debug   Trace   Plugins   Favourites   Options   Help   Sep 13 2018

  CPU      Graph      Log      Notes      Breakpoints      Memory Map      Call Stack

  004017A0    55                         push ebp
  004017A1    8BEC                       mov ebp,esp
  004017A3    81EC 18020000              sub esp,218
  004017A9    53                         push ebx
  004017AA    56                         push esi
  004017AB    57                         push edi
  004017AC    9C                         pushfd
  004017AD    60                         pushad
  004017AE    E8 18000000               call 4017CB
  004017B3    83C0 02                    add eax,2
  004017B6    50                         push eax
  004017B7    64:FF35 00000000           push dword ptr fs:[0]
  004017BE    64:8925 00000000           mov dword ptr fs:[0],esp
  004017C5    58                         pop eax
  004017C6    58                         pop eax
  004017C7    33DB                       xor ebx,ebx
  004017C9    8A03                       mov al,byte ptr ds:[ebx]
```

Now we are ready to press F8 over the `ResumeThread` line. But before doing that, it would be a good idea to create a snapshot of our running VM just in case something goes sideways:

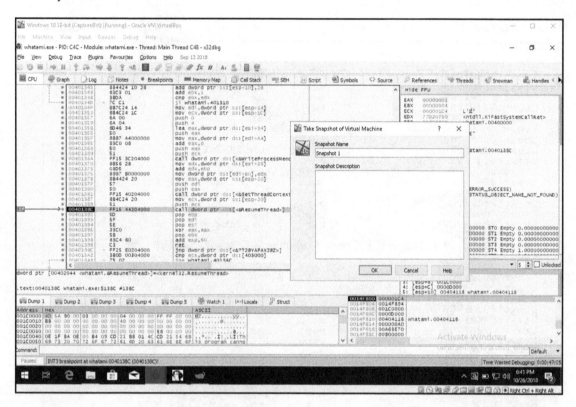

At this point, the only API left for `whatami.exe` to run is `ExitProcess`. This means that we can just press F9 to let this process die.

After `ResumeThread` has been called, the `calc` process is lifted from being suspended and begins to run. But since the unknown image is in a debugger paused state, we observe that the `calc` image is still at the attached breakpoint instruction pointer.

The unknown image

At this point, we have the memory dump opened in IDA Pro and have the same unknown image mapped into a Calculator process. We will work with both tools by using IDA Pro for viewing the disassembly code and `x86dbg` for debugging.

In `x86dbg`, we have placed a breakpoint at the `WinMain` address of the unknown image. However, the instruction pointer is still at an `NTDLL` address. Hit `F9` to make it continue and bring us to our `WinMain`.

Taking a detailed look at the disassembly codes from `WinMain`, we will notice an SEH anti-debug here:

```
.text:004017A1                     mov       ebp, esp
.text:004017A3                     sub       esp, 218h
.text:004017A9                     push      ebx
.text:004017AA                     push      esi
.text:004017AB                     push      edi
.text:004017AC                     pushf
.text:004017AD                     pusha
.text:004017AE                     call      sub_4017CB
.text:004017B3                     add       eax, 2
.text:004017B6                     push      eax
.text:004017B7                     push      large dword ptr fs:0
.text:004017BE                     mov       large fs:0, esp
.text:004017C5                     pop       eax
.text:004017C6                     pop       eax
.text:004017C7                     xor       ebx, ebx
.text:004017C9                     mov       al, [ebx]
.text:004017C9 _wWinMain@16        endp ; sp-analysis failed
.text:004017C9
.text:004017CB
.text:004017CB ; =============== S U B R O U T I N E =====================
.text:004017CB
.text:004017CB
.text:004017CB sub_4017CB          proc near                    ; CODE XREF: wWin
.text:004017CB                     call      $+5
.text:004017D0                     pop       eax
.text:004017D1                     retn
.text:004017D1 sub_4017CB          endp
.text:004017D1
.text:004017D2 ; --------------------------------------------------------
.text:004017D2                     mov       eax, [esp+8]
.text:004017D6                     mov       large fs:0, eax
.text:004017DC                     mov       esp, [esp+8]
.text:004017E0                     mov       eax, [esp]
.text:004017E3                     mov       large fs:0, eax
.text:004017E9                     lea       esp, [esp+8]
.text:004017ED                     popa
.text:004017EE                     popf
.text:004017EF                     call      sub_401730
.text:004017F4                     mov       dword ptr [ebp-4], 493E0h
```

`call sub_4017CB` goes to a subroutine that has a `call $+5`, `pop eax`, and then a `retn` instruction. `call $+5` calls the next line. Remember that when `call` is executed, the top of the stack will contain the return address. `call sub_4017CB` stores the return address, `0x004017B3`, at the top of the stack. And again, `call $+5` stores `0x004017D0` at the top of the stack. `0x004017D0` is placed in the eax register because of `pop eax`. The ret instruction returns to the `0x004017AD` address. A value of 2 is added to the address stored at the `eax` register. As a result, the address in `eax` points to `0x004017D2`. This must be the handler for the SEH being set up.

We can go through the SEH, or simply skip this in our debug session. Skipping it would be as simple since we can identify the pushf/pusha and popa/popf instructions and execute the same process as we did in the whatami.exe process.

Going through the SEH should also be simple. We can just place a breakpoint at the handler address, 0x004017D2, and press F9 until we reach the handler.

> We can choose either of these options. When it comes to decisions like this, it is always wise to take a snapshot of the VM. We can try both options by simply restoring the VM snapshot.

Our next stop is sub_401730. The following screenshot shows the code in sub_401730:

```
.text:00401730 sub_401730    proc near              ; CODE XREF: .text:004017EF↓p
.text:00401730
.text:00401730 ProcName      = byte ptr -0Ch
.text:00401730 var_8         = dword ptr -8
.text:00401730 var_4         = dword ptr -4
.text:00401730
.text:00401730               push    ebp
.text:00401731               mov     ebp, esp
.text:00401733               sub     esp, 0Ch
.text:00401736               mov     eax, ds:dword_409AF4
.text:0040173B               mov     ecx, ds:dword_409AF8
.text:00401741               mov     edx, ds:dword_409AFC
.text:00401747               push    ebx
.text:00401748               push    offset aUser32   ; "user32"
.text:0040174D               mov     dword ptr [ebp+ProcName], eax
.text:00401750               mov     [ebp+var_8], ecx
.text:00401753               mov     [ebp+var_4], edx
.text:00401756               call    ds:LoadLibraryA
.text:0040175C               lea     ecx, [ebp+ProcName]
.text:0040175F               push    ecx              ; lpProcName
.text:00401760               push    eax              ; hModule
.text:00401761               call    ds:GetProcAddress
.text:00401767               push    0
.text:00401769               push    offset aPackt    ; "Packt"
.text:0040176E               push    offset aLearningRevers ; "Learning reversing is fun.\nFor educati"...
.text:00401773               push    0
.text:00401775               call    eax
.text:00401777               add     esp, 10h
.text:0040177A               push    ebx
.text:0040177B               mov     ebx, esp
.text:0040177D               sub     esp, 4
.text:00401780               push    eax
.text:00401781               xor     eax, eax
.text:00401783               mov     al, ah
.text:00401785               mov     eax, 0FACEB00Ch
.text:0040178A               pop     eax
.text:0040178B               add     esp, 4
.text:0040178E               mov     esp, ebx
.text:00401790               pop     ebx
.text:00401791               mov     al, 1
.text:00401793               pop     ebx
.text:00401794               mov     esp, ebp
.text:00401796               pop     ebp
.text:00401797               retn
.text:00401797 sub_401730    endp
```

Debugging through this code reveals that `LoadLibraryA` and `GetProcAddress` is used to retrieve the address of `MessageBoxA`. Afterward, it just displays a message.

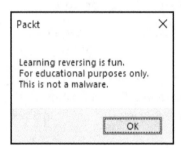

The next lines of code is an anti-automated analysis trick. We can see that the difference of the results of two `GetTickCount` is being compared to a value `0x0493e0` or `300000`. Between the calls to `GetTickCount`, a Sleep function is also called.

```
.text:004017F4          mov       dword ptr [ebp-4], 493E0h
.text:004017FB          call      ds:GetTickCount
.text:00401801          mov       [ebp-8], eax
.text:00401804          mov       eax, [ebp-4]
.text:00401807          push      eax
.text:00401808          call      ds:Sleep
.text:0040180E          call      ds:GetTickCount
.text:00401814          sub       eax, [ebp-8]
.text:00401817          cmp       eax, [ebp-4]
.text:0040181A          jb        loc_4018A9
```

A Sleep for 300000 means 5 minutes. Usually, automated analysis systems would turn a long Sleep to a very short one. The preceding code wants to make sure that 5 minutes really elapsed. As analysts debugging this code, we can simply skip this trick by setting our instruction pointer after the jb instruction.

Next is a call to `sub_401500` with two parameters: "`mcdo.thecyberdung.net`" and `0x270F` (`9999`). The routine contains socket APIs. As we did before, let us list down the sequence of APIs we will encounter.

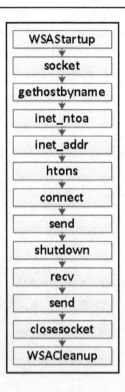

For network socket behaviors, what we will be looking into are the parameters and results for `gethostbyname`, `htons`, `send` and `recv`. Again, before we proceed, taking a VM snapshot would be recommended at this point.

Keep on step debugging until we reach the call to `gethostbyname`. We can get the server to which the program is connecting to by looking at `gethostbyname`'s parameters. And that would be "`mcdo.thecyberdung.net`". Proceeding with the call, we might encounter a problem with gethostbyname's result. The result in register EAX is zero. This means `gethostbyname` failed because it was not able to resolve "`mcdo.thecyberdung.net`" to an IP address. What we need to do is setup `FakeNet` to mimic the internet. Revert the VM snapshot to take us back before executing `WSAStartup`.

Before running `FakeNet`, disconnect the cable by selecting Machine->Settings->Network from the VirtualBox menu. Expand the Advanced menu and uncheck Cable connected. We are doing this procedure to make sure that there will be no interference for `FakeNet` reconfiguring the network.

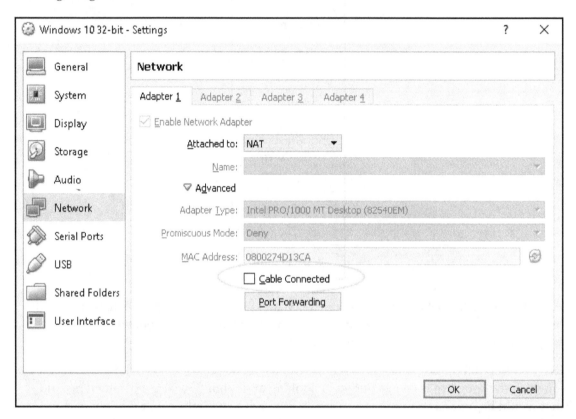

The following screenshot shows `FakeNet` running successfully. `FakeNet` might require running in administrative privileges. If that happens, just run it as an Administrator:

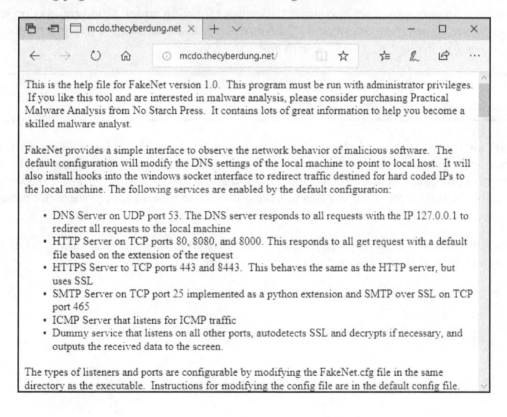

Restore cable connection by checking the VM Network settings' Cable Connected check box. To verify that everything works fine, open up Internet Explorer and visit any website. The resulting page should be similar to the following screenshot:

Now, we can go back to our debugging at the `gethostbyname` address. We should now get a result in register `EAX` with `FakeNet` running.

The next API we are after is `htons`. This should give us information about the server's network port the program is going to connect to. The parameter passed to `htons` is stored in register `ECX`. This is the port number that will be used, `0x270F` or `9999`.

Going on with debugging, we encounter the connect function where actual connection to the server and given port commences. The connect function returns zero to register `EAX` if it was successful. In our case, this fails with a −1 return value.

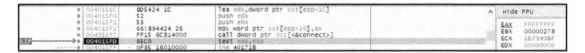

The reason for this is that FakeNet only supports commonly used and few known malware ports. Fortunately, we can edit FakeNet's configuration and add port 9999 to the list. FakeNet's configuration file, FakeNet.cfg, is found at the same directory where FakeNet's executable is. But before updating this file, we will have to revert again to snapshot before `WSAStartup` is called.

Using Notepad, edit `FakeNet.cfg`. Look for the line that has the "`RawListner`" text. If not found, just append the following lines in the config file.

```
RawListener Port:9999 UseSSL:No
```

When this line is added, the config file should look like this:

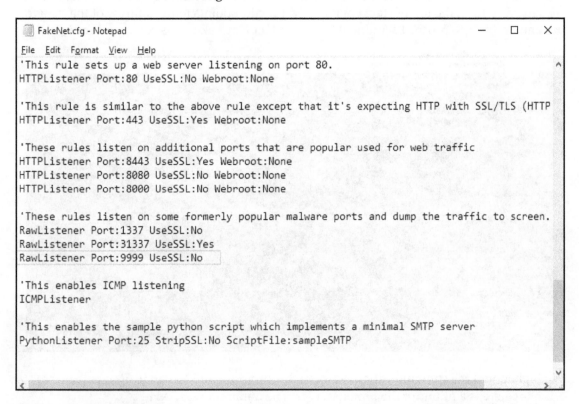

```
FakeNet.cfg - Notepad                                    —    □    ×
File  Edit  Format  View  Help
'This rule sets up a web server listening on port 80.
HTTPListener Port:80 UseSSL:No Webroot:None

'This rule is similar to the above rule except that it's expecting HTTP with SSL/TLS (HTTP
HTTPListener Port:443 UseSSL:Yes Webroot:None

'These rules listen on additional ports that are popular used for web traffic
HTTPListener Port:8443 UseSSL:Yes Webroot:None
HTTPListener Port:8080 UseSSL:No Webroot:None
HTTPListener Port:8000 UseSSL:No Webroot:None

'These rules listen on some formerly popular malware ports and dump the traffic to screen.
RawListener Port:1337 UseSSL:No
RawListener Port:31337 UseSSL:Yes
RawListener Port:9999 UseSSL:No

'This enables ICMP listening
ICMPListener

'This enables the sample python script which implements a minimal SMTP server
PythonListener Port:25 StripSSL:No ScriptFile:sampleSMTP
```

Take note of the added `RawListener` line. After this, restart `FakeNet` then debug again until we reach the `connect` API. This time we are expecting the connect function to become successful.

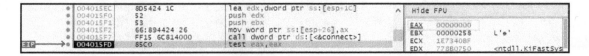

```
  004015EC    8D5424 1C        lea edx,dword ptr ss:[esp+1C]
  004015F0    52               push edx
  004015F1    53               push ebx
  004015F2    66:894424 26     mov word ptr ss:[esp+26],ax
  004015F7    FF15 6C814000    call dword ptr ds:[<&connect>]
EIP→ 004015FD    85C0             test eax,eax
```

Hide FPU

EAX 00000000
EBX 00000258   L's'
ECX 1E7340BF
EDX 773B0750   <ntdll.KiFastSys

Continue debugging until we reach the send function. The second parameter (look at the second entry from the top of stack) of the send function points to the address of the data to be sent. Press F8 to proceed sending the data and look at FakeNet's command console.

```
FN C:\Users\refun\Desktop\FakeNet2.0_beta\FakeNet.exe                    -  □  ×

[Listening for SSL traffic on port 31337.]
[Listening for traffic on port 9999.]
[Listening for traffic on port 25.]
[Listening for ICMP traffic.]

[DNS Query Received.]
  Domain name: mcdo.thecyberdung.net
[DNS Response sent.]


[Received new connection on port: 9999.]

[DNS Query Received.]
  Domain name: arc.msn.com
[DNS Response sent.]

[DNS Query Received.]
  Domain name: client.wns.windows.com
[DNS Response sent.]

[DNS Query Received.]
  Domain name: cdn.onenote.net
[DNS Response sent.]


[Received new connection on port: 443.]
[New request on port 443 with SSL.]
  [Received unsupported HTTP request.]
  [Received NON-SSL data on port 9999.]
  OLAH
```

We highlighted the communication between this program and FakeNet. Remember that FakeNet here is a mimic of the remote server. The data sent was "OLAH".

Continue debugging until we reach another send or recv function. The next function is a recv.

The second parameter is the buffer that receives data from the server. Apparently, we are not expecting FakeNet to send any data back. What we can do is monitor succeeding code that will process the data in this recv buffer. But to make the recv call successful, the return value should be a non-zero number. We will have to change register EAX's value after stepping on the recv call, as we did in the following screenshot:

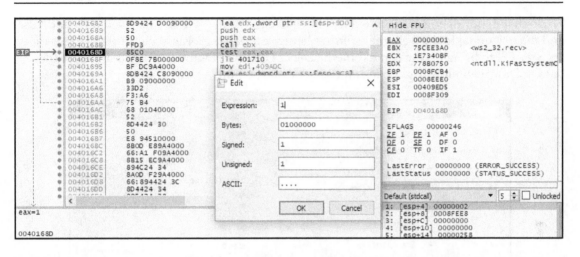

The next lines of code compare the data received with a string. See the following disassembly using the `repe cmpsb` instruction to compare the strings. This instruction compares the text string stored at the address pointed to by registers ESI and EDI. The number of bytes to compare is stored in register ECX. The supposedly received data is located at the address pointed to by register ESI. And the address of the string, "jollibee", is stored in register EDI. What we want to happen here is make both strings equal.

```
.text:00401674                 mov     eax, [esp+0DDCh+s]
.text:00401678                 add     esp, 0Ch
.text:0040167B                 push    0               ; flags
.text:0040167D                 push    401h            ; len
.text:00401682                 lea     edx, [esp+0DD8h+buf]
.text:00401689                 push    edx             ; buf
.text:0040168A                 push    eax             ; s
.text:0040168B                 call    ebx ; recv
.text:0040168D                 test    eax, eax
.text:0040168F                 jle     loc_401710
.text:00401695                 mov     edi, offset aJollibee ; "jollibee"
.text:0040169A                 lea     esi, [esp+0DD0h+buf]
.text:004016A1                 mov     ecx, 9
.text:004016A6                 xor     edx, edx        |
.text:004016A8                 repe cmpsb
.text:004016AA                 jnz     short loc_401660
```

To do that in our debug session, we will have to edit the bytes at the received data address and make it equal to the 9 character string being compared to. Right click on the value of register ESI to bring up the context menu, select Follow in Dump. At the first byte of the data in Dump window, right click and select **Binary->Edit**.

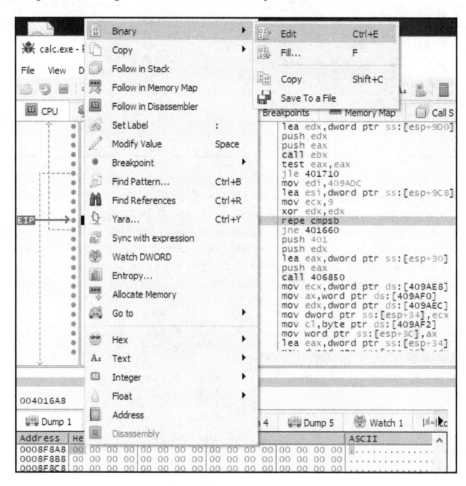

This pops up a dialog box (shown in the following) where we can enter the string
"jollibee":

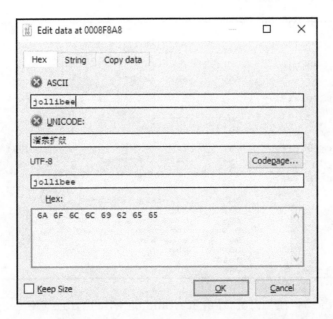

Hit F8 to proceed with the comparison. This should not go to the address where the
conditional jump points to. Continue debugging until we reach another send function.
Again, look at the data to be sent, which is the address that the second parameter points to.
However, irrespective of whether this succeeds or fails, the result is not processed. The
succeeding API closes the connection with `closesocket` and WSACleanup functions, sets
EAX to 1, and returns from the current function. EAX will only be set to 1 after the last send
function.

We've highlighted `var_DBD` in the disassembly code shown below to see that a value of 1 was stored after the sending data back to the server.

```
.text:00401703                         push    0                       ; s
.text:00401705                         call    ds:send
.text:0040170B                         mov     [esp+0DD0h+var_DBD], 1
.text:00401710
.text:00401710 loc_401710:                                            ; CODE XREF: sub_401500+18F↑j
.text:00401710                         mov     ebx, [esp+0DD0h+s]
.text:00401714
.text:00401714 loc_401714:                                            ; CODE XREF: sub_401500+13D↑j
.text:00401714                                                         ; sub_401500+14F↑j
.text:00401714                         push    ebx                     ; s
.text:00401715                         call    ds:closesocket
.text:0040171B
.text:0040171B loc_40171B:                                            ; CODE XREF: sub_401500+FF↑j
.text:0040171B                         call    ds:WSACleanup
.text:00401721
.text:00401721 loc_401721:                                            ; CODE XREF: sub_401500+29↑j
.text:00401721                                                         ; sub_401500+43↑j
.text:00401721                         mov     al, [esp+0DD0h+var_DBD]
.text:00401725                         pop     edi
.text:00401726                         pop     esi
.text:00401727                         pop     ebx
.text:00401728                         mov     esp, ebp
.text:0040172A                         pop     ebp
.text:0040172B                         retn
.text:0040172B sub_401500              endp
```

After returning to the `WinMain` function, it would be wise to do a VM snapshot.

Keep on debugging until we reach a call to address `0x00401280`. There are two parameters that will be passed to the function with values stored in the EAX and ECX registers . The data is dumped under `Dump 1`, demonstrated as follows:

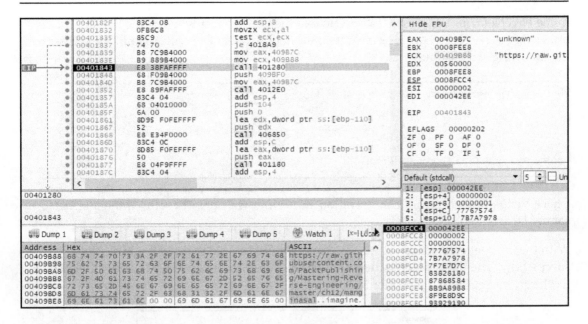

After entering function `0x00401280`, we will only encounter a URLDownloadToFile function. The function downloads
`https://raw.githubusercontent.com/PacktPublishing/Mastering-Reverse-Eng
ineering/master/ch12/manginasal` and stores it to a file named `unknown`, as can be
seen in the following screenshot:

```
.text:00401280 ; int __thiscall sub_401280(LPCSTR)
.text:00401280 sub_401280      proc near               ; CODE XREF: .text:00401843↓p
.text:00401280                 push    0               ; LPBINDSTATUSCALLBACK
.text:00401282                 push    0               ; DWORD
.text:00401284                 push    eax             ; LPCSTR
.text:00401285                 push    ecx             ; LPCSTR
.text:00401286                 push    0               ; LPUNKNOWN
.text:00401288                 call    URLDownloadToFileA
.text:0040128D                 retn
.text:0040128D sub_401280      endp
```

Doing this, we get to encounter an error that fails to download the file. The reason is that
we are still under a mimicked internet. This time, we will need to get a connection to the
live internet. We will have to revert back to the snapshot before the `URLDownloadToFile`
function happens.

In the FakeNet console, press *CTRL + C* to exit the tool. To test whether the live internet is up, visit `http://testmyids.com` from the internet browser. The result should be similar to the following screenshot:

Check VirtualBox's network configuration and Windows' network setup if the internet cannot be accessed.

With the internet connection up, the program should be able to download the file successfully. The file is downloaded with the filename `unknown`. If we load this file in CFF Explorer, we get these file properties:

unknown	
Property	Value
File Name	C:\Users\refun\Desktop\unknown
File Type	Unknown format
File Info	Unknown format
File Size	2.94 KB (3008 bytes)
PE Size	Not a Portable Executable.
Created	Saturday 27 October 2018, 03.16.39
Modified	Saturday 27 October 2018, 03.16.39
Accessed	Saturday 27 October 2018, 03.17.15
MD5	05213A14A665E5E2EEC31971A5542D32
SHA-1	7ECCD8EB05A31AB627CDFA6F3CFE4BFFA46E01A1

The following screenshot shows the file's content by selecting the CFF Explorer's Hex Editor:

Offset	0	1	2	3	4	5	6	7	8	9	A	B	C	D	E	F	Ascii
00000000	CD	E7	47	D4	5D	A0	96	10	50	4D	EA	77	F6	98	E4	92	ÍçGÔ] ▯ PMêwö▮ä´
00000010	99	B4	00	16	D4	4C	9B	8D	40	53	D6	44	71	C1	0A	09	▮´.▯ÔL▮ ▮@SÖDqÁ..
00000020	87	D1	86	E4	5B	49	02	7A	21	5C	D7	BB	E4	EA	12	CE	▮Ñ▮ä[I z!\×»äê▮ Î
00000030	F3	2C	52	E0	72	D2	65	C8	63	C1	5B	36	37	4A	E7	80	ó,RàrÒeÈcÁ[67Jç▮
00000040	8B	36	82	0F	EF	1C	63	A6	57	16	3A	BB	72	94	20	A7	▮6▮▯ï c¦W▯ :»r▮ .§
00000050	9D	0B	F7	22	80	3C	AF	13	21	B7	A4	0E	C8	86	C3	FB	▯÷"▮<¯▯ !·¤▯È▮Ãû
00000060	28	31	28	50	87	A4	6E	96	77	B6	FA	B2	16	39	A7	FA	(1(P▮¤n▮w¶ú▮²▯ 9§ú
00000070	DF	B8	89	B5	BE	1F	56	FC	63	89	54	94	47	FB	11	64	ß¸▮µ¾ Vüc▮T▮Gû▯ d
00000080	9F	62	36	EA	04	D0	1B	2A	54	4B	1E	F3	39	44	12	27	▮b6ê▯ Ð▯ *TK ó9D▯ '
00000090	F6	91	93	99	93	2E	2B	20	B2	FA	DB	0F	C6	E8	FA	5C	ö´▮▮▮.+. ²úÛ▯ Æèú\
000000A0	5C	86	C3	30	53	4D	DB	38	84	A5	10	3F	96	06	A4	99	\▮Ã0SMÛ8▮¥▯ ?▮▯ ¤▮
000000B0	7E	50	9C	32	5D	E6	3B	FC	4B	36	65	9C	CE	26	30	AF	~P▮2]æ;üK6e▮Î&0¯
000000C0	4E	4B	75	73	89	AE	61	D0	5D	0F	40	30	86	6A	43	F0	NKus▮®aÐ]▯@0▮jCð
000000D0	2F	1A	10	81	07	6F	F5	22	89	9C	A0	86	2C	38	8F	E7	/▯▯ ▮o õ"▮▮ ▮,8 ç
000000E0	C8	5F	7C	22	EA	44	91	1F	F3	25	E8	8F	75	88	54	64	È_|"êD´ ó%è u▮Td
000000F0	AB	AD	3E	16	78	C9	D7	D1	22	6F	09	EA	95	83	4E	F8	«>▯ xÉ×Ñ"o.ê▮▮Nø
00000100	6A	ED	D3	F3	BF	C8	AF	8E	01	4E	DD	A5	AD	51	0F	2D	jíÓ ó¿È¯▮ NÝ¥Q▯ -
00000110	EE	8C	03	B0	02	7C	2C	F0	CB	B1	CA	BA	5B	FF	FF	F0	î▮▯ ° |,ðˆ±Êº[ÿÿð
00000120	B1	77	E3	90	C5	D4	79	1D	40	5A	5E	82	BF	32	2C	1F	±wã ÅÔy @Z^▮¿2,
00000130	83	10	F1	15	BF	43	B2	4A	4E	50	39	2F	4D	F5	6F	AD	▮▯ ñ▯ ¿C²JNP9/Mõo
00000140	8B	58	39	50	B4	CE	20	57	7A	65	DF	D6	73	A0	53	65	▮X9P´Î WzeßÖs Se
00000150	7A	40	43	A3	3E	4B	33	CD	29	01	1D	A4	9E	C0	FB	7A	z@C£>K3Í)▯ ¤▮Àûz

The file seems to be encrypted. We should expect that the next behavior will process this file. Keep on debugging until we reach a call to address `0x004012e0`. This function accepts two parameters, an address stored in EAX, and another address pushed to the stack. The function receives these `imagine` parameter strings from the top of the stack and `unknown` from the register EAX.

Entering the function reveals reading the content of the file "unknown". The disassembly code that reads the file in a newly allocated memory space is as follows:

```
.text:004012E7          push    0               ; hTemplateFile
.text:004012E9          push    0               ; dwFlagsAndAttributes
.text:004012EB          push    4               ; dwCreationDisposition
.text:004012ED          push    0               ; lpSecurityAttributes
.text:004012EF          push    0               ; dwShareMode
.text:004012F1          push    80000000h       ; dwDesiredAccess
.text:004012F6          push    eax             ; lpFileName
.text:004012F7          call    ds:CreateFileA
.text:004012FD          mov     esi, eax
.text:004012FF          push    0               ; lpFileSizeHigh
.text:00401301          push    esi             ; hFile
.text:00401302          call    ds:GetFileSize
.text:00401308          mov     edi, eax
.text:0040130A          lea     ebx, [edi+edi]
.text:0040130D          push    ebx             ; Size
.text:0040130E          call    ??2@YAPAXI@Z    ; operator new(uint)
.text:00401313          push    ebx             ; Size
.text:00401314          mov     ebp, eax
.text:00401316          push    0               ; Val
.text:00401318          push    ebp             ; Dst
.text:00401319          call    _memset
.text:0040131E          add     esp, 10h
.text:00401321          push    0               ; lpOverlapped
.text:00401323          lea     ecx, [esp+5Ch+NumberOfBytesRead]
.text:00401327          push    ecx             ; lpNumberOfBytesRead
.text:00401328          push    edi             ; nNumberOfBytesToRead
.text:00401329          push    ebp             ; lpBuffer
.text:0040132A          push    esi             ; hFile
.text:0040132B          mov     [esp+6Ch+NumberOfBytesRead], 0
.text:00401333          call    ds:ReadFile
.text:00401339          push    esi             ; hObject
.text:0040133A          call    ds:CloseHandle
```

Keep on pressing F8 until after the CloseHandle call. The next set of code shows the use of Cryptographic APIs. Let's list the sequence of APIs here once again:

```
.text:0040137A call ds:CryptAcquireContextA
.text:0040139B call ds:CryptCreateHash
.text:004013C8 call ds:CryptHashData
.text:004013EC call ds:CryptDeriveKey
.text:004013FF call sub_401290
.text:0040147B call ds:CryptDecrypt
.text:0040149D call ds:CreateFileA
.text:004014AF call ds:WriteFile
.text:004014B6 call ds:CloseHandle
.text:004014BE call ds:Sleep
.text:004014D9 call ds:CryptDestroyKey
.text:004014E4 call ds:CryptDestroyHash
.text:004014F1 call ds:CryptReleaseContext
```

Based on the list, it would seem that whatever is decrypted gets stored in a file. What we would want to know about this are the following:

- The cryptographic algorithm used
- The cipher key used
- The name of the file it stores data into

To identify the algorithm used, we should monitor the parameters used in either `CryptAcquireContextA` function. Keep on debugging until `CryptAcquireContextA`. The fourth parameter, `dwProvType`, should tell us what algorithm was used. `dwProvType` here is `0x18` or `24`. For the list of provider type values, we can reference `https://docs.microsoft.com/en-us/dotnet/api/system.security.permissions.keycontainerpermissionattribute.providertype`. In this case, 24 is defined for the value of `PROV_RSA_AES`. Thus, the cipher algorithm here uses `RSA AES`.

The cipher key used for this algorithm should be the third parameter of the `CryptHashData` function. Look at the second parameter of the `CryptHashData` function in the following screenshot:

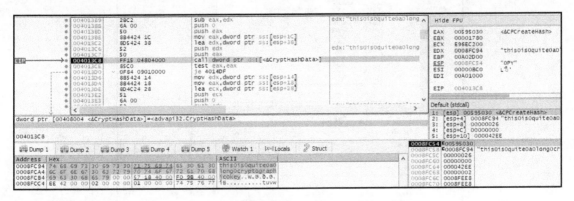

The key is `this0is0quite0a0long0cryptographic0key`.

For the final piece of information, we need to monitor `CreateFileA` to get the filename of where the decrypted data will possibly be placed. After debugging to `CreateFileA`, we should see the first parameter as the output filename, `"imagine"`. The `CryptDecrypt` function accepts the location of encrypted data, the fifth parameter, and decrypts it at the same location. The process runs in a loop where every piece of decrypted data gets appended to the "imagine" file.

The following screenshot, an IDA Pro graphical view, shows decrypted data being appended to the output file:

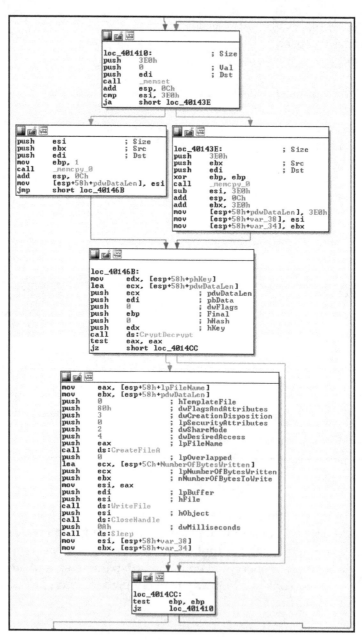

The decryption ends by closing the cryptographic handles with `CryptDestroyKey`, `CryptDestroyHash`, and `CryptReleaseContext`.

Curious enough, let's use CFF Explorer to extract information from the "`imagine`" file:

imagine	
Property	Value
File Name	C:\Users\refun\Desktop\imagine
File Type	Unknown format
File Info	Unknown format
File Size	2.94 KB (3007 bytes)
PE Size	Not a Portable Executable.
Created	Saturday 27 October 2018, 04.04.16
Modified	Saturday 27 October 2018, 04.37.11
Accessed	Saturday 27 October 2018, 04.37.57
MD5	7AAF7D965EF8AEE002B8D72AF6855667
SHA-1	4757E071CA2C69F0647537E5D2A6DB8F6F975D49
Property	Value
Empty	No additional info available

Using the TrID tool, we get a more meaningful file type, as shown in the following screenshot:

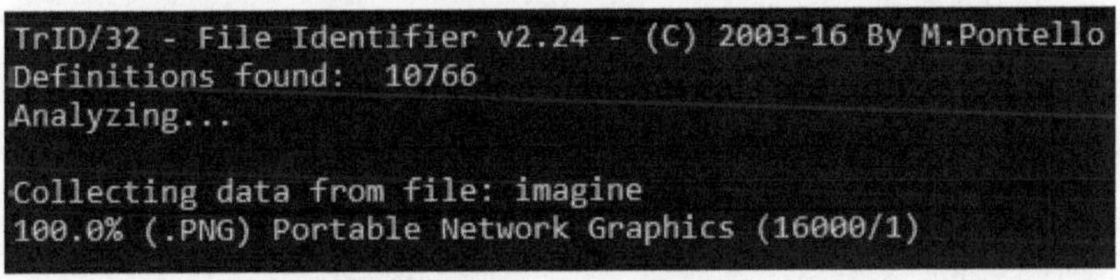

```
TrID/32 - File Identifier v2.24 - (C) 2003-16 By M.Pontello
Definitions found:  10766
Analyzing...

Collecting data from file: imagine
100.0% (.PNG) Portable Network Graphics (16000/1)
```

The file is a PNG image file.

Continuing with the debug session, keep on pressing F8 until we reach a call to address `0x00401180`. Press F7 to enter this function. This reveals the utilization of registry APIs in this sequence:

```
.text:004011BF call ds:RegOpenKeyExA
.text:004011E6 call esi ; RegQueryValueExA
```

```
.text:004011F3 call edi ; RegCloseKey
.text:00401249 call ds:RegOpenKeyA
.text:0040126A call esi ; RegQueryValueExA
.text:00401271 call edi ; RegCloseKey
```

Basically, the registry functions here only retrieve certain values that exist in the registry. The disassembly codes shown below shows that the first query retrieves the data value of `ProgId` from the `HKEY_CURRENT_USER\Software\Microsoft\Windows\Shell\Associations\UrlAssociations\http\UserChoice` registry key:

```
lea     ecx, [esp+118h+phkResult]
push    ecx                  ; phkResult
push    20019h               ; samDesired
push    0                    ; ulOptions
push    offset SubKey        ; "Software\\Microsoft\\Windows\\Shell\\As"...
push    80000001h            ; hKey
mov     [esp+12Ch+cbData] ; CHAR SubKey[]
call    ds:RegOpenKeyEx  SubKey  db 'Software\Microsoft\Windows\Shell\Associations\UrlAssociations\htt'
mov     esi, ds:RegQuer                          ; DATA XREF: sub_401180+2D↑o
lea     edx, [esp+118h+          db 'p\UserChoice',0
push    edx
mov     edx, [esp+11Ch+phkResult]
lea     eax, [esp+11Ch+Data]
push    eax                  ; lpData
lea     ecx, [esp+120h+Type]
push    ecx                  ; lpType
push    0                    ; lpReserved
push    offset ValueName     ; "ProgId"
push    edx                  ; hKey
call    esi ; RegQueryValueExA
mov     eax, [esp+118h+phkResult]
mov     edi, ds:RegCloseKey
push    eax                  ; hKey
call    edi ; RegCloseKey
```

If we take a look at the registry, this location points to the ID of the default internet browser used by the logged-in user. The following screenshot shows an example of the ID of the default internet browser set in `Progid`, which is `FirefoxURL-308046B0AF4A39CB`:

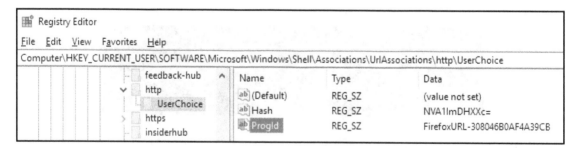

For the next registry query, `RegOpenKeyExA` opens the `HKEY_CLASSES_ROOT\FirefoxURL-308046B0AF4A39CB\shell\open\command` registry key, where `FirefoxURL-308046B0AF4A39CB` is the ID of the default internet browser:

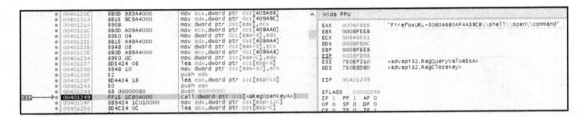

The succeeding `RegQueryValueExA` has the second parameter, `lpValuename`, equal to zero. Refer to the disassembly as follows:

```
call    ds:RegOpenKeyA
mov     edx, [esp+118h+lpData]
lea     ecx, [esp+118h+cbData]
push    ecx                 ; lpcbData
mov     ecx, [esp+11Ch+phkResult]
push    edx                 ; lpData
lea     eax, [esp+120h+Type]
push    eax                 ; lpType
push    0                   ; lpReserved
push    0                   ; lpValueName
push    ecx                 ; hKey
call    esi ; RegQueryValueExA
mov     edx, [esp+118h+phkResult]
push    edx                 ; hKey
call    edi ; RegCloseKey
```

If `lpValuename` is equal to 0, the data being retrieved will be taken from the default value.

Looking at the registry, this is displayed as (Default), demonstrated as follows:

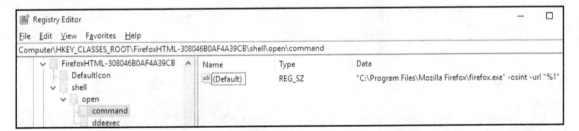

Hence, the action performed by the function was retrieval of the command line for the default internet browser.

The following lines of code resolve the full file path of the "imagine" file, and then pass the path to the final function, sub_401000, before exiting the process:

```
.text:0040187F                      push    0
.text:00401881                      lea     ecx, [ebp-218h]
.text:00401887                      push    ecx
.text:00401888                      push    104h
.text:0040188D                      push    offset aImagine ; "imagine"
.text:00401892                      call    ds:GetFullPathNameA
.text:00401898                      lea     eax, [ebp-218h]
.text:0040189E                      lea     ecx, [ebp-110h]
.text:004018A4                      call    sub_401000
.text:004018A9
.text:004018A9 loc_4018A9:                          ; CODE XREF: .text:0040181A↑j
.text:004018A9                                      ; .text:00401837↑j
.text:004018A9                      push    0
.text:004018AB                      call    ds:ExitProcess
```

Debugging into sub_401000, we encounter more than a hundred lines of code that pretty much moves test strings around. But the bottomline is that it will run another process using the CreateProcessA. Taking a look at the parameters that will be passed to CreateProcess, the second parameter, which is the command line, that it will execute contains the path of the default browser passed with the full path of the "imagine" file as its argument. From the following screenshot, it can be seen that we dumped the command line in Dump 1:

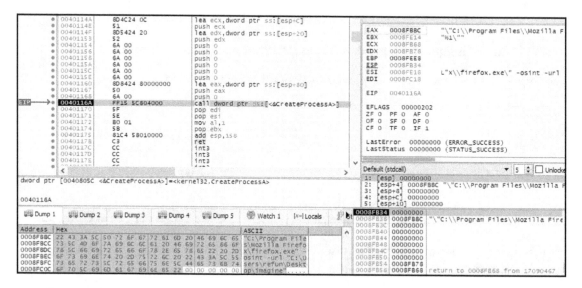

As a result, this opens the "imagine" file using the default internet browser. The following screenshot is displayed:

Analysis summary

The following table concerns the file elements we found.

The original file is a UPX-packed Win32 executable file.

Filename	whatami.exe
File size	28,672 bytes
MD5	F4723E35D83B10AD72EC32D2ECC61091
SHA-1	4A1E8A976F1515CE3F7F86F814B1235B7D18A231
File type	Win32 PE file – packed with UPX v3.0

The UPX unpacked version gives us this new information about the file:

Filename	whatami.exe
File size	73,728 bytes
MD5	18F86337C492E834B1771CC57FB2175D
SHA-1	C8601593E7DC27D97EFC29CBFF90612A265A248E
File type	Win32 PE file – compiled by Microsoft Visual C++ 8

The program maps an unknown PE file using process hollowing. This PE file contains the following information:

File size	53,248 bytes
MD5	DD073CBC4BE74CF1BD0379BA468AE950
SHA-1	90068FF0C1C1D0A5D0AF2B3CC2430A77EF1B7FC4
File type	Win32 PE file – compiled by Microsoft Visual C++ 8

A file downloaded from `https://raw.githubusercontent.com/PacktPublishing/ Mastering-Reverse-Engineering/master/ch12/manginasal` is stored in a file as unknown. Here is the file's information:

Filename	unknown
File size	3,008 bytes
MD5	05213A14A665E5E2EEC31971A5542D32
SHA-1	7ECCD8EB05A31AB627CDFA6F3CFE4BFFA46E01A1
File type	Unknown file type

The unknown file was decrypted and stored using the filename "imagine", containing the following file information:

Filename	imagine
File size	3,007 bytes
MD5	7AAF7D965EF8AEE002B8D72AF6855667
SHA-1	4757E071CA2C69F0647537E5D2A6DB8F6F975D49
File type	PNG file type

To recap what behaviors it executed, here is a step-by-step process:

1. Displays a message box: "How did you get here?"
2. Decrypts a PE image from the resource section
3. Uses process hollowing to replace "calc" with a decrypted PE image

4. Displays a message box: "Learning reversing is fun. For educational purposes only. This is not a malware."
5. Sleeps for 5 minutes
6. Checks the connection to the "`mcdo.thecyberdung.net:9999`" server
7. Downloads the file from `raw.githubusercontent.com`
8. Decrypts the downloaded file and outputs of result to a PNG image file.
9. Retrieves the default internet browser path
10. Displays the PNG image file using the default internet browser

Summary

Reversing a software takes time and patience. It may take days to analyze just one piece of software. But with practice and experience, the time it takes to analyze a file improves.

In this chapter, we dealt with a file that can be reversed using the tools we learned. With the help of a debugger, a disassembler, and tools such as CFF Explorer and TriD, we were able to extract file information and behaviors. In addition, we also learned to use FakeNet to mimic the network and the internet, which became very useful for us when generating network information for the socket functions.

There are a lot of obstacles, including anti-debugging tricks. However, familiarity with these tricks enabled us to skip these codes.

One of the most important tips when reversing is to keep on making snapshots just in case we encounter obstacles. We can experiment on every piece of data that functions require.

Again, reversing is a patience game that you can cheat by saving and loading snapshots.

Further Reading

DLL Injection - `https://en.wikipedia.org/wiki/DLL_injection`

Process Hollowing - `https://github.com/m0n0ph1/Process-Hollowing`

Reversing Various File Types

13

So far, we have been dealing with binary executables. In this chapter, we will also look at other ways in which code can be executed. Visiting websites (HTML) and receiving emails (that have documents attached to them) are some of the mediums where malware can easily enter a target system.

In this chapter, we will learn about the following topics:

- Debugging scripts in HTML
- Understanding Macro in Office documents
- Performing PDF analysis
- SWF analysis

Analysis of HTML scripts

Almost every website we visit contains scripts. Most commonly, it contains JavaScript code that is triggered by clicking on the OK button on a website or by those artistic bubbles and stars that roam around with the mouse pointer. JavaScript is one of the most powerful tools that can be used by a site developer. It can be used to control elements that an internet browser contains.

Besides JavaScript, Visual Basic scripts (VBScripts) can also be embedded in HTML websites. However, VBScript has been disabled by default in recent web browsers. This is due to the fact that VBScript has been exposed to a lot of vulnerabilities in the past. In addition, JavaScript is the default language used by many internet browsers.

There are two sides for a website to work, that is, the server side and the client side. When visiting a website, we are looking at the client side page. All backend scripts are running at the server side. For example, when visiting a website, the server-side programs send the HTML contents, including text, scripts, images, Java applets, and flash files. Only the browser elements, like HTML, JavaScript, Java applets, and SWF flash, that can be supported by internet browsers, are the objects that are crafted and sent by server-side programs. In essence, what we can analyze are these browser elements.

Fortunately, scripts are readable text files. We can perform static analysis for HTML scripts. But like any other code, reversing requires that we have learn scripting language used. The bottom line is, we need to learn the basics of the JavaScript programming language.

Let's try reversing a simple HTML file. You can download this HTML file from the following link: `https://github.com/PacktPublishing/Mastering-Reverse-Engineering/blob/master/ch13/demo_01.html`.

Only do this if you have time. When reversing a HTML file, it is recommended that you set it up to run as though it's being viewed in a website and not as an HTML file.

Using a text editor, such as Notepad, we can perform static analysis on the HTML file. Other text editors, such as Notepad++ (`https://notepad-plus-plus.org/`), would be better since it can show script syntax in color. This helps us to distinguish between the script functions from the data, as shown in the following screenshot:

```
1   <html>
2   <script>
3       alert("Hello reverser! --from a javascript code");
4   </script>
5   hi there<br/>
6   <script>
7       alert("1 + 2 is equal to");
8       x = 1
9       y = 2
10  </script>
11  reversing is fun!<br/>
12  <script>
13      alert(x + y);
14  </script>
15  m'kay bye!
16  </html>
```

To understand this code, a lot of references about HTML programming are available in the internet. One of these reference sites is `https://www.w3schools.com/html/default.asp`. What we are after here are the scripts that are defined in the `script` tags. There are a total of three JavaScript script codes here. The first script contains the following code:

```
alert("Hello reverser! --from a javascript code");
```

The `alert` function is used to display a message box. The message should be enclosed with quotes.

The second script contains the following code:

```
alert("1 + 2 is equal to");
x = 1
y = 2
```

Again, the script displays a message, and then assigns the value 1 to variable `x` and the value 2 to variable `y`.

The last script contains the following code:

```
alert("x + y");
```

This shows another message. This time, the message is the sum of the `x` and `y` variables, which should give us the value of 3. Even with the script code being located in separate tags, values in variables from the last running script should be reflected in succeeding scripts.

To prove this behavior, let's dynamically analyze the file by running it in an internet browser.

Open Internet Explorer. We can also use Firefox or Chrome. Drag and drop `demo_01.html` into Internet Explorer. This should show the following message box once it has loaded:

The message may not show up if the internet browser has disabled running JavaScript content. Usually, a security message appears, asking if we want to allow running script codes. Just allow the script to run:

The following message boxes will come up afterwards:

Now that the page has completely been loaded, press F12 to bring up the debugger console. Select the **Debugger** pane. This should show the HTML script, as follows:

In the debugger, place a breakpoint at line 3, which is the first `alert` function. To place a breakpoint, click on the empty gray space at the left of the line number. This should create a red dot that indicates a breakpoint line. The following screenshot shows all three scripts with their first lines marked with a breakpoint:

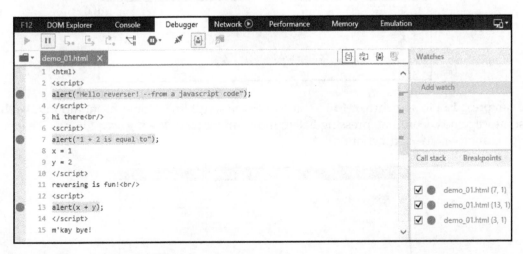

Refresh the browser by focusing on the internet browser's page and pressing **F5.** We may end up debugging the `browsertools` script, which is an Internet Explorer initialization script. This is shown in the following screenshot:

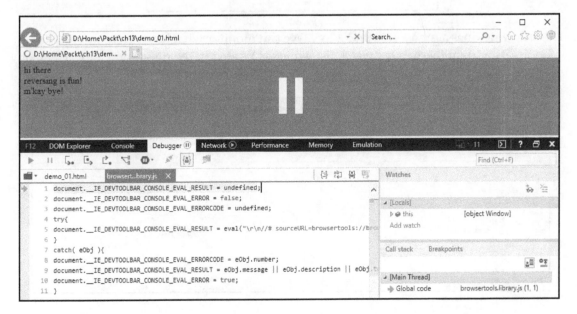

Just press *F5* again to make the debugger continue until we reach our breakpoint. We should now be at the first `alert` function, as follows:

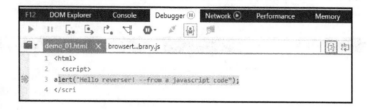

We can press **F11** to step into or **F10** to Step over the script line. Doing so should invoke the first message box. Continue pressing **F10** to move on to the following script lines. The next script is another `alert` function:

The following lines assign 1 to x and 2 to y. We can monitor what happens to these variables by adding these in the watch list, which is located in the right-hand pane. Click on **Add watch** to add the variables that we can monitor:

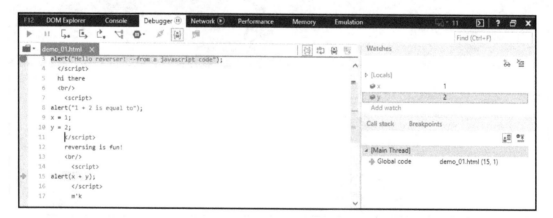

The last function is another `alert` function that displays the sum of x and y.

Let's try this with `demo_02.html` (https://github.com/PacktPublishing/Mastering-Reverse-Engineering/blob/master/ch13/demo_02.html).

If we debug this, it performs the same behavior that we encountered in `demo_01.html`. The difference is that it looks obfuscated when we look at it from the text editor:

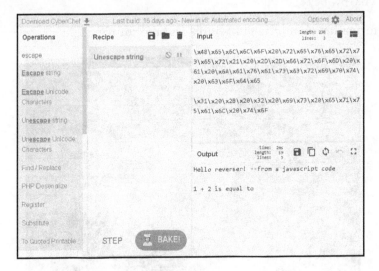

The message was converted to escaped format using each ASCII character's hexadecimal equivalent. In the previous chapter, we learned about `Cyberchef`, an online tool that we can use to de-obfuscate these types of data. Since this type of data is escaped, we should use an `unescape` operation to decode this data. Using `Cyberchef`, search for the `unescape` operation, and then copy and paste the escaped data in the **Input** window. We should get a decoded output showing the exact text we saw in the messages, like so:

Analyzing HTML scripts is not that complicated, especially since everything is almost human readable. All we need to understand is the syntax and the functions of the script language. Plus, this a way to dynamically analyze the script using debugging tools that are fortunately available in internet browsers.

MS Office macro analysis

Microsoft Office has a way for automating simple tasks such as creating formatted tables or inserting letterheads. This is called an MS office macro. MS Office macro makes use of the Visual Basic for Application language, which uses the same language as Visual Basic scripts. However, these can be abused to do more like download a file, create files, make registry entries, and even delete files.

First off, we need static tools to read information and extract the macro source from a given Office file. To open MS Office documents, we need to have Microsoft Office installed. The other tool that we could use would be OLE tools, which can be downloaded from `http://www.decalage.info/en/python/oletools`. These set of tools are Python scripts, and will require Python 2.7 to be installed on your system. The Python installer can be downloaded from `https://www.python.org/`.

The file we are going to analyze first is `https://github.com/PacktPublishing/Mastering-Reverse-Engineering/blob/master/ch13/demo_01.doc`. Type in the following code into the command line to use `olevba.py` on `demo_01.doc`:

```
python olevba.py demo_01.doc
```

This extracts information about the VBA source and the source itself:

We can see from the preceding screenshot that the source has two subroutines: `autoopen()` and `autoclose()`. `olevba.py` also describes these subroutines that are tied to events when the document is opened and closed.

The source contains code that pops up messages. Now, let's try to open the document in Microsoft Word. By doing this, we may end up with Microsoft Word showing us a security warning about the document containing code. Click on **Enable Content** so that we can see what the macro can do:

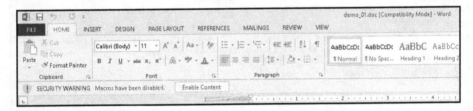

The first message immediately appears:

To debug the code, we need to open up the VBA editor. Select **View->Macro**. This opens up the **Macro** dialog box where you can select any **Macro name** and click on the **Edit** button:

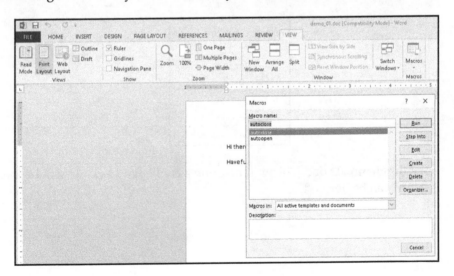

We are currently using Microsoft Office 2013, so the user interface for the VBA Editor may be different for other versions. In the VBA Editor, we should now see the source code. Pressing **F9** on a line of code enables or disables a breakpoint. Pressing **F8** does step debugging. **F5** is for continuing to run the code. We can start debugging from any of the subroutines. Select the **Debug** menu to view more debug features that are available:

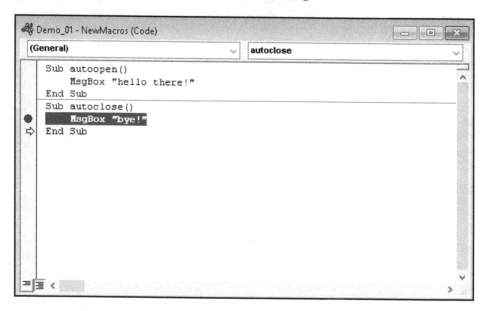

Closing the document will bring up the following message box:

Now, try analyzing **demo_02.doc**. This will be quite a challenge since we will be looking at how the password can be derived.

Remember that the VBA Editor is the macro developer's console. This is where the macro program was developed and debugged. Thus, to reverse what we are looking for, we can manipulate the source code.

```
================================================================================
FILE: demo_02.doc
Type: OpenXML
--------------------------------------------------------------------------------
VBA MACRO ThisDocument.cls
in file: word/vbaProject.bin - OLE stream: u'VBA/ThisDocument'
- - - - - - - - - - - - - - - - - - - - - - - - - - - - - - - - - - - - - - - -
(empty macro)
--------------------------------------------------------------------------------
VBA MACRO NewMacros.bas
in file: word/vbaProject.bin - OLE stream: u'VBA/NewMacros'
- - - - - - - - - - - - - - - - - - - - - - - - - - - - - - - - - - - - - - - -
Function Rot13(str)
    Dim rotorg
    Rot13 = ""
    str = LCase(str)
    rotorg = "nopqrstuvwxyzabcdefghijklm"
    rotequ = "abcdefghijklmnopqrstuvwxyz"
    For i = 1 To Len(str)
        c = Mid(str, i, 1)
        n = InStr(rotequ, c)
        o = Mid(rotorg, n, 1)
        Rot13 = Rot13 & o
    Next

End Function

Sub autoopen()
    spassword = InputBox("What is the password?", "password", "")
    MsgBox "You entered " + spassword
    realpassword = StrReverse(spassword)
    realpassword = Rot13(realpassword)
    If realpassword = "xnrgferteho" Then
        MsgBox "Congratulations!"
    Else
        MsgBox "Sorry! Try Again Later."
    End If
End Sub
Sub autoclose()
    MsgBox "bye!"
End Sub
```

Type	Keyword	Description
AutoExec	AutoOpen	Runs when the Word document is opened
AutoExec	AutoClose	Runs when the Word document is closed
Suspicious	StrReverse	May attempt to obfuscate specific strings
Suspicious	Base64 Strings	Base64-encoded strings were detected, may be used to obfuscate strings (option --decode to see all)

The password for demo_02.doc can be found in the Summary section of this chapter.

PDF file analysis

PDF files have evolved to run specific actions and allow for the execution of JavaScript. For PDF analysis, what we can do is extract event information and analyze what the JavaScript will do. We can use Didier Stevens' PDF Tools to help us analyze PDFs. This toolset runs using Python, so we will again need that installed. PDF Tools can be downloaded from `https://blog.didierstevens.com/programs/pdf-tools/`. If you go to the site, you will get a description about each tool in the package.

Let's try using the tool with `https://github.com/PacktPublishing/Mastering-Reverse-Engineering/blob/master/ch13/demo_01.pdf`. Using `pdfid.py`, execute the following line:

```
python pdfid.py demo_01.pdf
```

The following screenshot shows the result of `pdfid` on `demo_01.pdf`:

```
PDFiD 0.2.5 demo_01.pdf
 PDF Header: %PDF-1.0
 obj                    8
 endobj                 8
 stream                 1
 endstream              1
 xref                   1
 trailer                1
 startxref              1
 /Page                  0
 /Encrypt               0
 /ObjStm                0
 /JS                    1
 /JavaScript            2
 /AA                    0
 /OpenAction            1
 /AcroForm              0
 /JBIG2Decode           0
 /RichMedia             0
 /Launch                0
 /EmbeddedFile          0
 /XFA                   0
 /URI                   0
 /Colors > 2^24         0
```

Here, we can see that there is JavaScript code embedded to it. Let's now try the `pdf-parser.py` file so that we can extract more information. Some elements in the PDF file can be compressed and will not be readable. The `pdf-parser` tool is able to decompress these streams. Execute the following command to redirect output from `pdf-parser` to `demo_01.log`:

```
python pdf-parser.py demo_01.pdf > demo_01.log
```

The output given by `pdf-parser` is basically the same as the contents of `demo_01.pdf`. The reason for this is that there were no PDF objects that got decompressed. If we look closer at the output, we can easily identify where the script code is:

```
<<
    /JS (app.alert({cMsg: "Reversing is fun!", cTitle: "Mastering Reverse
Engineering"})
    ; )
    /S /JavaScript
>>
```

As a result, using Chrome as our PDF reader, the PDF displays the following message box:

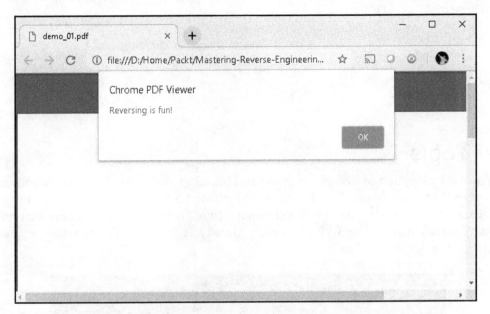

To debug the JavaScript, we would need to copy this into a separate JavaScript or HTML file. We may also need to fix the syntax of running JavaScript operators. The JavaScript code from the PDF can be converted into the following HTML code:

```
<html>
<script>
    alert("Reversing is fun!", "Mastering Reverse Engineering");
</script>
</html>
```

SWF file analysis

ShockWave Flash files can also contain code. Basically, flash files are legitimately written to follow a sequence of tasks. But just like any other code, it can be abused to carry out malicious activities.

The SWF file we are going to analyze can be downloaded from `https://github.com/PacktPublishing/Mastering-Reverse-Engineering/blob/master/ch13/demo01.swf`.

The main tool used for analyzing SWF at the time of writing this book is the JPEXS SWF decompiler. Besides this let's first talk about other existing tools that are able to parse SWF files. These tools are as follows:

- SWFTools
- FLASM
- Flare
- XXXSWF

SWFTools

SWFTools is a collection of tools for reading and building SWF files. It can be downloaded from `http://www.swftools.org/`. To successfully install SWFTools, it should be run as administrator. The tools are used at the command line. There are two tools here that can extract information about the SWF file: `swfdump` and `swfextract`. Here's what `swfdump` gives us:

```
C:\Program Files\SWFTools>swfdump.exe C:\Users\refun\Desktop\demo01.swf
[HEADER]        File version: 32
[HEADER]        File is zlib compressed. Ratio: 70%
[HEADER]        File size: 1299
[HEADER]        Frame rate: 30.000000
[HEADER]        Frame count: 1
[HEADER]        Movie width: 800.00
[HEADER]        Movie height: 600.00
[045]         4 FILEATTRIBUTES usenetwork as3 symbolclass
[04d]       459 METADATA
[040]        14 ENABLEDEBUGGER2
[03f]        16 MX4
[041]         4 SCRIPTLIMITS
[009]         3 SETBACKGROUNDCOLOR (ff/ff/ff)
[029]        26 SERIALNUMBER
[02b]         5 FRAMELABEL "Main"
[052]       706 DOABC "Main", lazy load
[04c]         9 SYMBOLCLASS
                exports 0000 as "Main"
[001]         0 SHOWFRAME 1 (00:00:00,000) (label "Main")
[000]         0 END
```

The result tells us that the file is `zlib` compressed. There is also a `DOABC` method labeled `Main`. The existence of a `DOABC` also means that there is an embedded action script. Using `HxD`, we can verify that the file is compressed. The magic header `CWS` indicates that the `SWF` is indeed compressed. An uncompressed `SWF` starts with `FWS` magic bytes:

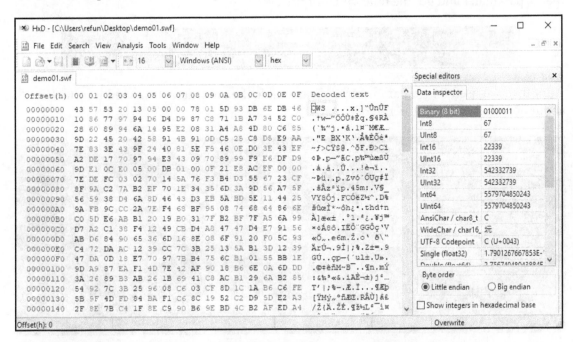

The other tool, `swfextract`, is capable of extracting embedded videos or images. `demo01.swf` doesn't contain any media, as we can see from the following screenshot:

```
C:\Program Files\SWFTools>swfextract.exe C:\Users\refun\Desktop\demo01.swf
Objects in file C:\Users\refun\Desktop\demo01.swf:
 [-f] 1 Frame: ID(s) 0
```

The other tools in `SWFTools` are used to build `SWF`s from PDFs, images, and videos.

FLASM

FLASM is a tool that is capable of decompressing and disassembling SWF files. It can be downloaded from http://nowrap.de/flasm.html. We decompressed demo01.swf using the -x parameter and got the following output:

```
C:\Users\refun\Downloads\flasm16win>flasm -x demo01.swf
demo01.swf successfully decompressed, 1299 bytes
```

After that, we used the -d parameter to disassemble the file where it showed information about how the SWF was structured:

```
C:\Users\refun\Downloads\flasm16win>flasm -d demo01.swf
movie 'demo01.swf' // flash 32, total frames: 1, frame rate: 30 fps, 800x600 px

  fileAttributes attrUseNetwork,attrActionScript3,attrHasMetadata

  metadata '<rdf:RDF xmlns:rdf=\'http://www.w3.org/1999/02/22-rdf-syntax-ns#\'><rdf:Description rdf:about=\'\' xmlns:dc=
\'http://purl.org/dc/elements/1.1\'><dc:format>application/x-shockwave-flash</dc:format><dc:title>Adobe Flex 4 Applicati
on</dc:title><dc:description>http://www.adobe.com/products/flex</dc:description><dc:publisher>unknown</dc:publisher><dc:
creator>unknown</dc:creator><dc:language>EN</dc:language><dc:date>Oct 29, 2018</dc:date></rdf:Description></rdf:RDF>'

  enableDebugger2 'NO-PASSWORD'

  // unknown tag 63 length 16

  scriptLimits recursion 1000 timeout 60

  // unknown tag 82 length 706

  // unknown tag 76 length 9
end
```

We can't see any disassembled nor decompiled action scripts here.

Flare

This is a tool that is capable of decompiling ActionScript code. It can be downloaded from http://nowrap.de/flare.html. However, it may not be able to fully support AS2 and AS3 code. Just pass the SWF file to the Flare tool and it will generate an FLR file. We can executed Flare using the following command:

```
flare.exe demo01.swf
```

The result placed in demo01.flr contained the following output:

```
movie 'demo01.swf' {
// flash 32, total frames: 1, frame rate: 30 fps, 800x600 px, compressed,
network access alowed
```

```
    metadata <rdf:RDF
xmlns:rdf=\'http://www.w3.org/1999/02/22-rdf-syntax-ns#\'><rdf:Description
rdf:about=\'\'
xmlns:dc=\'http://purl.org/dc/elements/1.1\'><dc:format>application/x-shock
wave-flash</dc:format><dc:title>Adobe Flex 4
Application</dc:title><dc:description>http://www.adobe.com/products/flex</d
c:description><dc:publisher>unknown</dc:publisher><dc:creator>unknown</dc:c
reator><dc:language>EN</dc:language><dc:date>Oct 29,
2018</dc:date></rdf:Description></rdf:RDF>
    // unknown tag 82 length 706
    // unknown tag 76 length 9
}
```

It had the same result as FLASM. No action scripts were disassembled.

XXXSWF

This tool can be downloaded from https://github.com/viper-framework/xxxswf. It is a Python script that accepts the following parameters:

```
Usage: xxxswf.py [options] <file.bad>

Options:
  -h, --help show this help message and exit
  -x, --extract Extracts the embedded SWF(s), names it MD5HASH.swf &
                      saves it in the working dir. No addition args
needed
  -y, --yara Scans the SWF(s) with yara. If the SWF(s) is
                      compressed it will be deflated. No addition args
                      needed
  -s, --md5scan Scans the SWF(s) for MD5 signatures. Please see func
                      checkMD5 to define hashes. No addition args needed
  -H, --header Displays the SWFs file header. No addition args needed
  -d, --decompress Deflates compressed SWFS(s)
  -r PATH, --recdir=PATH
                      Will scan a directory for files that contain SWFs.
                      Must provide path in quotes
  -c, --compress Compress SWF using Zlib
  -z, --zcompress Compress SWF using LZMA
```

We tried using this tool with `demo01.swf`. After using the `-H` paramater, the tool tells us that it is compressed. We then decompressed the file using the `-d` option. This resulted in a decompressed SWF version in the `243781cd4047e8774c8125072de4edb1.swf` file. Finally, we used the `-H` parameter on the decompressed file:

```
C:\Users\refun\Downloads\xxxswf-master\xxxswf>python xxxswf.py -H demo01.swf

[SUMMARY] Potentially 1 SWF(s) in MD5 aab42616d58a6f2067470c7bcece3510:demo01.swf
        [ADDR] SWF 1 at 0x0
- CWS Header

C:\Users\refun\Downloads\xxxswf-master\xxxswf>python xxxswf.py -d demo01.swf

[SUMMARY] Potentially 1 SWF(s) in MD5 aab42616d58a6f2067470c7bcece3510:demo01.swf
        [ADDR] SWF 1 at 0x0
- CWS Header
                [FILE] Carved SWF MD5: 243781cd4047e8774c8125072de4edb1.swf

C:\Users\refun\Downloads\xxxswf-master\xxxswf>python xxxswf.py -H 243781cd4047e8774c8125072de4edb1.swf

[SUMMARY] Potentially 1 SWF(s) in MD5 243781cd4047e8774c8125072de4edb1:243781cd4047e8774c8125072de4edb1.swf
        [ADDR] SWF 1 at 0x0
- FWS Header
```

So far, what comes in useful for this without the `yara` and `md5` features is its ability to search for embedded flash files. This comes in useful for detecting SWF malware with embedded SWFs in it.

JPEXS SWF decompiler

One of the most used tool for analyzing SWF files is the JPEXS SWF decompiler. Nightly builds can be downloaded from `https://github.com/jindrapetrik/jpexs-decompiler`. This tool is capable of decompiling ActionScript that supports AS3. The following screenshot shows the JPEXS console:

Besides being able to decompile, it has an interface that can be set up with Adobe Flash Player's debugger. After installing JPEXS, we need to download the *flash player projector content debugger* from `https://www.adobe.com/support/flashplayer/debug_downloads.html`.

Open JPEXS and then select **Settings->Advanced Settings->Paths**. Then, browse to the downloaded flash executable to fill up the Flash Player projector content debugger path. Click **OK** when you're done:

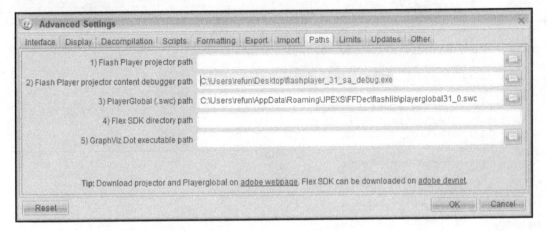

This is an important setup that enables us to debug the decompiled ActionCcript. You can also fill up the Flash Player projector path by downloading the Flash Player projector from `https://www.adobe.com/support/flashplayer/debug_downloads.html`.

Open the SWF file and expand the tree of objects in the left window pane. Select **Main** under the `scripts` object. This displays the decompiled ActionScript, as shown in the following screenshot:

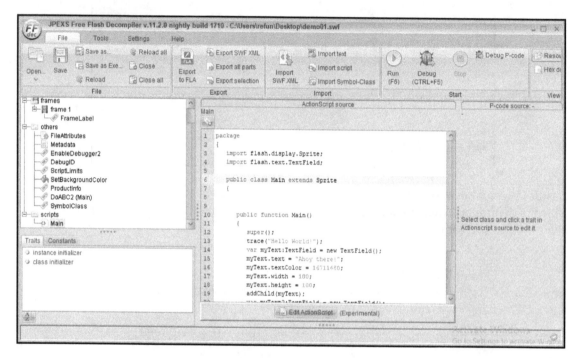

And here is the decompiled code for `demo01.swf`:

```
package
{
    import flash.display.Sprite;
    import flash.text.TextField;
    public class Main extends Sprite
    {
        public function Main()
        {
            super();
            trace("Hello World!");
            var myText:TextField = new TextField();
            myText.text = "Ahoy there!";
            myText.textColor = 16711680;
```

```
        myText.width = 100;
        myText.height = 100;
        addChild(myText);
        var myText2:TextField = new TextField();
        myText2.text = "Reversing is fun!\n--b0yb4w4n9";
        myText.y = 100;
        addChild(myText2);
    }
  }
}
```

Click the **Debug** button or **Ctrl+F5**, this should bring us to the debugger console. In the left-most window, the byte-code equivalent of the decompiled Actionscript is shown.

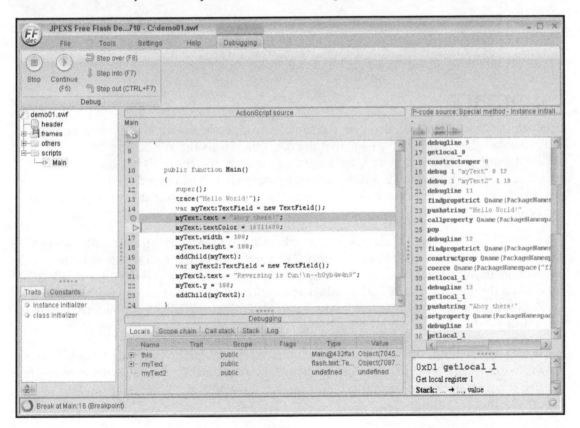

What the code does is create two TextFields containing text that gets displayed on the SWF display space.

Reversing is fun!
--b0yb4w4n9

Ahoy there!

JPEXS is a tool that has the important feature we want to analyze code in a flash file. It has a byte-code disassembler, source decompiler, and a debugger.

Summary

Analyzing various file types also uses the same concept as reversing. In this chapter, we learned about the scripting language that the file format is using. We could gather additional information if we were also inclined to understand the file's header and structure. We also learned that as long as executable code can be embedded into a file, there is a way to analyze it. It may not be dynamically analyzed easily, but at least static analysis can be performed.

We tackled how to debug JavaScript that is embedded in HTML scripts. Virtually, we can analyze any website we visit. We also learned about the tools that we can use to extract macro code in Microsoft Office documents. It also happens that we can debug this macro code using the VBA Editor. We also looked at a variety of tools that we can use to extract JavaScript from a PDF file. Then we analyzed an SWF file using JPEXS, a powerful tool that has a disassembler, decompiler, and debugger.

Reversing engineering software is a concept at hand. We research what the software is and how it works. We also get to learn the low-level language beneath the code that executes in the file. It may take time to learn this language, but it is worth the knowledge and experience that we gain from it.

Have a fun day reversing!

P.S. The password for `demo_02.doc` is burgersteak.

Further reading

`https://www.w3schools.com/html/default.asp` : a good tutorial site for learning HTML scripting

`http://www.javascriptobfuscator.com` – this is an online site that can obfuscate javascript code

Other Books You May Enjoy

If you enjoyed this book, you may be interested in these other books by Packt:

Hands-On Cybersecurity for Architects
Neil Rerup

ISBN: 9781788830263

- Understand different security architecture layers and their integration with all solutions
- Study SWOT analysis and dig into your organization's requirements to drive the strategy
- Design and implement a secure email service approach
- Monitor the age and capacity of security tools and architecture
- Explore growth projections and architecture strategy
- Identify trends, as well as what a security architect should take into consideration

Cybersecurity - Attack and Defense Strategies
Yuri Diogenes

ISBN: 9781788475297

- Learn the importance of having a solid foundation for your security posture
- Understand the attack strategy using cyber security kill chain
- Learn how to enhance your defense strategy by improving your security policies, hardening your network, implementing active sensors, and leveraging threat intelligence
- Learn how to perform an incident investigation
- Get an in-depth understanding of the recovery process
- Understand continuous security monitoring and how to implement a vulnerability management strategy
- Learn how to perform log analysis to identify suspicious activities

Leave a review - let other readers know what you think

Please share your thoughts on this book with others by leaving a review on the site that you bought it from. If you purchased the book from Amazon, please leave us an honest review on this book's Amazon page. This is vital so that other potential readers can see and use your unbiased opinion to make purchasing decisions, we can understand what our customers think about our products, and our authors can see your feedback on the title that they have worked with Packt to create. It will only take a few minutes of your time, but is valuable to other potential customers, our authors, and Packt. Thank you!

Index

B

bases
  about 56, 57
  converting between 57, 58
basic analysis lab setup 16, 18, 19, 20
basic instructions
  about 66
  arithmetic operations 69
  bitwise algebra 73
  control flow 75, 76, 77
  data, copying 67
  opcode bytes 67
  stack manipulation 77, 78
BEYE
  about 144
  reference 144
binary analysis tools 12
binary arithmetic 59
binary numbers
  about 56
  bases 56, 57
  signed numbers 60
BinText 142
bintext
  reference 130
bitwise algebra
  about 73
  AND 73
  NOT 73
  OR 73
  ROL 74
  ROR 74
  SHL/SAL 74
  SHR/SAR 74
  XOR 73
Bless 147
Bochs
  about 241
  MBR debugging 244, 246, 247, 249, 250, 251, 252
Buster Sandbox Analyzer (BSA) 150

C

Capstone

about 144
  reference 144
CaptureBAT 143
CFF Explorer
  about 141
  download link 209
code assembly 257, 258
Complex Instruction Set Computing (CISC) 240
compressors 279
control flow 75, 76, 77
CPU architectures 240
CPUID
  reference 325
crypters 281, 282
Cryptographic Service Provider (CSP) 200
Cuckoo 120, 149
Cyberchef 309

D

data assembly
  in memory regions 262, 263
  on stack 255, 256
deadlisting 119
debuggers
  about 15, 144
  GDB 145
  IDA Pro 144
  Immunity Debugger 145
  OllyDebug 145
  Radare 145
  Windbg 145
  x86dbg 144
debugging
  about 97, 349, 350, 352, 353, 354, 355, 357, 359
  analysis summary 383
  unknown image 359, 361, 362, 364, 365, 366, 368, 370, 371, 373, 375, 377, 379, 380, 381, 383
decompilers
  about 15, 120, 145
  dotPeek 146
  Hex-Rays 146
  ILSpy 120
  iLSpy 146

CPSIA information can be obtained
at www.ICGtesting.com
Printed in the USA
LVHW041150091222
734813LV00005B/265